In Defence of a Billion Hindus

BY THE SAME AUTHOR

Arise Again, Ô India!

A Western Journalist on India: The Ferengi's Columns

A New History of India

A History of India as it Happened

Hindu Power in the 21st Century

In Defence of a Billion Hindus

one of the most marvelous people on this planet-ever ...

François Gautier

HAR-ANAND PUBLICATIONS PVT LTD
E-49/3, Okhla Industrial Area, Phase-II, New Delhi-110020
Tel.: 41603490
E-mail: info@haranandbooks.com/haranand@rediffmail.com
Shop online at: www.haranandbooks.com

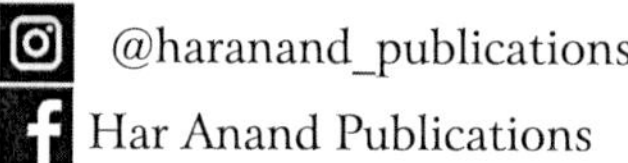

Reprint, 2025

Published by Ashok Gosain and Ashish Gosain for
Har-Anand Publications Pvt Ltd

Printed in India at Megha Enterprises

Prologue

Every 6th person on this Planet is a Hindu and Hindus still constitute the overwhelming majority in India—nearly 80% of the population. Humanity needs thus to re-discover the wonder that is Hinduism, the oldest spirituality still in practice in the world.

Hindus have been the most tolerant people on this planet, accepting the fact that the Divine manifests Himself or Herself at different times of the history of humanity using different names and different scriptures. This is why Hindus have always welcomed in their midst all the persecuted religious minorities of the world—from the Syrian Christians, the Jews (India is the only country in the world where Jews were never persecuted), from the Parsis to the Tibetans today.

In 5000 years of existence, Hindus have never militarily invaded another country, never tried to impose their religion on others by force or induced conversions, contrary to Islam and Christianity. You cannot find anybody less fundamentalist than a Hindu in the 21st century.

Yet it has been one-way traffic, as Hindus have been the most persecuted people of this planet. In fact in terms of genocide, there is no greater holocaust than that of the Hindus—it has been estimated than more than a hundred million Hindus have been killed from the Hindu Kush, till today....

This book is then about the story of the Hindus, their scriptures, their history, the bloody invasions that they faced over the centuries and the menaces that still threaten their very survival.

Hope you will enjoy it.

Contents

CHAPTER 1

Who are the Hindus?

Let's say it right away: there are no Hindus.... This word was invented by European colonizers to designate a people which lived in the valley of the Indus. The exact appellation should be *Indu*, a term which was actually used for centuries by outsiders, to name all India's inhabitants, be they Muslims, Christians, Buddhists or Hindus. But when *Indus* became *Hindus* at the hands of western colonizers, it grew to be a source of confusion and had catastrophic consequences for Indian history: it brought indirectly the terrible partition of the subcontinent and is partly responsible today for the inter-religious strife in India.

Who are the Hindus then—or shall we say *Indus*? Western (and unfortunately also Indian) historians have often reduced Hinduism to a code of moral conduct and a set of rites and rituals, or have even negated Hinduism by associating it only with the hated system of castes, forgetting that Hinduism was not only a wonderful system of thought, which influenced many of the philosophical systems of our planet, but that it was—and hopefully still is today, even if it has lost some of its early purity—a unique spirituality, which went beyond all religions in the true spirit of *Induity*. It may be necessary then—even for Indians, who often seem to have very little idea of the greatness of their culture—to remind the readers of a few of the lasting principles of Hinduism.

In the beginning for the Hindus, the world was only the Being without duality: *Sat*. Certain sects of Hinduism even said that before man, before any living organism, there was only Non-Being: *a-sat*. But how could the Being emerge from Non-Being? In the beginning then, this world must have been Pure Being, unique, without past, present or future:

It was the hour before the Gods awake.
Across the path of the divine Event
The huge foreboding mind of Night, alone
In her unlit temple of eternity,
Lay stretched immobile upon Silence's marge....

(Sri Aurobindo, Savitri, page 1)

And then, « something » happened:

Then Something in the inscrutable darkness stirred;
A nameless movement, an unthought Idea,
Insistent, dissatisfied, without an aim,
Something that wished but knew not how to be,
Teased the Inconscient to wake Ignorance....

(Idem, page 2)

Human evolution had started; the Non-Manifest had descended into Matter. And all the forms of life as we know them, were going to blossom during the millions of years which followed, until the *homo sapiens* of today.

And for the Hindus, the symbol, the unalterable proof of this descent of the Non-Manifest on our earth is *jiva*, the soul, a spark of the Infinite which is hidden in every thing. It is through *jiva* that the flower finds its infinite exquisiteness; it is because of *jiva* that the animal moves with such beauty, it is by the grace of *jiva* that man always aspires higher. "As tiny as an atom, as vast as the universe, *jiva* is unfathomable and cannot be seized; eternal, *jiva* cannot be destroyed; without attachments, free, nothing can touch it," says the Taittirîya Upanishad.

Hinduism has always maintained that *jiva* reincarnates itself from life to life, thus perfecting itself throughout the ages. Everything is valuable for *jiva* and there is nothing that it neglects, as each experience enriches the soul: sufferings and joys, honors and disgrace, king in this life, untouchable in the next, criminal yesterday, saint today.... When we die, the physical body goes back to the universal Earth, the intellect dissolves itself in the larger universal Mind, and the vital, or Life Force, which is the mass of the impulsions and desires which we have formed in the course of a lifetime, return to the universal Vital. And then *jiva* is reborn, again and again, until we become fully conscious of the Supreme Being from which we all emanate: "Old and feeble, he becomes young again and again," says the Rig Veda.

This concept of reincarnation, without which it is difficult to understand the why of our often painful lives, or accept the inevitability (and immense cruelty) of death, has been lost in the West and most other parts of the world and religions, whereas it was prevalent nearly everywhere during Antiquity. "Which sadist God has decreed that we would have only one life to realize ourselves and through which colossal ignorance Islam and Christianity have decided that we shall go to Heaven, or to Hell, according to the deeds, bad or good, which we have committed in a single life?" asks French writer Satprem.

The ancient Hindus were intensely secular in spirit, as their spirituality was absolutely non-sectarian—and still is today in a lesser measure. Seven thousand years ago, Vedic sages, to define the Universal Law which they had experienced within themselves on an occult and supra-spiritual plane, had invented the word *dharma*. In a nutshell, *dharma* is all that which helps you to become more and more aware of *jiva* inside yourself. In fact, *dharma* defines good and bad: what helps you on the path of spiritual discovery can be considered good = *dharmic*; and what impedes, you can be taken it as bad = *a-dharmic*. And to help the seeker progress in his *sadhana*, the sages of ore had codified a series of systems called *yogas*. There is *hatha-yoga*, or the yoga of the body, the only Indian spiritual discipline which the West knows about and which has been copied by all the gymnastics and aerobics systems of the world; *karma-yoga,* or yoga of work; *jnana-yoga,* that of knowledge; *bhakti yoga*, the path of devotion ... and so on. The Masters had also discovered that the personality of each human being is composed of three main "psychological" elements, or *gunas*: *tamas*, which is the principle of inertia, of heaviness and indolence; *rajas*, the more dynamic energy of our desires and impulsions; and *sattwa*, the most spiritualized and refined element in us. All yogas have thus attempted to promote *sattwa*, while taming *rajas* and uplifting *tamas.*

Karma is another very important tenet of Hinduism which has been perverted in modern times, not only because of its fashionable misuse in the West, but also in India itself where, because of influences during three centuries by missionaries and secular thought, it is often mixed-up in varying degrees with the Christian concept of sin and virtue. Hindus (and Buddhists) have always maintained that all actions, good or bad, which we perform during a lifetime, carry automatically consequences for the next lives to come. But there is absolutely no moral implication, no notion of Good or Evil, as for Hinduism there is a mathematical and immutable logic in our actions: "Whatever the seed you planted, you will harvest its fruit sooner or later," says the Buddha. Consequently, there is never any absolute injustice: suffering in this life could be the consequence of a "bad" karma sown in another life; and today's happiness, might result from a "good" karma performed in another body. With this knowledge, one can understand a little better the sufferings of humanity, even though many of them still look so unjust; but true compassion is always accompanied by right knowledge.

The concept of the *avatar* is also indispensable to the understanding of induism—Hinduism or true *dharma*. Hindus have always believed that the Infinite, the Immanent, the Supreme, or whatever name you want to give to That which is beyond us, has manifested Himself throughout the ages in human bodies—particularly at crucial stages during the history of humanity. Christ, Krishna, Buddha, Confucius, Mohamed, are all *avatars* in the eyes of Hindus. Each of these "sons of God" explained and developed their messages in the terms and with the images of their times, which fitted into the understanding and culture of the country where they had incarnated themselves. None of them, except maybe Mohamed, ever said that he was "the only" son of God and that his religion was the only true one; it is their disciples and followers who later perverted their messages and converted what was essentially spiritual teachings into fixed religions with their intolerant and exclusive credos. It is these followers who today refuse to adapt their religions to modern times.

Finally, it is difficult to understand Hinduism if you do not grasp the concept of *shakti*, the divine feminine energy. Because of the influence of British thought, it is nowadays fashionable in India to always to highlight the downtrodden condition of Indian women and its underprivileged place in Indian society. As a result, Western correspondents are always keen to do stories on female infanticides in Bihar, child marriages, or *sati* cases in Rajasthan. But who knows that no country in the world has granted such an important place to women in its spirituality and social ethos? "Without Him I exist not, without Her I am unmanifest," says a great Indian yogi. Thus in India—and it is true that it is often a paradox, as women, because of later Muslim influences, have often been relegated to the background—the feminine concept is a symbol of dynamic realization. She is the eternal Mother, who is all Wisdom, all Compassion, all Force, Beauty and Perfection. It is in this way that since the dawn of times, Hindus have venerated the feminine element under its different manifestations: *Makalaxmi, Mahakali, Mahasaraswati, Maheshwari*—and even India is feminine: "Mother India." She is the consciousness transcending all things, she is the emptiness beyond all emptiness, the smile beyond all smiles, the divine beauty beyond all earthly beauties. India has had many great female figures, whether warriors such as the Rani of Jhansi, or saints like Anandamai. And even today, behind all appearances—arranged marriages, submission to men, preference of male children in some rural areas (but girls are loved in India like nowhere in the world)—the role of women in India is essential and it can be safely said that very often, from the poorest to the richest classes, they control—even if behind the scenes—a lot of the family affairs: the education of their children (men in India are often "mama's boys"), monetary concerns, and men often refer to them for important decisions. Countries such as France or the United States, who are often preaching India on "women's rights" never had a woman as their top leader, whereas India had Indira Gandhi ruling with an iron hand for nearly twenty years; and proportionately they have less MP's than India, which is considering earmarking 33% of seats in

Parliament for women, a revolution in human history! And finally this *shakti* concept is so rooted in the subcontinent, that you have had women Prime Ministers, such as Benazir Bhutto or Kaleda Zia, in Islamic countries (Pakistan and Bangladesh) which are predominantly male-controlled in a much stricter way than India.

1.1 The myth of Polytheism

Throughout its long history, the concept of *dharma*, or the universal Law, gave such a freedom to Indians that all kind of branches and sects developed within Hinduism, which sometimes even went against each other. Indeed, Hinduism was never static, it never barred its followers from experimenting new techniques and spiritual paths: everything that helps you on the way is *dharmic*. It is this fundamental principle which allowed India to survive all over the ages with a prodigious continuity, whereas other civilizations saw their cultures and their religions systematically destroyed. Unfortunately, this enormous tolerance of Hinduism—or Induism, if you prefer—is not recognized in the world today, or even acknowledged by Indians themselves, for two reasons. The first one are the Muslim invasions and the second the European colonization. It is the immense shock between these two great monotheist religions and Hindu polytheism, which has completely perverted our perception of India.

Yet, Hinduism, whether you want to call it a religion or a spiritual system, is without doubt the most monotheist religion in the world, because it always recognized that the Supreme can only be diverse and that he incarnates Himself in many forms—hence the million of gods in the Hindu pantheon. Vedic Sages had understood that man has to be given a multiplicity of different approaches, if you want him to fathom the Unfathomable. And truly, for the Hindus, the Divine cannot be "this" or "that," *neti, neti*; in its essence He cannot be several—or even one—and thus can never be perfectly seized by the human mind. Indeed, Hindus, who were once upon a time the best dialecticians in the world (and this is maybe why they are today the best software programmers of this planet), were able to come-up with this kind of equation: (a) God is in the world; (b) the world is in God; (c) the world is God; (d) God and the world are distinct; (e) God is distinct from the world, but the world is not distinct from God; (f) it is impossible to discern if the world is distinct from God or not.... Never has the unique nature of Hindu polytheism been better defined.

Hindus have also always recognized the divinity of other religions, as their concept of the *avatar* helped them to accept the reality of other prophets, masters or gurus. It is, for instance, perfectly acceptable for an ordinary Hindu to have on his wall the image of Krishna, alongside the one of Buddha, one of the Christ, with a few photos of the Mecca or even John Fitzgerald Kennedy! And Hindus have always worshipped at non-Hindu places, such as Velangani, the Christian place of pilgrimage of South India, or some Sufi shrine in Kashmir or Rajasthan. Not only that, but Hindus never tried to convert others to their own religion, not even by peaceful means, as the Buddhists did all over Asia; and their armies never set to conquer other nations to impose their own culture and religion. Yet for the Muslims and later European invaders, who were both persuaded that their God was the only true one, Hinduism with its myriad of Gods, represented the Infidel, the *Kafir* par excellence, not only did they set upon, by violence, coercion, or devious means, to convert Hindus to their own "true" religion, but they also propagated in the world the image of the "Pagan" Hindus, which has survived even up to today in many ways, subtle—and not so subtle.

1.2. European Cartesianism and Hinduism

"Only believe what you experience on yourself," said the Buddha 2500 years ago. Indian philosophy and spiritual thought was thus always very down to earth and attempted to define scientifically and logically the different means and ways to reach the goal: "If you do this, this is what will happen; if you breathe in this way, this is what may result; if you practice this particular posture, these are the results you will gain...."

Yet the West is today wary of anything which has a Hindu flavor and is quick to label as "sects" everything that does not spring from the larger conventional family of Christianity. It is true that gurus teaching in the West can be a mixed lot, and some of them might have brought a bad name to Hinduism, but the ordinary Indian meditating every morning, or doing his *pujas*, practicing his *asanas*, chanting *bhajans*, or doing *pranayama*, does not feel he is doing anything out of the ordinary. There is no sectarism here, no fake mysticism, no pagan obscure rites.

To understand India and Hinduism, one then has to go beyond the *clichés* of paganism and the accusations of sects that have been applied to Hindus, particularly after the coming of Christian missionaries to India who had a vested motive to show Hinduism in a bad light. It is true that Hindus adore Gods made out of stone or cast in brass. But is it less rational or Cartesian to think, as the Catholics do, that Mary conceived a child while remaining a virgin, or that Christ came back from the dead and ascended physically to heaven (and not in his subtle body, which is more likely)? Muslim invaders were also immensely shocked by this worshipping of images and gods and set upon destroying hundreds of thousand of temples and idols. But Alexandra David-Neel, the remarkable French explorer, writer and mystic, had remarked that the role that Gods play in India is remarkable "because the images or statues are like a battery which is charged over the ages by the adoration of the devotees, who in turn can draw energy, inspiration, or grace from these statues." She goes on: "As a battery, the energy in the statue will not get discharged, as long as the faithful continue worship it by their cult and adoration." And she concludes: "Gods are thus created by the energy given out by the faith in their existence."

At any rate, Hindus are great rationalists: they have discovered for instance that the sound *Aum*, "Amen" for the Christians, possesses very strong vibrations which take you to the deepest level and that the Creator is the Original Verb: *Shabda Brahman;* that the *ragas*, these few notes of music on which one can improve indefinitely, have also a strong inner power; or that the breath is the physical conduit to the Divine, which they have codified into *pranayama*, the Indian science of breathing. But nothing, without any doubt, is more scientific, more logical, more Cartesian, more noble and prophetic than the Vedas, the most ancient and sacred Scriptures of Hinduism, which are nearly totally ignored in the West and misunderstood in India.

CHAPTER 2

The Secret of the Vedas

"One finds two theorems in modern science which have a profound spiritual echo, wrote in 1926 Sri Aurobindo, India's avatar of the Modern Age: first that atoms are masses of swirling structures, like the solar system; and then that all the atoms are constituted of the same elements. If one considered these two theorems under their true light, they could lead science to new discoveries which are today unfathomable and in comparison of which the present realisations would look very primitive."

And Sri Aurobindo to add: "our ancient vedic*rishis* knew of a triple fire, which they had named *agni*: the ordinary fire—*jada agni*; the electric fire—*vaidyuta agni*; and the solar fire—*saura agni*. Modern science knows only these first two fires and the fact that the atom is like a solar system could lead them to the third discovery." This prophecy of course, came to be fulfilled when the Americans exploded their first nuclear device in the Nevada desert in 1944. But how could Sri Aurobindo have guessed twenty years before this momentous event, that solar heat is the result of a nuclear fusion and that nuclear power is locked in the atoms ?

Because seven thousand years ago, the Vedic rishis had experienced within themselves the different subtle properties of *agni*, the inner fire, which becomes solar, *saura-agni*, when one reaches the supra-mental levels of consciousness and of which nuclear energy is only the most material manifestation. "It is through *agni* that man can reach superior states of being and come into contact with the Gods: *agni* is the mouth of the Gods and it is through this mouth that they breathe," says the Shatapâ-brâhmana. Who then were these "sages" who may have already pierced the secrets of our universe many thousands of years ago?

"I seek not science, not religion, not Theosophy, but Veda—the truth about Brahman, not only about His essentiality, but also about His manifestation, not a lamp on the way to the forest, but a light and a guide to joy and action in the world, the truth which is beyond opinion, the knowledge which all thought strives after—'yasmin vijnate sarvam vijnatam' (which being known, all is known). I believe that Veda be the foundation of the Sanatana Dharma; I believe it to be the concealed divinity within Hinduism,—but a veil has to be drawn aside, a curtain has to be lifted. I believe it to be knowable and discoverable. I believe the future of India and the world depends on its discovery and on its application, not to the renunciation of life, but to life in the world and among men." (India's Rebirth, page 90)

Sri Aurobindo contended that Europeans have seen in the Vedas "only the rude chants of an antique and pastoral race sung in honor of the forces of nature and succeeded in imposing them on the Indian intellect." But he insisted that a time must come "when the Indian mind will shake off the darkness that has fallen upon it, cease to think or hold opinions at second and third hand and reassert its right to judge and enquire in perfect freedom into the meaning of its own scriptures." He argued that the Veda remains the foundation of Indian culture: "the Veda was the beginning of our spiritual knowledge, the Veda will remain its end. The recovery of the perfect truth of the Veda is therefore not merely a desideratum for our modern intellectual curiosity, but a practical necessity for the future of the human race. For I firmly believe that the secret concealed in the Veda, when entirely discovered, will be found to formulate perfectly that knowledge and practice of divine life to which the march of humanity, after long wanderings in the satisfaction of the intellect and senses, must inevitably return." (India's rebirth, 94)

What is the Secret of the Vedas? First we have to discard the ridiculously early dates given by historians and bring it back to at least 4000 BC. Why did historians show such an eagerness in post-dating the Vedas and making of them just a mumble-jumble of pagan superstition? Because it would have destroyed the West's idea of its own supremacy: primitive barbarism could not possibly have risen to such high conceptions so early, particularly when the Westerners have started our era after the birth of Christ and decreed that the world began on 23rd October 4004 B.C...! Secondly, the Vedic seers, who had attained the ultimate truth, *had clothed their oral findings in symbols and images, so that only the initiated would understand the true meaning of their aphorisms*. For the more ordinary souls, "those who were not yet twice born," it meant only an outer worship which was fit for their level of spiritual evolution. The Vedic rituals, has lost its profound meaning to us. Therefore, as Sri Aurobindo elucidates, when we read: "Sarama by the path of the Truth discovers the herds," the mind is stopped and baffled by an unfamiliar language. It has to be translated to us..into a plainer and less figured thought: "Intuitions by the way of Truth arrive at the hidden illuminations." (India's rebirth, 109) Lacking the clues, we only see in the Vedas a series of meaningless mouthings about the herds or the Sun. Sri

Aurobindo remarks that the Vedic rishis "may not have yoked the lighting to their chariots, nor weighed sun and star, nor materialized all the destructive forces of Nature to aid them in massacre and domination, but they had measured and fathomed all the heavens and earth within us, they had cast their plummet into the inconscient and the subconscient and the supraconscient; they had read the riddle of death and found the secret of immortality; they had sought for and discovered the One and known and worshipped Him in the glories of His light and purity and wisdom and power." (India's rebirth, 116)

Ah, these are the two secrets of the Vedas, then, the reason why they have remained so obscure and lost their original meaning. Firstly, the Vedic rishis had realized that God is One, but He takes many faces in His manifestation; this is the very foundation of Hinduism. And Secondly, the Vedic rishis had gone down in their minds and their bodies all the way to the roots of Death, to that eternal question which haunts humanity since the beginning of times: why death? What is the purpose of living if one has always to die? Why the inevitable decay and oblivion? And there, in their own bodies, at the bottom rock of the Inconscient, they had discovered the secret of immortality, which Sri Aurobindo called later the Supramental and which he said was the next step in humanity's evolution.... "Not some mysterious elixir of youth, but the point, the spring where All is One and death disappears in the face of the Supreme Knowledge and Ananda." (India's rebirth, 95)

Is this then the work of a few uncivilized shepherds, who had colonized the poor Dravidians? No wonder the West cannot recognize the Vedas for what they are, the whole foundation of their moral domination would then collapse.

All the subsequent scriptures of Hinduism derive from the

Vedas, even though some of them lost sight of the original Vedic sense. *The Vedas are the foundations of Indian culture;* the greatest power of the Vedic teaching, that which made it the source of all later Indian philosophies, religions, systems of yoga, lay in its application to the inner life of man. Man lives in the physical cosmos, subject to death and the falsehood of mortal existence. To rise beyond death, to become one of the immortals, he has to turn from the falsehood to the Truth; he has to turn onto the Light, to battle with and conquer the powers of Darkness. This he does by communion with the Divine Powers and their aid; ***the way to call down these aids was the secret of the vedic mystics***. "The symbols of the outer sacrifice are given for this purpose in the manner of the Mysteries all over the world an inner meaning; they represent a calling of the Gods into the human being, a connecting sacrifice, an intimate interchange, a mutual aid, a communion." (Foundations of Indian Culture. p 145). Sri Aurobindo also emphasizes that the work that was done in this period became the firm bedrock of India's spirituality in later ages and from it "gush still the life-giving waters of perennial never failing inspiration."

David Frawley, who is today the best Vedic specialist in the West, could not agree more: Ô Indians, your spiritual tradition, as it is encoded in the Vedas, represents the most precious treasure of the human race. Cherish it, support it, and above all share it with the entire world. For the Vedas are like a sun: in them you will find the key of all light, all life, all love and there is no individual or collective problem which cannot be solved by them (Arise Arjuna 221).

CHAPTER 3

The Influence of Indu India on the Western World

It was always thought that India was a melting pot of different influences coming from the West, either by trade or through invasions, and that she owes many of her achievements—her sciences, philosophy, or religion—to outside influences, whether it is by the way of the Aryan invasions for the Vedas, or via the Greek incursions, which are supposed to have influenced her architecture and philosophies. But more and more discoveries, both archeological and linguistic, are pointing to exactly the opposite direction: In the millenniums before Christ, it is Indian civilization which went gradually westwards (we shall not speak of its march eastwards, as there is hardly any controversy about it) and influenced the religions, the sciences and the philosophies of many of the civilizations which are considered today by the West as the cradle of its culture and thought.

3.1 The influence of the Hindus on Egypt, the Greeks and Palestine

American mathematician A. Seindenberg has demonstrated that the *Sulbasutras*, the ancient Vedic mathematics, have inspired all the mathematic sciences of the antique world from

Babylonia to Egypt and Greece. "Arithmetic equations from the *Sulbatras* were used in the observation of the triangle by the Babylonians and the theory of contraries and of inexactitude in arithmetic methods, discovered by Hindus, inspired Pythagorean mathematics," writes Seindenberg. In astronomy too, Indus were precursors: XVIIth century French astronomer Jean-Claude Bailly had already noticed that "the Hindu astronomic systems were much more ancient than those of the Greeks or even the Egyptians and the movement of stars which was calculated by the Hindus 4500 years ago, does not differ from those used today by even one minute." American Vedic specialist David Frawley has also demonstrated that the methods utilized in the building of Egyptian pyramids were also borrowed from the Hindus. "The funeral altars, for instance, he writes, which are also in the shape of pyramids, were known in the Vedic world under the name of *smasana-cit*."

What about philosophy? Hindu Shivaism seems to have had a tremendous influence in the indo-mediterranean world and reincarnated itself under different names, at different places, during Antiquity. French historian Alain Danielou noted as early as 1947 that "the Egyptian myth of Osiris seemed directly inspired from a Shivaïte story of the Puranas and that at any rate, Egyptians of those times considered that Osiris had originally come from India mounted on a bull (*nandi*), the traditional transport of Shiva." But it is mainly Greece that was most influenced by the myth of Shiva: many historians have noted that the cult of Dionysus (later known as Bacchus in the Roman world), definitely looks like an offshoot of Shivaism. Danielou thus remarks that "the Greeks were always speaking of India as the sacred territory of Dionysus and historians working under Alexander the Great clearly mention chronicles of the Puranas as sources of the myth of Dionysus."

There is also no doubt that the impact of the Vedas and subsequent Hindu scriptures, such as the Vedanta and Upanishads, was tremendous on the different philosophical sects which flourished at different times in Greece, such as the eleatic, orphic, platonician, stoic, gnostic or neoplatonician movements. We know that the Greek Demetrios Galianos had translated the Bhagavad-Gita and French philosopher and historian Roger-Pol Droit writes in his classic *L'oubli de l'Inde* (*India forgotten*) "that there is absolutely not a shadow of a doubt that the Greeks knew all about Indian philosophy." Alain Danielou quotes Clement of Alexandria who admitted that "we the Greeks have stolen to the Barbarians their philosophy." And even William Jones, the XVIIIth century linguist of British India, noted that "the analogies between Greek Pythagorean philosophy and the Sankhya school, are very obvious." German philosopher Shroeder had also remarked in his book *Pythagoras und die Inder* that nearly all the philosophical and mathematical doctrines attributed to Pythagoras are derived from India, particularly the Sankhya school.

It also seems very clear that Hinduism played an immense role in the making of Christianity, particularly the writings of the Gospel. Alain Danielou point outs that "quite a few events surrounding the birth of Christ as they are related in the Gospels, are strangely similar to Buddhist and Krishnaite legends." And it is true that the resemblances existing between Buddhism and Christianity cannot be simple coincidences. Buddhism was flourishing in northern and north-east India during the times of Christ and there are many legends that he came to India to be enlightened (and supposedly died in Srinagar). Even if we discount these stories, there is no doubt that many Buddhist and Hindu teachers traveled to Palestine in the beginning of our era. Alain Danielou thus notes that the structure of the Christian church resembles that of the Buddhist Chaitya, that the rigorous asceticism of certain early Christian sects reminds one of jaïna practices, that the veneration of relics, or the usage of rosaries are all Hindu customs." Sri Sri Ravi Shankar, the founder of the Art of Living, which is practiced in more than eighty countries, also remarks that Jesus sometimes wore an orange robe, the Hindu symbol of renunciation in the world, which was not a usual practice in Judaism. "In the same way, he continues, the worshipping of the Virgin Mary in Catholicism is probably borrowed from the Hindu cult of Devi." Bells too, which cannot be found today in synagogues, the temples of Judaism, are used in churches and we all know their importance in Buddhism and Hinduism for thousands of years. There are many other similarities between Hinduism and Christianity: incense, sacred bread (*Prasadam*), the different altars around churches (which recall the manifold deities in their niches inside Hindu temples); reciting the rosary (*japamala*), the Christian Trinity (the ancient *Sanatana Dharma*: Brahma, Vishnu and Mahesh), Christian processions, the sign of the cross (*Anganyasa*) etc...

This Buddhist and Hindu influences started worrying later Christians: Saint Hyppolitus is know to have treated Brahmans of "heretics" and later, Saint Gregory even destroyed himself some of the pagan Gods of a colony of Hindus who had settled on the river Tigris.

3.2. The Secret Links between Hindus and Celts

India often exercises a fascination on French people, which is strange, as not only huge distances separate both countries, but also their cultures are utterly dissimilar. Yet, points out Guy Deleury, a French historian specialist of India, there is no doubt that quite a few Hindu tribes (the Gypsies being the remnants of one of them), emigrated westwards, about two millenniums before Christ, through Iran, Greece and Eastern Europe, to finally reach western Europe and the Celtic domains of Gaul and Ireland. "There was a time, which cannot be yet exactly determined with precision, writes Deleury, when Celtic and Vedic tribes lived together and blended their customs."

And it is true that the similarities between the two cultures are striking: both Celts and Gauls utilized the same chariots and both described them in the same poetic terms, as the chariot to them was not only an instrument of war, but also an occult symbol of spiritual progress:

The four directions of the earth are the four horses of the Gods
Earth and sky the two flanks of the horse;
The seasons, the reins; the intermediary space, the harness;
The year is the chariot; the cycle is the caisson of the chariot.
Indra is the warrior, the moon the charioteer ...

(Atharva Veda)

Compare this to an old Celtic ballad:

As the spokes of a chariot's wheel,
Everything is in the Breath:
Hymns and melodies, rituals,
The power of the priests and the force of the warrior...

Deleury also notes that in Sanskrit the chariot of war is called *Ratha*, while the Gallic name is *Reda*, which is found in the name of a famous Gallic tribe, the *Redones* and survives today in the name of *Rennes*, a French town which used to be the capital of *Bretagne*, where Celtic culture flourished in the first millennium before Christ. The prefix *red* is also found in the Latin name for the horse: *paraveredus*, *palefroi* in French, *pferd* in

German, or in the name of a famous Gallic chieftain who fought Cesar: *Eporedorix*. We also know that the name *Ann* is an ancient Shivaite name and that the Celtic legends of Saint Ann seem derived from Shivaite stories. British Professor Calvert Watkins has also shown that ancient Celtic versification, such as the one used in the Ballad of the four sons of *Cu'Shorbb*, has the same metric rhythm than Vedic poetry. "All French history books, concludes Deleury, should quote some of the Vedic chants of which we know many thousands and which bear an important part in the making of the Gallic ethos of today."

3.3 Hindu Influence on Western Civilization

Western philosophy and culture trace its sources to ancient Greece ... which in turn was greatly influenced by Hinduism. Famous Indianist Jean Herbert reminds us that "many many centuries before us, India had devised most of the philosophical systems which Europe experienced with later. They contained, at least in its essence, the philosophy of the Greeks, the Alexandrine mystique, the religious speculation of the Middle Ages, the rationalism of the XIXth century and even the most recent incarnations of modern pantheism." In 1782, already, French philosopher Pierre Sonnerat had written: "Ancient India gave to the world its religions and philosophies: Egypt and Greece owe India their wisdom and it is known that Pythagoras went to India to study under Brahmins, who were the most enlightened of human beings."

But it is in XIXth century Europe that an open admiration for ancient India's culture flourished best, particularly in Germany, where philosophers, such a Frederich Shlegel, y said that "there is no language in the world, even Greek, which has the clarity and the philosophical precision of Sanskrit," adding "that India is not only at the origin of everything, she is superior in everything, intellectually, religiously or politically—and even the Greek heritage seems pale in comparison...." The great Shopenhauer agrees with him and writes in the preface of his "*The World as a Will and as a Representation*": "According to me, the influence of Sanskrit literature on our time will not be lesser than what was in the XVIth century Greece's influence on Renaissance. One day, India's wisdom will flow again on Europe and will totally transform our knowledge and thought." And Nietzsche himself had read the Vedas, which he admired profoundly, could quote from the Law of Manu and thought that "Buddhism and Brahmanism are a hundred times deeper and more objective than Christianity."

France itself had in the XIXth century a great India-tradition. Anquetil-Duperron had translated the Upanishads in 1801, Eugene Burnouf published in 1844 an *Introduction to Indian Buddhism* and it is in Paris that was created the first Chair of Sanskrit in Europe. Schools and universities were teaching Indian philosophy and famous writers and philosophers, such as Edgar Quinet, Ernest Renan, Hippolyte Taine, or Charles Renouvier, were devoting pages and pages to India. One of the last great French Romantics, the remarkable historian Michelet, wrote: "From India comes to us a torrent of light, a river of Right and Reason...."

3.4. The forgetting of India

When Nietzsche collapsed in January 1889, the India of philosophy, of the Vedas and spirituality, seems to disappear with him from the consciousness of Europeans and the references to Indian culture disappear gradually from all schools and universities. Since then, Europe (and the United States) practice what French philosopher and journalist Roger-Pol Droit calls "helleno-centrism" (Greece-centered) education, which means that the West believes that all philosophical systems started with Greece and that there was nothing worth the name before them. In his a remarkable book mentioned ealier, *L'oubli de l'Inde (the forgetting of India*) Droit explains the reasons of this "intellectual amnesia." Firstly, he says, the great responsible for this forgetting of India is German philosopher Hegel. "Hegel, he writes, did not discover the Greeks, he *created* them and made up for them a destiny and thoughts which they did not always have." And it is true that it is Hegel who immortalized the myth that the Spirit of Europe, her philosophy and her history are eternally rooted in Greece. But Hegel had much more words for India: "As to the Indians, he wrote, their life and thoughts are solely an opium of foolish superstitions, which explain their utterly lethargic and dazed appearance...."

But the two main culprits for this forgetting of India in Europe are the British colonizers and the Christian missionaries. How could the English, they who had come to civilize the Barbarians, admit that their very culture was derived from these very savages? And how could the missionaries, they who had come to bring the True God to the Pagans, admit that their own religion was influenced by these very heathens? And it is this neo-colonialist spirit which makes Max Mueller, the so-called Sankritist of the late XIXth century say that "The Vedas are just a mixture of jumble-mumble," or Barthelemy de Saint Hilaire the Education Minister of the French Government of 1883, declare "that the Hindu system of thought is hideous, without any intellectual rigor and coherence and cannot be compared with those of ancient

Greece or modern Europe." Thus, even today, one can hardly find a single reference to Indian philosophy in modern text books. "For instance, writes Roger-Pol Droit, one cannot come across a single mention, in the Dictionary of Philosophers, of the Buddhist philosopher Asanga, whose works are probably as important as those of Aristotle, nor his books can be found in libraries, while some letters that Nietzsche wrote to his mother when he was six years old, are treated as intellectual marvels."

American Indianist David Fawley considers that this breaking away between the West and the East is totally artificial and was created by Europe to prove its material and intellectual superiority. "Everything that then came from the East, he writes, took an inferior, or pagan value." And yet, we know that the European scientific spirit found its roots in Greece, whose religion was also definitely pagan and was inspired by Hindu practices. Thus he concludes: "if only the West knew that the philosophical and religious framework from which emerged later European science, partakes much more with eastern religions such as Hinduism and Buddhism, than with the Judeo-Christian tradition, they would look at India differently."

CHAPTER 4

The Wonder that «was» India

Like A.L. Basham, the author of the classic "The Wonder that was India," most Europeans have often seen at best in India an exalted civilisation of « religious » and artistic achievements. But India's greatness encompassed ALL aspects of life, from the highest to the most material, from the most mundane to the supremely spiritualised. As Sri Aurobindo emphasises: "The tendency of the West is to live from below upward and from out inward.... The inner existence is thus formed and governed by external powers. India's constant aim has been on the contrary, to find a basis of living in the higher spiritual truth and to live from the inner spirit outwards." (India's Rebirth, 109) The old Vedic seers said the same thing in a different form: "their divine foundation was above even while they stood below. Let its rays be settled deep within us."

The foundations of the Indian society were thus unique, because all the aspects of life were turned towards the spiritual. The original social system was divided in four "varnas," or four castes, which corresponded to each one's inner capacities. In turn the life of a man was separated in four ashramas. That of the student, the householder, the recluse and the yogi. The elders taught the student that "the true aim of life is to find your soul." The teaching was always on the guru-chelas principle, and the teacher being considered as a representative of God, he got profound respect and obedience from his pupils. Everything was taught to the students: art, literature, polity, the science of war, the development of the body—all this far away from the cities, in an environment of nature, conducive to inner growth, which was ecological, long before it became imperative and fashionable.

Indian society of that time was neither dry nor ascetic: it satisfied the urges, desires and needs of its ordinary people, particularly of the husband and wife -the beauty and comfort of Mohenjo-Daro is testimony to that fact. It taught them that perfection could be attained in all spheres of life, even in the art of physical love, where Indians excelled, as vouched so powerfully and artistically by Khajurao and the Kama-sutra. And when man had satisfied his external being, when he had paid his debt to society and grown into wisdom, it was time to discover the spirit and roam the width and breadth of India, which at that period was covered by forests. In time he would become a yogi, young disciples would gather around him and he would begin imparting all the knowledge, worldly and inner, gathered in a lifetime—and the cycle would thus start again. That the great majority did not go beyond the first two stages is no matter; this is the very reason why Indian society provided the system of castes, so that each one fitted in the mould his inner development warranted.

"It is on this firm and noble basis that Indian civilisation grew to maturity and became rich and splendid and unique, writes Sri Aurobindo. It lived with a noble, ample and vigorous order and freedom; it developed a great literature, sciences, arts, crafts, industries; it rose to the highest possible ideals of knowledge and culture, of arduous greatness and heroism, of kindness, philanthropy and human sympathy and oneness. It laid the inspired basis of wonderful spiritual philosophies; it examined the secret of external nature and discovered and lived the boundless and miraculous truths of the inner being; it fathomed self and understood and possessed the world...." (Foundations of Indian Culture, p.116-117) How far we are from A.L. Basham's vision of a militant Hinduism and evil Aryans, however brilliant the social and artistic civilisation he describes! For not only did the Hindus (not the Indians, but the Hindus), demonstrate their greatness in all fields of life, social, artistic, spiritual, but they had also developed a wonderful political system.

4.1 The Genius of (Hindu) Indian Politics

Another of these great prejudices with which Indians had to battle for centuries, is that whatever the spiritual, cultural, artistic, even social greatness of India, it always was disunited, except under Ashoka and some of the Mughal emperors—just a bunch of barbarian rulers, constantly fighting themselves—and that it was thanks to the Mughals and the British, that India was finally politically united. This is doing again a grave injustice to India. The Vedic sages had devised a monarchical system, whereby the king was at the top, but could be constitutionally challenged. In fact, it even allowed for men's inclination to war, but made sure that it never went beyond a certain stage, for only professional armies fought and the majority of the population remained untouched. Indeed, at no time in ancient India, were there great fratricidal wars, like those between the British and the French, or even the Protestants and the Catholics within France itself. Moreover, the system allowed for a great federalism: for instance, a long time after the Vedic fathers, the real power lay in the village panchayats. Sri Aurobindo refutes the charge (which Basham levels), that India has always shown an incompetence for any free and sound political organisation and has been constantly a divided nation. « There always was a strong democratic element in pre-Muslim India, which certainly showed a certain similarity with Western parliamentary forms, but these institutions were **INDIAN** ». The early Indian system was that of the clan, or tribal system, founded upon the equality of all members of the tribe. In the same way, the village community had its own assembly, the "visah," with only the king above this democratic body. The priests, who acted as the sacrifice makers and were poets, occultists and yogis, had no other occupation in life and their positions were thus not hereditary but depended on their inner abilities. And it was the same thing with warriors, merchants, or lower class people. "Even when these classes became hereditary, remarks Sri Aurobindo, from the king downwards to the Shudra, the predominance, say of the Brahmins, did not result in a theocracy, because the Brahmins in spite of their ever-increasing and finally predominant authority, did not and could not usurp in India the political power." (Foundations of Indian Culture p. 326). The Rishi had a peculiar place, he was the sage, born from any caste, who was often counsellor to the King, of whom he was also the religious preceptor. Later it seems that it was the Republican form of government which took over many parts of India. In some cases these "Republics" appear to have been governed by a democratic assembly and some came out of a revolution; in other cases, they seem to have had an oligarchic senate. But they enjoyed throughout India a solid reputation for the excellence of their civil administration and the redoubtable efficiency of their armies. It is to be noted that these Indian Republics existed long before the Greek ones, although the world credits the Greeks with having created democracy; but as usual History is recorded through the prism of the Western world and is very selective indeed. One should also add that none of these Indian republics developed an aggressive colonising spirit and that they were content to defend themselves and forge alliances amongst them.

But after the invasion of Alexander's armies, India felt for the first time the need to unify its forces. Thus the monarchical system was raised-up again; but once more, there was no despotism as happened in Europe until the French revolution: the Indian king did enjoy supreme power, but he was first the representative and guardian of Dharma, the sacred law; his power was not personal and there were safeguards against abuses so that he could be removed. Furthermore, although the king was a Hindu, Hinduism was never the state religion, and each cult enjoyed its liberties. Thus could the Jews and the Parsis and the Jains and the Buddhists, and even the early Christians (who abused that freedom), practised their faith in peace. Which religion in the world can boast of such tolerance?

As in a human being, a nation has a soul, which is eternal; and if this soul, this idea-force, is strong enough, it will keep evolving new forms to reincarnate itself constantly. "And a people, maintains Sri Aurobindo, who learn consciously to think always in terms of Dharma, of the eternal truth behind man, and learn to look beyond transient appearances, such as the people of India, always survives » (Foundations of Indian Culturc, p.334).

And in truth, Indians always regarded life as a manifestation of Self and the master idea that governed life, culture and social ideals of India has been the seeking of man for his inner self-everything was organised around this single goal. Thus, Indian politics, although very complex, always allowed a communal freedom for self-determination. In the last stages of the pre-Muslim period, the summit of the political structure was occupied by three governing bodies: the King in his Ministerial Council, the Metropolitan Assembly and the General Assembly of the kingdom. The members of the Ministerial Council were drawn from all castes. Indeed the whole Indian system was founded upon a close participation of all the classes; even the Shudra had his share in the civic life. Thus the Council had a fixed number of Brahmin, Kshatrya, Vaishya and Shudra representatives, with the Vaishya having a greater preponderance. And in turn, each town, each village, had its own Metropolitan Civic Assembly allowing a great amount of autonomy. Even the great Ashoka was defeated in his power tussle with his Council and he had practically to abdicate.

It is this system which allowed India to flower in an unprecedented way, to excel perhaps as no other nation had done before her, in all fields, be it literature, architecture, sculpture, or painting and develop great civilisations, one upon the other and one upon the other, each one more sumptuous, more grandiose, more glittering than the previous one.

4.2. The Greatest (Hindu) Literature ?

Basham feels that "much of Sanskrit literature is dry and monotonous, or can only be appreciated after a considerable effort of the imagination" (Wonder that Was India, page 401), which shows a total misunderstanding of the greatness of the genius of that « Mother of all languages ». Sri Aurobindo evidently disagrees with him: "the ancient and classical literature of the Sanskrit tongue shows both in quality and in body an abundance of excellence, in their potent originality and force and beauty, in their substance and art and structure, in grandeur and justice and charm of speech, and in the heightened width of the reach of their spirit which stands very evidently in the front rank among the world's great literatures." (Foundations of Indian Culture p. 255)

Four masterpieces seem to embody India's genius in literature: the Vedas, the Upanishads, the Ramayana, the Mahabharata. As seen earlier, the Vedas represent "a creation of an early and intuitive and symbolic mentality" (Foundations of Indian Culture, p.260). It was only because the Vedic rishis were careful to clothe their spiritual experiences in symbols, so that only the initiated would grasp them, that their meaning has escaped us, particularly after they got translated in the last two centuries. "The Veda is the **WORD** discovering truth and clothing in image and symbol, the mystic significance of life," wrote again Sri Aurobindo. (India's Rebirth, p.95)

As to the Upanishads, asserts the Sage from Pondichery, "they are the supreme work of the Indian mind, that of the highest self-expression of genius, its sublimest poetry, its greatest creation of the thought and word ... a large flood of spiritual revelation..." (Foundations of Indian Culture p.269). The Upanishads are Philosophy, Religion and Poetry blended together. They record high spiritual experiences, are a treaty of intuitive philosophy and show an extraordinary poetic rhythm. It is also a book of ecstasy: an ecstasy of luminous knowledge, of fulfilled experience, « a book to express the wonder and beauty of the rarest spiritual self-vision and the profoundest illumined truth of Self and God and the Universe », writes Sri Aurobindo (Found. of Indian Culture, 269). The problem is that the translations do not render the beauty of the original text, because these masterpieces have been misunderstood by foreign translators, who only strive to bring out the intellectual meaning without grasping the soul contents of it and do not perceive the ecstasy of the seer "seeing" his experiences.

But without doubt, it is the Mahabarata and the Ramayana, which are dearest to all Indians, even today. Both the Mahabarata and the Ramayana are epical, in the spirit as well as the purpose. The Mahabarata is on a vast scale, maybe unsurpassed even today, the epic of the soul and tells a story of the ethics of India of that time, its social, political and cultural life. It is, notes Sri Aurobindo, "the expression of the mind of a nation, it is the poem of itself written by a whole nation.... A vast temple unfolding slowly its immense and complex idea from chamber to chamber" (Foundations of Indian Culture, p 287). More than that even, it is the **HISTORY OF DHARMA**, of deva against asura, the strife between divine and titanic forces. You find on one side, a civilisation founded on Dharma, and on the other, beings who are embodiments of asuric egoism and misuse of Dharma. It is cast in the mould of tales, legends, anecdotes, telling stories of philosophical, religious, social, spiritual values: « as in Indian architecture, there is the same power to embrace great spaces in a total view and the same tendency to fill them with an abundance of minute, effective, vivid and significant detail ». (Foundations of Indian Culture, p 288).

The Baghavad Gita must be the supreme work of spiritual revelation in the whole history of our human planet, for it is the most comprehensive, the most revealing, the highest in its intuitive reach. No religious book ever succeeded to say nearly everything that needs to be known on the mysteries of human life: why death, why life, why suffering? why fighting, why duty? Dharma, the supreme law, the duty to one's soul, the adherence to truth, the faithfulness to the one and only divine reality which pertains all things in matter and spirit. « Such then is the divine Teacher of the Gita, the eternal Avatar, the Divine who has descended into human consciousness, the Lord seated within the heart of all beings, He who guides from behind the veil all our thought and action ». (Sri Aurobindo; Essays on the Gita, page 17)

The Ramayana's inner genius does not differ from the Mahabharata's, except by a greater simplicity of plan, a finer glow of poetry maybe. It seems to have been written by a single hand, as there is no deviation from story to story.... But it is, remarks Sri Aurobindo, "like a vastness of vision, an even more winged-flight of epic in the conception and sustained richness of minute execution in the detail (289). For Indians, the Ramayana embodies the highest and most cherished ideals of manhood, beauty, courage, purity, gentleness. The subject is the same as in the Mahabharata: the struggle between the forces of light and darkness; but the setting is more imaginative, supernatural and there is an intensification of the characters in both their goodness and evil. As in the Mahabharata too, we are shown the ideal man with his virtues of courage, selflessness, virtue and spiritualised mind. The asuric forces have a near cosmic dimension of super-human egoism and near divine violence, as the chased angels of the Bible possessed after them. « The poet makes us conscious of the immense forces that are behind our life and sets his action in a magnificent epic scenery, the great imperial city, the mountains and the ocean, the forest and wilderness, described with such largesse as to make us feel that the whole world were the scene of his poem and its subject the whole divine and titanic possibility of man, imagined in a few great or monstrous figures ». (Found of Indian Culture page 290)

Does India's literary genius end with the Ramayana? Not at all. It would take too long here to jot down all the great figures of Indian literature and this is not a literary treatise. But we may mention Kalidasa, whose poetry was imitated by all succeeding generations of poets, who tried to copy the perfect and harmoniously designed model of his poetry. The Puranas and the Tantras, « which contain in themselves, writes Sri Aurobindo, the highest spiritual and philosophical truths, while embodying them in forms that are able to carry something of them to the popular imagination and feeling by way of legend, tale, symbols, miracles and parables » (Found of Indian Culture P.312). The Vaishnava poetry, which sings the cry of the soul for God, as incarnated by the love stories of Radha and Krishna, which have struck forever Indian popular imagination, because they symbolise the nature in man seeking for the Divine soul through love. Valmiki, also moulded the Indian mind with his depiction of Rama and Sita, another classic of India's love couples and one that has survived through the myth of enduring worship, in the folklore of this country, along with the popular figures of Hanuman and Laksmanan. "His diction, remarks Sri Aurobindo, is shaped in the manner of the direct intuitive mind as earlier expressed in the Upanishads."

But Indian literature is not limited to Sanskrit or Pali. In Tamil, Tiruvalluvar, wrote the highest ever gnomic poetry, perfect in its geometry, plan and force of execution. In Hindi, Tulsidas, is a master of lyric intensity and the sublimity of epic imagination. In Marathi, Ramdas, poet, thinker, yogi, deals with the birth and awakening of a whole nation, with all the charm and the strength of a true bhakti. In Bengal, there is Kashiram, who retold in simple manner the Mahabharata and the Ramayana, accompanied by Tulsidas who did the same thing in Hindi and who managed to combine lyric intensity, romantic flight of imagination, while retaining the original sublimity of the story. One cannot end this short retrospective without mentioning Chaitanya, Nanak, Kabir, Mirabai.... All these remarkable writers have often baffled the Western mind, which could never understand the greatness of Indian literature, forgetting that in India everything was centred around the spiritual.

4.3 Indian Art: Turned Towards the Essential

"The highest business of Indian art has always been to describe something of the Self, of the soul, contrary to Western art, which either harps at the superficially beautiful or dwells at the vital-unconscious level." (Sri Aurobindo. Foundations of Indian Culture p.208)

This is indeed the great difference between Indian art and other art forms. For the Indian artist first visualises in his inner being the truth of the element he wants to express and creates it in his intuitive mind, before externalising it. Stories of how Indian sculptors of ancient times used to meditate for one year before starting on their particular work, are common. Not the idea of the intellect or mental imagination, but the essence, the emotion, the spirit. Thus, for the Indian artist, material forms, colour, line, design, are only physical means of expression, **NOT** his first preoccupation. So he will not attempt, as in Western art, which in its heydays continuously recreated scenes of Christ's life or that of saints, to reconstitute some scene of Buddha's life, but instead, he will endeavor to **REVEAL** the calm of Nirvana. And every accessory is an aid, a **MEANS** to do so. "for here spirit carries the form, while in western art, form carries whatever they think is spirit." (Foundations p.211)

In effect, Indian art, its architecture for instance, demands an inner eye to be appreciated, otherwise its truth will not reveal itself. Great temples in India are an architectural expression of an ancient spiritual culture. Its many varied forms express the manifestation of the infinite multiplicity which fills the oneness of India. And indeed even the Moslem architecture was taken up by India's creative genius and transformed into something completely Indian.

Indian sculpture also springs from spiritual insight and it is unique by *its total absence of ego*. Very few of India's sculptures masterpieces are signed for instance; they are rather the work of a collective genius whose signature could be "INDIA." "Most ancient sculptures of India embody in visible form what the Upanishads threw out into inspired thought and the Mahabaratha and the Ramayana portrayed by the word in life," observes Sri Aurobindo (Foundations, p.230). The Gods of Indian sculpture are cosmic beings, embodiments of some great spiritual power. And every movement, hands, eyes, posture, conveys an INNER meaning, as in the Natarajas for example. Sri Aurobindo admired particularly the Kalasanhara Shiva, about which he said: « it is supreme, not only by the majesty, power, calmly forceful controlled dignity and kinship of existence which the whole spirit and pose visibly incarnates ... but much more by the concentrated divine passion of the spiritual overcoming of time and existence which the artist has succeeded in putting into eye and brow and mouth ... (Foundations P. 233)

Indian painting, has unfortunately been largely erased by time, as in the case of the Ajanta caves. It even went through an eclipse and was revived by the Mughal influence. But what remains of Indian paintings show the immensity of the work and the genius of it. The paintings that have mostly survived from ancient times are those of the Buddhist artists; but painting in India was certainly pre-Buddhist. Indeed in ancient

India, there were six "limbs," six essential elements "sadanga" to a great painting: The first is "rupabheda," distinction of forms; the second is "pramana," arrangement of lines; the third is "bhava," emotion of aesthetic feelings; the fourth is "lavanya," seeking for beauty; the fifth is "sadrsya," truth of the form; and the sixth is "varnikashanga," harmony of colours. Western art always flouts the first principle "rupabheda," the universal law of the right distinction of forms, for it constantly strays into intellectual or fantasy extravagances which belong to the intermediate world of sheer fantasia. On the other hand in the Indian paintings. Sri Aurobindo remarks that: "the Indian artist sets out from the other end of the scale of values of experience which connect life and the spirit. The whole creative force here comes from a spiritual and psychic vision, the emphasis of the physical is secondary and always deliberately limited so as to give an overwhelmingly spiritual and psychic impression and everything is suppressed which does not serve this purpose." (Foundations, p.246). It is unfortunate that today most Indian painting imitates Western modern art, bare for a few exceptions. And it is hoped that Indian painters will soon come back to the essential, which is the vision of the inner eye, the transcription, not of the religious, but of the spiritual and the occult.

4.4 THE GREAT CIVILISATIONS

It is upon this great and lasting foundations, cultural, artistic, social and political, that India, Mother India, Sanatana Dharma, produced many wonderful periods. We are not here to make an historical review of them; a few of their glorious names will suffice, for with them still rings the splendour and towering strength of the eternal spirit of the Vedic fathers....

The Kashi kingdom of Benares, which was founded upon the cult of Shiva and was the spiritual and cultural capital of India, was, we are told, a great show of refinement and beauty, and that at least ten centuries before Christ was born, according to conservative estimates. Remember that Gautama the Buddha preached his first sermon in the suburbs of Benares at Sarnat. « Kashi, eulogises Alain Danielou, was a kind of Babylon, a sacred city, a centre of learning, of art and pleasures, the heart of Indian civilisation, whose origins were lost in prehistoric India and its kings ruled over a greater part of northern and even southern India ».

We may also mention the Gandhara kingdom, which included Peshawar, parts of Afghanistan, Kashmir and was thus protecting India from invasions, as Sri Aurobindo points out: « the historic weakness of the Indian peninsula has always been until modern times its vulnerability through the North-western passes. This weakness did not exist as long as ancient India extended northward far beyond the Indus and the powerful kingdoms of Gandhara and Vahlika presented a firm bulwark against foreign invasion ». (Found. 373)

But soon these kingdoms collapsed and Alexander's armies marched into India, the first foreign invasion of the country, if one discounts the Aryan theory. Henceforth, all the theoricians and politicians thought about the unifying of India and this heralded the coming of the first great Emperor: Chandra Gupta, who vanquished the remnants of Alexander's armies and assimilated some of the Greek civilisation's great traits. Thus started the mighty Mauryan empire, which represents the first effort at unifying India politically. A little of that time is known through the Arthashastra of Kautilya, or Chanakya, Minister of Chandragupta, who gives us glimpses of the conditions and state organisation of that time. Chandragupta, who was the founder of the Maurya dynasty, came from a low caste, liberated Punjab from the Greeks and managed to conquer the whole of the Indian subcontinent except for the extreme South. The administrative set-up of Chandragupta was so efficient that later the Muslims and the English retained it, only bringing here and there a few superficial modifications. Chandragupta in true Indian tradition renounced the world during his last years and lived as an anchorite at the feet of the jain saint Bhadrabahu in Shravanabelagola, near Mysore. Historians, such as Alain Danielou, label Chanakya and Chandragupta's rule as Machiavellian: «It was, writes Danielou, a centralised despotism, resting on military power and disguised into a constitutional monarchy ». (Histoire de l'Inde p. 114) This again is a very westernised view of post-vedic India, which cannot conceive that Hindustan could have devised constitutional monarchy before the Europeans.

And Sri Aurobindo obviously disagrees: « The history of this empire, its remarkable organisation, administration, public works, opulence, magnificent culture and the vigour, the brilliance, the splendid fruitfulness of life of the peninsula under its shelter, ranks among the greatest constructed and maintained by the genius of earth's great peoples. India has n o reason, from this point of view, to be anything but proud of her ancient achievement in empire-building or to surrender to the hasty verdict that denies to her antique civilisation a strong practical genius or high political virtue (Found. 373)

In the South the Andhras were dominating from Cape Comorin to the doors of Bombay. Then came the Pallavas, who were certainly one of the most remarkable dynasties of medieval India. The first Pallavas appeared near Kanchi in the 3rd century, but it is only with king Simhavishnu that they reached their peak. Simhavishnu conquered the Chera, the Cholas, the Pandya dynasties of the South and annexed Ceylon. It is to this period that belong the magnificent frescoes of Mahabalipuram which have survived until today. During the Pallavas' rule, great cities such as Kanchi flourished, busy ports like Mahabalipuram sprang-up, and arts blossomed under all its forms. So did the sanskrit language, which went through a great revival period and the dravidian architecture style of Southern India, famous for its mandapams, which has passed down, from generation to generation until today. The Bhakti movement, also developed in South India during the Pallavas and it gave a new orientation to Hinduism.

At the same time, the dynasty of the Vardhamana was establishing his might in the Centre of India. Founded by King Pushyabhuti, « who had acquired great spiritual powers by the practice of shivaite tantrism », writes Jean Danielou, it reached its peak under king Harsha, who, starting with Bengal and Orissa, conquered what is today UP, Bihar, extending his empire northwards towards Nepal and Kashmir and southwards to the Narmada river. Jean danielou feels « that King Harsha symbolised all that was right in Hindu monarchy, wielding an absolute power, but each sphere of administration was enjoying a large autonomy and the villages were functioning like small republics ». The Chinese traveller, Hiuen Tsang, another admirer of Harsha, writes that he was an untiring man, just and courageous, constantly surveying all parts of his kingdom.

India's influence was then at its highest, her culture and religions expanded all the way to Burma, Cambodia, Siam, Ceylon and in the other direction to the Mecca, where Shiva's black lingam was revered by Arabians.

But In 570 AD, the Prophet Mohammed was born and by the year 632, a few years before the death of King Harsha, the Muslim invasions started overtaking India, wave after destructive wave.

CHAPTER 5

Islam and the Muslim Invasions

5.1 An apology of Islam

Before going into the Muslim invasions in India, it would be worthwhile to cast a sympathetic look at Islam: why it sprang-up; how it immediately went out in the world with a missionary zeal, unsurpassed in the history of religions; its genius, its beauty, its relevance today; but also the limitations and drawbacks of the world's most militant faith. These are questions best answered by Muslims themselves, although the author does not necessarily agree with all the views expounded here.

Why Islam? Islam was a cry against the tortured atmosphere of Christianity, an answer to its perpetual ethos of suffering and its propensity to nail its saviours on the cross. Christianity is the first enemy of Islam, although in a sense, both religions are complementary.

Why did Europeans succeed in stopping the Arab onslaught, while at the same time Arabs managed to enter India again and again and again? (French King Charles Martel beat Arab armies in 732 in Poitiers, 300 kms away from Paris. If this battle has been lost, the whole of Europe, might have been Muslim today)

Because the Kshatryia class had become weak. The warriors of India had become arrogant, degenerate in their clinging to power and the true spirit of the Kshatriyas had been lost for the centuries to come, except in a few Rajput, Sikh or Mahrattis, like Shivaji. But the Arabs were khsatriyas: they were fired by the zeal to do Allah's work, unafraid of death. They were a young warrior class.

But why this extraordinary ferocity of Arabs in India?

This brutal zeal to conquer, this militancy to convert by the scimitar is « Jihad », holy war. It is the giving of oneself to the expansion of the Infinite, Allah, the only one. There is also a beauty in that kind of violence.

What is the genius of Islam? Islam does not kill the soul of a country. It assimilates its culture, as it did in India; take the zero for instance, which was invented by Hindus: Arabs took it up, developed it and made of it a full-fledged mathematics system, which from India travelled all through the Arab empire and reached Europe, thanks to Arab colonisation. Or take the Advaita, which they blended with Islam and transformed into Sufism, probably the most enlightened, mystical branch of Islam. You know, each Muslim has a direct contact with his God, each one is a servant of god and there are no intermediaries like in Hinduism with its idols and gods. **It is a religion of the individual, for the individual**; each one can thus lead prayers and become in effect a mullah; thus there is no Brahmin class in Islam, no monasteries, no churches. And this is what makes it so popular in the 20th century, why so many Muslims and non-Muslims, disillusioned with western society and its evils are going back to the fundamentals of Islam. *What is the strength of Islam?*

Islam is a religion of force, it is in the Arab temperament, borne out of the hardship and beauty of the desert and its nomad life. Muslims are devout soldiers; their savagery is not gratuitous, it is the fire of Allah which burns in them. Not the meekness of the Buddhist, which opened India to invasions;

not the guiltiness of the Christians which has hampered all western civilisation, **but the spirit of might**.

Why did Islam crush Hinduism so mercilessly?

Hindus adore images and stone Gods and it makes them the number one enemy of Islam. For did not the Prophet say: « thou shalt not worship stone idols »? Thus Arabs, when they invaded India, did not feel guilty when they killed Hindus; on the contrary, it was an obligation, a holy duty.

Why the hardening of Islam today, the harping on returning to the shariat, which seems maladjusted to today's modern world ?

It is the refusal by the Muslim world to be swallowed by the grey uniform, soul-killing materialism of the West. The unconscious fear of losing one's Muslim identity in the face of the onslaught of the modern, atheist world. Even the burqua is a returning to a fundamental that have baffled all religion: the mystery of the woman, its destabilising effects on men. Hindus themselves forbid women in certain temples; or consider them impure when they are menstruating; or even do not allow them to read the Veda. Why should Islam be judged on the Burqa issue? It may be something that shocks the West, but Islam is not the burqa alone! And look at what happened in the West with the liberalisation of women: it led to the break-up of the family system and brought in a perverse sexuality. And finally, which is better: wearing a burqa while maintaining one's identity, or finishing as a servant in some western bourgeois home with no dignity left?

Moreover, Muslims all over the world feel they are attacked from every corner, whether in Bosnia, Kashmir, Palestine, or Chechnya. And this leads to an entrenched paranoia.

What are the qualities of Islam today? Charity first and foremost. Contrary to the Hindus, who although they are generous people individually, are not concerned by the welfare of their less fortunate brethren—witness the abject poverty in India—Islam cares for their own. It is enough for a Muslim to say « Salam u alli kum » anywhere in the world and be treated like a brother, fed, clothed and sometimes helped financially. They all belong to the **Ouma**, the great universal Muslim brotherhood. Also the pure of Islam do not smoke, do not take drugs, do not drink alcohol; and this also encourages Muslims leaders all over the world to reimpose the shariat in their countries. After all, if India imposes dry law in some of her states, nobody has anything to says. Islam does it in the name of Allah instead of that of N.T. Rama Rao!

The motto of Islam?

You deal with your material life as if you're going to live eternally; and with your spiritual life as if you are going to die tomorrow».

The best of Islam today?

Without doubt the great mosque of Casablanca, completed in the early nineties, symbolises what is most luminous in Islam today and stands as an example of a Muslim nation which has (so far) managed to retain the positive qualities of Islam, while adapting itself to the western world.

Each artisan has recreated the splendour of ancient Muslim handicrafts: sculpture, paintings, marble inlay... It's a people's work; every Moroccan has contributed money, however small an amount, for the finishing of the mosque; it is thus a collective work which embodies all the love of beauty inherent in Islam and its moderation. There, after having washed oneself, one can in pray in an atmosphere of peace.

What Islam borrowed from Hinduism?

Sufism of course, which adopted some of the beauty of Indu India. Mogol architecture, which retained the perfect symmetry of Muslim linear design, while achieving infinite humanity. Hindustan music, enchanting to the ear.... But overall, above everything, Islam in India borrowed the **Shakti** concept of Hinduism. Look at the Islamic countries surrounding India today. They are all governed by women! Is it not a proof that deep inside him, the Bangladeshi or the Pakistani (or the Sri Lankan for that matter), are still worshipers of the eternal shakti principle: « without her you do not manifest ». Is it not also proof that deep at heart they are still Indians, Indus?

About Indian Muslims

They can never really be integrated to India, because the philosophy of Islam the essence of its message is in **total contradiction with what Hinduism represents.** Nevertheless, they are there to stay

About Pakistan.

Pakistan embodies the fundamental contradiction of the subcontinent, for it symbolises the fact that Islam always refused to be synthesised synthesized, absorbed, transmuted by Hinduism as all other religions in India were over a period of time, whether Christianity, Buddhism or Jainism. But Pakistan also prepares the future greatness of India, because the day where the two nations are reunited they will stand as individual entities, with their own culture, own religion; own soul. But for that, Pakistan and Bangladesh will have to recognise their fundamental « Indianness ».

The limitations of Islam?

This is the profession of faith of a Muslim: « I certify that there is no other God than Allah, of whom Mohammed is the only prophet » Which means in effect: « After (and before) Mohammed, there is nobody else, no more avatars ». Thus the whole religion of Islam is based on a **negation**: nobody but us, no other religion but ours. And if you disagree, you shall die ».

The 11th September attack on the World Trade Center in New York are nothing but an expression of that strong belief This puts a serious limitation to tolerance and from this strong belief sprang sprang all the horrors of the Muslim invasions of India.

5.2 Why the Muslim Invasions of India ?

Nobody will ever be able to estimate the incredible damage done to the Hindu culture, civilisation, human population and environment, during the Muslim invasions which spanned nearly ten centuries. But it should be interesting to see why these invasions happened, for no civilisation, if its inner core is strong and dynamic, can be trampled upon so mercilessly, as the Arabs trampled India. What ever happened to that great Vedic culture, which gave birth to so many wonderful dynasties, which in turn devised illustrious democratic systems and whose Kshatriyas were supposed to protect the land of Bharat against barbarian invaders?

Since the beginning of Human History, all civilisations have gone through the same cycle: birth-rise-peak maturity-decline-death. And so many great civilisations are no more but in the memories of our text-books: Mesopotamia; Egypt; Rome; Great Africa; Greece.... Yet, because of its extraordinary spirituality, because of the Dharma stored by its great Rishis, India always had the extra impetus to renew itself, to spring forward again, when it seemed she was on the brink of collapsing. It blossomed thus for at least five millenniums, more than any other civilisation before or ever after. Then India started faltering and Alexander was able to invade her sacred soil and later the Arabs raped her beloved land. Why?

Buddhists believe that each nation, like the human soul, packs karma in each of its lives or cycles. Good karma or Bad karma have one unique characteristics: they are like a tiny seed, bearing their fruits ages or cycles later, often giving the impression to the ignorant mind of total injustice done to innocent souls. Thus the individual who seems to suffer unfair circumstances in this life, may be paying for a bad karma done dozens of lives ago. In the same manner, a nation which appears to suffer inexplicable hardships: persecution, earthquakes, great natural catastrophes, dictatorships, may be amending for a karma accomplished centuries ago. The Tibetan people's plight seems to be a good example of this phenomenon. Here is one of the most harmless, peaceful, adorable culture on earth, spiritualised on top of that, who suffered and is still suffering the worst ignominies at the hands of the Chinese communists, who have eradicated their culture, razed to the ground hundreds of ancient and marvellous temples, killed either directly or indirectly—concentration camps, torture, famine—more than one million of this adorable people! Why? **WHY**? The Dalai-Lama, himself, one of the last great spiritual figures of this era, admits that it was because of an ancient "black karma," bad deeds. Was it feudalism? Was it not opening itself to the world for so long? Or misuse of Tantrism? Who knows and who can judge? But it's a good bet to say that there is probably **NO** total injustice in this world. Everything springs from a *mathematical*, ultra-logical system, where one gets the *exact* reward one deserves, which bears **NO** moral connotation like in Christianity.

Thus for India, the Muslims invasions and later the European ones, must be the result of a bad karma. But the difference with Tibet, is that India's soul is so strong, so old, so vibrant, that she has managed so far to survive the terrible Muslims onslaughts and later the more devious British soul-stifling occupation.

There seemed to be two reasons for the decline of Indian civilisation. The foremost is that in India, Spirit failed Matter. At some point, Her yogis started withdrawing more and more in their caves, Her gurus in their ashrams, Her sannyasins in their forests. Thus slowly, a great *tamas* overtook matter, an immense negligence towards the material, an intense inertia set in, which allowed for the gradual degradation of the physical, a slackening of the down to earth values, an indifference towards the worldly, which in turn permitted successive invasions, from Alexander to the Muslim and finally the European, the rape the land of the Vedas.

The second reason and the one which has been most commonly invoked, including by Muslim apologists—see beginning of this chapter—because is it so obvious, is the fossilisation of the caste system and the gradual take-over of India by an arrogant Brahmin and kshatriya society. What used to be a natural arrangement—a Kshatriya became a warrior to express heroic tendencies in him developed from countless births on earth—turned-out to be an inherited legacy, which was not merited by chivalrous deeds. A Brahmin who used to deserve his status by his scholarship and piety, and was twice-born in the spiritual sense, just inherited the charge from his father. And the shudras were relegated to a low status, doing the menial chores, when in their heyday, they fulfilled an indispensable role, which granted them recognition from the king himself. Thus Hindu religion lost its immense plasticity, which allowed her to constantly renew herself—and India became ripe for invasions.

And finally, Buddhism and its creed of non-violence, however beautiful and noble, opened India's gates wide. Buddhists forgot the eternal principle of the Gita: « protecting one's country from death, rape, mass slaughter, is « dharma »;

and the violence you then perform is not only absolved, karma-free, but it also elevates you.

5.3 The Muslim invasions of India

Let it be said right away: the massacres perpetuated by Muslims in India are unparalleled in history, bigger than the Holocaust of the Jews by the Nazis; or the massacre of the Armenians by the Turks; more extensive even than the slaughter of the South American native populations by the invading Spanish and Portuguese.

We shall quote from the French historian Alain Danielou, as well as the Dutch scholar Koenraad Elst who has written a very interesting book called "Negationism in India (see next chapter), and finally from Sri Aurobindo, who was one of the very few amongst Indian revolutionaries, who had the courage to say the truth about what was called then « the Mahomedan factor ».

"From the time when Muslims started arriving, around 632 AD, remarks Alain Danielou, the history of India becomes a long monotonous series of murders, massacres, spoliations, destructions. It is, as usual, in the name of "a holy war" of their faith, of their sole God, that the Barbarians have destroyed civilisations, wiped-out entire races. Mahmoud Ghazni, continues Danielou, was an early example of Muslim ruthlessness, burning in 1018 of the temples of Mathura, razing Kanauj to the ground and destroying the famous temple of Somnath, sacred to all Hindus. His successors were as ruthless as Ghazini: in 1030 the holy city of Benares was razed to the ground, its marvellous temples destroyed, its magnificent palaces wrecked. Indeed, the Muslim policy "vis à vis" India, concludes Danielou, seems to have been a conscious systematic destruction of everything that was beautiful, holy, refined." (Histoire de l'Inde, p.222)

In the words of another historian, American Will Durant:

"the Islamic conquest of India is probably the bloodiest story in history. It is a discouraging tale, for its evident moral is that civilisation is a precious good, whose delicate complex order and freedom can at any moment be overthrown by barbarians invading from without and multiplying within."

But more horror was to come, for without any doubt the bloodiest Muslim deeds in India were done from the 14th century onwards, thanks to the Mughals, who today have been nearly raised to the ranks of great art patrons and benevolent rulers, bringing to India such treasures as the art of miniature painting, ghazals and Sufism.

For instance, Danielou points out that the sack of the magnificent city of Vijayanagar, which was like an island of civilisation, chivalry, and beauty, in the midst of a shattered and bleeding India, by Husain Nizam Shah, was an horror: "During nearly **FIVE** months, reminisces Danielou, the Muslims set themselves to the task of destroying everything, the temples, the palaces, the magnificent residences. The scenes of terror and massacre were unparalleled and mightier than the imagination can ever fathom. The victors grabbed so much richness in gold, jewels, precious furniture, camels, tents, girls, boys, slaves, weapons, armours, that there was not a single plain soldier who did not depart a rich man. And nothing remained after their departure of the most beautiful and prosperous city of that time, but smoking ruins." (Histoire de l'Inde, p.251)

Babur was another ferocious conqueror, indulging in unnecessary massacres and his ultimate goal was the destruction and the enslaving of the Hindus. His successor, Sher Khan, was no better, ravaging Punjab, betraying his word to the

Rajputs of Malwa, who were all massacred one by one after they had honourably surrendered. Women and children were killed by the Rajput themselves, knowing what would happen to them if they fell in Muslims hands. As for Humayun, History has treated him well, forgetting that he too, was a staunch Muslim. Under his reign, a terrible famine ravaged India, people were killed, erring miserably in their land. What happened to the beautiful land of Bharat, where once honey and wine flowed like an Himalayan delight?

Akbar was the exception in a sea of monsters, although he had his preceptor Bairam, and the regent Adam Khan killed, and was responsible for the great massacre of Chittor. In his 40 years of conquests, he too must have slaughtered his fair share of Hindus. Nevertheless, he was better than the average lot, maybe because his mother was Persian and he married Hindu wives. His intelligence, his love of arts, his interest for his people, his religious liberalism, make of him a unique emperor. Through his Rajput spouses, Akbar had a close contact with Hindu thought and he dreamed of a new religion that would be a synthesis of all creeds—and under him the Hindus were allowed some breathing space.

Unfortunately, his successors started again their policy of massacre and persecution of the Hindus. Jahangir, Akbar's son, had Guru Arjun Singh killed. Jehangir was a warped personality, "he was moved by the shivering of elephants in winter, says Danielou, but had people he disliked whipped in front of him until they died. The story of how he had Husain Beg and Abdul Aziz, two enemies, sewn in the skins of a donkey and a cow and paraded in the city, has never been forgotten." (Danielou, Histoire de l'Inde, p.269)

But the worst of the Mughal emperors must be Aurangzeb. He had his father imprisoned till the end of his life, ordered his brothers executed and his own son imprisoned for life. Aurangzeb's religious fanaticism plunged India again in chaos, famine and misery. Aurangzeb was foremost a Sunni Muslim, puritan, unbending; he had the koranic law applied in its strictest sense, chased from the court all musicians and poets, banned all Hindu religious festivals and imposed the very heavy "jizya" tax on unbelievers. He thus made once more the Mughal monarchy highly unpopular and everywhere revolts sprang-up, such as the one of the Satnamis of Alwar. "Aurangzeb had them massacred *until the last one*, leaving an entire region empty of human beings." (Danielou p. 278). Aurangzeb also battled the Sikhs and the Rajpouts. But it's against the great Mahrattas, who spearheaded a Hindu renaissance in India, that Aurangzeb was most ferocious: he had Shambuji, Shivaji's son and his Minister Kavi-Kulash tortured scientifically for **THREE** weeks and after that they were cut in small pieces till they died on 11 march 1689. Aurangzeb was also the first Mughal who really attempted to conquer the South. By the end of his reign, there was nothing left in the coffers, culture and arts had been erased and the Hindus were once more haunted by persecution.

Fortunately, by then the Mughal empire was already crumbling; but the woes of Hindus were not finished. Nadir Shah, of Iran attacked Delhi in 1739 and for one whole week his soldiers massacred everybody, ransacked everything and razed the entire countryside, so that the survivors would have nothing to eat. He went back to Iran taking with him precious furniture, works of arts, 10,000 horses, the Kohinoor diamond, the famous Peacock throne and 150 million rupees in gold, (Danielou p.290). After that blow, the Mughal dynasty was so enfeebled, that India was ready for its next barbarians: the Europeans.

CHAPTER 6

Negationism and the Muslim Conquests

It is important to stop a moment and have a look at what the Belgian scholar Koenraad Elst, has called *negationism in India.* In his foreword to the book of the same title, Koenraad explains that negationism, which means in this context *the denial of historical crimes against humanity*, is not a new phenomenon. In modern history, the massacre by the Turks of 1.5 millions Armenians, or that of the 6 million Jews by the Nazis, the several millions of Russians by Stalin, or again the 1 million Tibetans by the Chinese communists, are *historical* facts which have all been denied by their perpetrators....

But deny is not the exact word. They have been **negated** in a thousand ways: gross, clever, outrageous, subtle, so that in the end, the minds of people are so confused and muddled, that nobody knows anymore where the truth is.

Sometimes, it is the numbers that are negated or passed under silence: the Spanish conquest of South America has been one of the bloodiest and most ruthless episodes in history. Elst estimates that out of the population of native Continental South America of 1492, which stood at 90 million, only 32 million survived; terrible figures indeed but who talks about them today?

"But what of the conquest of India by Muslims," asks Elst?

In other parts of Asia and Europe, the conquered nations

quickly opted for conversion to Islam rather than death. But in India, because of the staunch resistance of the 4000 year old Hindu faith, the Muslim conquests were for the Hindus a pure struggle between life and death. Entire cities were burnt down and their populations massacred. Each successive campaign brought hundreds of thousands of victims and similar numbers were deported as slaves. Every new invader made often literally his hill of Hindu skulls. Thus the conquest of Afghanistan in the year 1000, was followed by the annihilation of the entire Hindu population there; indeed, the region is still called Hindu Kush, 'Hindu slaughter.' The Bahmani sultans in central India, made it a rule to kill 100,000 Hindus a year. In 1399, Teimur killed 100,000 Hindus **in a single day**, and many more on other occasions. Koenraad Elst quotes Professor K.S. Lal's "Growth of Muslim population in India," who writes that according to his calculations, the Hindu population decreased by **80 million** between the year 1000 and 1525. **Indeed probably the biggest holocaust in the whole world history**. (Negat, 34)

But the "pagans" were far too numerous to kill them all; and Hinduism too well entrenched in her people's soul, never really gave up, but quietly retreated in the hearts of the pious and was preserved by the Brahmins' amazing oral powers. Thus, realising that they would never be able to annihilate the entire Indian population and that they could not convert all the people, the Muslims rulers, particularly under the Hanifite law, allowed the pagans to become "zimmis" (protected ones) under 20 humiliating conditions, with the heavy "jizya," the toleration tax, collected from them.

"It is because of Hanifite law, writes Elst, that many Muslim rulers in India considered themselves exempted from the duty to continue the genocide of Hindus." The last "jihad" against the Hindus was waged by the much glorified Tipu Sultan, at the end of the 18th century. Thereafter, particularly following the crushing of the 1857 rebellion by the British, Indian Muslims fell into a state of depression and increasing backwardness, due to their mollah's refusal of British education (whereas the elite Hindus gradually went for it) and their nostalgia for the "glorious past." It is only much later, when the British started drawing them into the political mainstream, so as to divide India, that they started regaining some predominance.

Negationism means that this whole aspect of Indian history has been totally erased, not only from history books, but also from the memory, from the consciousness of Indian people. Whereas the Jews have constantly tried, since the Nazi genocide, to keep alive the remembrance of their six million martyrs, the Indian leadership, political and intellectual, **has made a wilful and conscious attempt to deny the genocide perpetrated by the Muslims**. No one is crying for vengeance. Do the Jews of today want to retaliate upon contemporary Germany? **No**. It is only a matter of making sure **that history does not repeat its mistakes**, as alas it is able to do today: witness the persecution of Hindus in Kashmir, whose 250,000 Pandits have fled their 5000 year old homeland; or the 50,000 Hindus chased from Afghanistan; or the oppression of Hindus in Bangladesh and Pakistan. And most of all, to remember, is to **be able to look at today with the wisdom of yesterday**. No collective memory should be erased for appeasing a particular community.

Yet, what has happened in India, at the hand of Hindus themselves, is a constant denial and even a perversion of the genocide committed by Muslims in India. Hasn't the "radical humanist" M.N. Roy, written "that Islam has fulfilled a historic mission of equality and abolition of discrimination in India, and that for this, Islam has been welcomed in India by the lower castes." "If AT ALL any violence occurred, he goes on to say, it was a matter of justified class struggle by the progressive forces against the reactionary forces, meaning the feudal Hindu upper classes..."

Want to listen to another such quote? This one deals with Mahmud Ghaznavi, the destroyer of thousands of Hindu temples, who according to his chronicler Utbi, sang the praise of the Mathura temple complex, sacred above all to all Hindus ... and promptly proceeded to raze it to the ground: "Building interested Mahmud and he was much impressed by the city of Mathura, where there are today a thousand edifices as firm as the faith of the faithful. Mahmud was not a religious man. He was a Mahomedan, but that was just by the way. He was in the first place a soldier and a brilliant soldier" ... Amazing eulogy indeed of the man who was proud of desecrating hundreds of temples and made it a duty to terrorise and humiliate pagans. And guess from whom is that quote? From Jawaharlal Nehru himself, the first Prime Minister of India and one of the architects of independence!

M.N. Roy, and Nehru in a lesser degree, represent the foremost current of negationism in India, which is Marxist inspired. For strangely, it was the Russian communists who decided to cultivate the Arabs after the First World War, in the hope that they constituted a fertile ground for future indoctrination. One should also never forget that Communism has affected whole generations of ardent youth, who saw in Marxism a new ideology in a world corrupted by capitalism and class exploitation. Nothing wrong in that; but as far as indoctrination goes, the youth of the West, particularly of the early sixties and seventies, were all groomed in sympathising with the good Arabs and the bad Jews. And similarly in India, two or three young generations since the early twenties, were tutored on negating Muslim genocide on the Hindus. In "Communalism and the writing of Indian history," Romila Thapar, Harbans Mukhia and Bipan Chandra, professors at the JNU in New Delhi, the Mecca of secularism and negationism in India, denied the Muslim genocide by replacing it instead with a conflict of classes. The redoubtable Romila Thapar in her "Penguin History of India," co-authored with Percival Spear, writes: "Aurangzeb's supposed intolerance, is little more than a hostile legend based on isolated acts such as the erection of a mosque on a temple site in Benares." How can one be so dishonest, or so blind? But it shows how negationism is perpetuated in India.

What are the facts? Aurangzeb (1658-1707) did not just build an isolated mosque on a destroyed temple, he ordered ALL temples destroyed, among them the Kashi Vishvanath, one of the most sacred places of Hinduism and had mosques built on a number of cleared temples sites. All other Hindu sacred places within his reach equally suffered destruction, with mosques built on them. A few examples: Krishna's birth temple in Mathura, the rebuilt Somnath temple on the coast of Gujurat, the Vishnu temple replaced with the Alamgir mosque now overlooking Benares and the Treta-ka-Thakur temple in Ayodhya. (Neg 60). The number of temples destroyed by Aurangzeb is counted in 4, if not 5 figures; according to his own official court chronicles: "Aurangzeb ordered all provincial governors to destroy all schools and temples of the Pagans and to make a complete end to all pagan teachings and practices." The chronicle sums up the destructions like this: "Hasan Ali Khan came and said that 172 temples in the area had been destroyed.... His majesty went to Chittor and 63 temples were destroyed. Abu Tarab, appointed to destroy the idol-temples of

Amber, reported that 66 temples had been razed to the ground." Aurangzeb did not stop at destroying temples, their users were also wiped-out; even his own brother, Dara Shikoh, was executed for taking an interest in Hindu religion and the Sikh Guru Tegh Bahadur was beheaded because he objected to Aurangzeb's forced conversions. As we can see Romila Thapar and Percival Spear's statement of a benevolent Aurangzeb is a flagrant attempt at negationism. Even the respectable Encyclopedia Brittannica in its entry on India, does not mention in its chapter on the Sultanate period any persecutions of Hindus by Muslims, except "that Firuz Shah Tughlaq made largely unsuccessful attempts at converting his Hindu subjects and sometime persecuted them."

The British, for their own selfish purpose, were of course greatly responsible for whitewashing the Muslims, whom they needed to counterbalance the influence of the Hindus and the Congress. It is sad that Jawaharlal Nehru and the Congress perpetuated that brand of negationism. But that is another story.

The happiest in this matter must be the Muslims themselves. What fools these Hindus are, they must be telling themselves: We killed them by the millions, we wrested a whole nation out of them, we engineer riots against them, and they still defend us!...

But don't the Hindus know that many orthodox Indian Muslims still cling to the Deoband school, which says that India was once "Dar-ul-Islam," the house of Islam, and should return to that status. Maulana Abul Kala Azad, several times Congress President, and Education Minister in free India, was a spokesman for this school. The Aligarh school on the contrary, led by Mohammed Iqbal, propounded the creation of Pakistan. What particularly interests us in the Aligarh school is the attempt by Muslim historians, such as Mohamed Habiib, to rewrite the Chapter of Muslim invasions in India. In 1920, Habib started writing his magnum opus, which he based on four theories: (1) that the records (written by the Muslims themselves) of slaughters of Hindus, the enslaving of their women and children and razing of temples were "mere exaggerations by court poets and zealous chroniclers to please their rulers." (2) That they were indeed atrocities, but mainly committed by Turks, the savage riders from the Steppe. (3) That the destruction of the temples took place because Hindus stored their gold and jewels inside them and therefore Muslim armies plundered these. (4) That the conversion of millions of Hindus to Islam was not forced, "but what happened was there was a shift of opinion in the population, who on its own free will chose the Shariat against the Hindu law (smriti), as they were all oppressed by the bad Brahmins...!!!" (Negationism p.42)

Unfortunately for Habib and his school, the Muslims invaders did record with glee their genocide on Hindus, because they felt all along that **they were doing their duty**; that killing, plundering, enslaving and razing temples **was the work of God**, Mohammed. Indeed, whether it was Mahmud of Ghazni (997-1030), who was no barbarian, although a Turk, and patronised art and literature, would recite a verse of the Koran every night after having razed temples and killed his quota of unbelievers; or Firuz Shah Tughlak (1351-1388) who personally confirms that the destruction of Pagan temples was done out of piety and writes: "on the day of a Hindu festival, I went there myself, ordered the executions of all the leaders **and practitioners** of his abomination; I destroyed their idols temples and built mosques in their places." Finally, as Elst points out, "Muslim fanatics were merely faithful executors of

Quranic injunctions. It is not the Muslims who are guilty but Islam." (Negationism in India, p. 44)

It is not only Indian historians, who are negationists, but also western historians and India-specialists. We know that the first historians of Indian—the Britishers—twisted India's history to suit their theory that they had come to civilize a race which was not only inferior to them, but also was supposed to have been heavily influenced in its philosophies or arts by European invaders—read the Aryans or Alexander the Great. But what is less known is that today many western historians not only still cling to these old outdated theories, but also actually more or less willfully mislead the general European public, who is generally totally ignorant and takes these "knowledgeable" comments about India as the absolute truth. One example is France, which has a long tradition of Indianists, who devote their time and life to the study of India. The main school of historic research in France is called the CNRS (National Center of Social Research), which has a very important South Asia section, of which India, of course, is the main component. Unfortunately, many of these India-specialists are not only Left-leaning, that is they are very close to the ideas of the JNU historians, with whom they are anyway in constant contact, but many of them are specialists of the Moghol period of India history, which is to say that they are sympathetic to Islam's point of view on India, while they often consider Hindus as fanatics....

Take for instance one of the recent Indian History books published in France "Histoire de l'Inde moderne" (1994 Fayard/Paris), the authors (there are seven of, all famous Indianists), having subscribed to the usual Aryan invasion theory, accuse Shiva "to incarnate obscure forces" (Introduction III) and of course use the word "fanatics" to describe the Hindus who brought down the Ayodhya mosque. Basically, the book does an apology of he moghol period in India; while keeping quiet about all their crimes. In the chapter dealing for instance with Vijaynagar, the last great empire of free India, which symbolized a Hindu Renaissance after nine centuries of savage Muslim conquests, one cannot but perceive the enmity of the authors for Hinduism. The two young princes, founder of Vijaynagar who were converted by force to Islam when in captivity, are accused of "duplicity," because they reverted back to Hinduism as soon as they were free; then the French historians highlight the "ambition of Brahmins, who used these two young princes to reconquer the power that at been lost at the hands of the conquering Muslims" (page 54); the book then mentions "the unquenchable exigencies of the (Hindu) central power in Vijaynagar," forgetting to say that that for the first time in centuries, Hindus could practice freely their faith, that they were not killed, their women raped, their children taken as slaves and converted to Islam. And all this to finally sum up in *seven* words the terrible end of Vijaynagar, which has left a wound in the Hindu psyche even up to today: "looting and massacres lasted for three days...."

But the authors of "Histoire de l'Inde moderne" do not only run down Hindus, they also glorify Muslims, particularly the Moghols. Babur for instance, this monster who killed hundreds of thousands of Hindus and razed thousands of temples becomes at their hands a gentle hero: "Babur did not like India and preferred to isolate himself in the exquisite gardens he had devised, with their geometrical design, their crossed canals, which evoked to him the rivers of paradise." Oh, God what a sensitive poet! And to make it sound even more glorious, the author adds: "there he translated a manual of Koranic law and a Sufi treaty of morals." Oh, what a saint and lover of humanity

... Aurangzeb, the cruelest of the Moghul emperors, has also the full sympathies of the authors: "Aurangzeb seems to have concentrated on himself the hatred of militant Hindus, who attribute to him systematic destruction of temples and massive conversion drives. But this Manichean impression has to be seriously countered (page 126)"... Unfortunately for the authors, as we have seen earlier, Aurangzeb was not only proud of what he was doing to the Hindus, but he had his scribes note each deed down for posterity....

These French Indianists have also a tradition of speaking against the BJP, which they have always labeled as "fundamentalist" and dangerous for the "secular" fabric of India, although the BJP has been in power for quite a few years and nothing dramatic has happened to the secular fabric of India. The problem is that these Indianists not only write lengthy and pompous articles in France's main newspapers, such as Left-leaning Le Monde, explaining to the ignorant reader why is India on the point of exploding because of fanatic Hindus, or how the Harijans in India are still the most downtrodden people on earth (this is why when President Narayanan visited France in April 2000, all the French newspapers chose to only highlight that he was an untouchable and that religious minorities in India were persecuted, nearly provoking a diplomatic incident between France and India), but unfortunately they also advise the French government, who like his citizens, is often shamefully ignorant and uninterested by India. This is why, although there has been a lot of sympathy for the French in India because of their tolerant response to the Indian nuclear tests of 1998 (whereas the whole western world reacted hysterically by imposing absurd sanctions), France has not yet bothered to capitalize on this sympathy and has not managed to realize that India is the ideal economic alternative to a very volatile China. Still today, one reads negative articles about Prime Minister Narendra Modi and how Indian minorities are 'persecuted', whereas Modi went out of his way to woo minorties....

It would be nice to say that Indian journalists are not blind to this influence of French Indianists and the adverse impact it has on Indo-French relations, but when Christophe Jaffrelot, for instance who wrote many a nasty books on Hindu fundamentalism and is most responsible for the bad image the BJP in France, comes to India to release the English translation of his book, he is feted by the Press corps, specially the Indian Express, where all kind of laudatory reviews are printed. So much for secularism in India.

And, ultimately, it is a miracle that Hinduism survived the onslaught of Muslim savagery; it shows how deep was her faith, how profound her karma, how deeply ingrained her soul in the hearts of her faithfuls. We do not want to point a finger at Muslim atrocities, yet they should not be denied and their mistakes should not be repeated today. But the real question is: **Can Islam ever accept Hinduism**? We shall turn towards the Sage, the yogi, who fought for India's independence, accepting the Gita's message of karma of violence when necessary, yet had a broad vision that softened his words: "You can live with a religion whose principle is toleration. But how is it possible to live peacefully with a religion whose principle is "I will not tolerate you? How are you going to havc unity with these people?... The Hindu is ready to tolerate; he is open to new ideas and his culture and has got a wonderful capacity for assimilation, but always provided India's central truth is recognised. (Sri Aurobindo India's Rebirth 161,173)

Or behold this, written on September 1909: "Every action for instance which may be objectionable to a number of

Mahomedans, is now liable to be forbidden because it is likely to lead to a breach of peace. And one is dimly beginning to wonder whether worship in Hindu temples may be forbidden on that valid ground (India's Rebirth p. 55). How prophetic! Sri Aurobindo could not have foreseen that so many Muslim countries would ban Rushdie's book and that Hindu processions would often be forbidden in cities, for fear of offending the Muslims. Sri Aurobindo felt that sooner or later Hindus would have to assert again the greatness of Hinduism.

And here we must say a word about monotheism, for it is the key to the understanding of Islam. Christians and Muslims (and Jews) have always harped on the fact that their religions sprang-up as a *reaction* against the pagan polytheist creeds, which adored many Gods. « There is only one real God they said (ours), all the rest are just worthless idols ». This « monotheism versus polytheism business » has fuelled since then the deep, fanatic, violent and murderous zeal of Islam against polytheist religions, particularly against Hinduism, which is the most comprehensive, most widely practiced of all them. It even cemented an alliance of sorts between the two great monotheist religions of the world, Christianity and Islam, witness the Britishers' attitude in India, who favoured Indian Muslims and Sikhs against the Hindus; or the King of Morocco who, even though he is one of the most moderate Muslim leaders in the world, recently said in an interview: « we have no fight with Christianity, our battle is against the Infidel who adores many gods ».

But as we have seen earlier, Hinduism is without any doubt *the most monotheist religion in the World,* for it recognises *divine unity in multiplicity*. It does not say: « there is only one God, which is Mohammed. If you do not believe in Him I will kill you». It says instead: « Yes Mohammed is a manifestation of

God, but so is Christ, or Buddha, or Krishna, or Confucius ». This philosophy, this way of seeing, which the Christians and Muslims call « impious », is actually the foundation for **a true monotheist understanding of the world**. It is because of this « If you do not recognize Allah (or Christ), I will kill you », that tens of millions of Hindus were slaughtered by Arabs and other millions of South Americans annihilated by the Christians. And ultimately the question is: Are the Muslims of today ready to accept Hinduism? Unfortunately no. For Muslims all over the world, Hinduism is **still** the Infidel religion « par excellence ». This what their religion tell them, at every moment, at every verse, at the beginning of each prayer : « Only Allah is great ». And their mollahs still enjoin them to go on fight « jihad » to deliver the world of the infidels. And if the armies of Babar are not there any longer; and if it is not done any more to kill a 100,000 Hindus in a day, there is still the possibility of planting a few bombs in Coimbatore, of fuelling separatisms in the hated land and eventually to drop a nuclear device, which will settle the problem once and for all. As to the Indian Muslim, he might relate to his Hindu brother, for whatever he says, he remains an Indian, nay a Indu; but his religion will make sure that he does not forget that his duty is to hate the Infidel. This is the crux of the problem today and the riddle if Islam has to solved, if it wants to survive in the long run.

We will never be able to assess the immense physical harm done to India by the Muslim invasions. Even more difficult is to estimate the moral and the spiritual damage done to Hindu India. But once again, the question is not of vengeance, or of reawakening old ghosts, *but of not repeating the same mistakes*. Unfortunately, the harm done by the Muslims conquest is not over. The seeds planted by the Moghols, by Babar, Mahmud, or Aurangzeb, have matured: the 125 million Indian Muslims of today have forgotten that they were once peaceful, loving Hindus, forcibly converted to a religion they hated. And they sometimes take-up as theirs a cry of fanaticism which is totally alien to their culture. Indeed, as Sri Aurobindo once said: "More than 90% of the Indian Muslims are descendants of converted Hindus and belong as much to the Indian nation as the Hindu themselves...." (Rebirth of India, p.237) The embryo of secession planted by the Mahomedans, has also matured into a poisonous tree which has been called Pakistan and comes back to haunt India through three wars and the shadow of a nuclear conflict embracing South Asia. And in India, Kashmir and Kargil are reminders that the Moghol cry for the house of Islam in India is not yet over.

CHAPTER 7

The European Invasions

Of the early European colonisers, the Portuguese seem to symbolise best the total disregard, ill will and destructive spirit of the West towards India. Whatever all the folklore today about the "relaxed atmosphere" of Portuguese Goa (the good life, the wine, the sensuous women), the Portuguese were a ruthless lot. In 1498, Vasco de Gama, the Portuguese "hero," was generously received by Zamorin, the Hindu king of Calicut, who granted him the right to establish warehouses for commerce. But once again, Hindu tolerance was exploited and the Portuguese wanted more and more: in 1510 Alfonso de Albuquerque seized Goa, where he started a reign of terror, burning "heretics," crucifying Brahmins, using false theories to forcibly convert the lower castes and encouraging his soldiers to take Indian mistresses. Indeed, the Inquisition in Goa had nothing to envy the Muslims, except in sheer number. Ultimately, the Portuguese had to be kicked out of India, when all other colonisers had already left.

There is no need to rewrite here the story of British India. From 1600, when the East India Company received its charter from Queen Elizabeth, to 1947, when Mountbatten packed up the Union Jack, the history of the British in India has been one of subtle treachery, crass commercial exploitation and sometimes of savagery. The English might have been totally ignorant of India's past greatness, when they set upon acquiring bit by bit their empire, but at least there was some early attempt at understanding each other between a few enlightened Britishers and some Indians. But after the mutiny of 1857, the English went into a frenzy of murder, revenge and atrocity and alienated themselves for ever from the "natives." Henceforth they would live separately in their forts, or their cantonments, and would be totally segregated from Indians, ending for ever any chance of bridging the gap between the two cultures. Indeed, Danielou feels that the crushing of the revolt, "was to trigger the slow and insidious destruction of one of the greatest civilisations of the world, of its philosophy, its arts, its sciences and its techniques now despised and discouraged. This was disaster for universal culture, he concludes." (Histoire de l'Inde p. 329)

Another question should also be asked: was the European conquest a unifying factor in India? According to Western historians, such as A.L. Basham, yes. For prior to the British conquest, they label India as a nation of feudal kings, constantly infighting each other. But as seen earlier, when one discounts the theory of an Aryan invasion, when one understands the genius of Vedic India, the greatness of it institutions, the unparalleled tolerance and spiritual vision of Hinduism and how it had devised a remarkable political system adapted to its own needs and psychology, this theory does not stand under scrutiny.

In truth, the British divided India; they exploited the schism between Hindus and Muslims and aggravated a small discontentment in the Sikh community. Dividing India to them was only a practical need to further their imperial dream - it was not done out of sheer fanatical conviction. But does that make it more acceptable?

Nevertheless, when History will be rewritten, the British will have to share the blame for the harm that was done to India. And their share has four names: **Missionaries, Secularism, Indian Elite, Repression.**

7.1. The Missionaries pre-Independence

The missionaries arrived in India on the heels of the British. As mentioned in the first chapter, their first prey were the Adivasis, the tribal people, which they promptly proceeded to name as the "original" inhabitants of India, who were colonised by the « bad » Brahmins, during the mythical Aryan invasion. "Was it not right, they said, to free them from the grip of their masters, who had enslaved them both socially and religiously"? Thus they set the Advisees against the mainstream of Hindu society and sowed the seeds of an explosive conflict which is ready to blow-up today, particularly in UP, where the caste conflict is exploited politically by politicians like Mulayam Singh, Kanshi Ram, or Laloo Prasad.

The missionaries in India were always supporters of colonialism; they encouraged it and their whole structure was based on "the good Western civilised world being brought to the Pagans." In the words of Charles Grant (1746-1823), Chairman of the East India Company: "we cannot avoid recognising in the people of Hindustan a race of men lamentably degenerate and base ... governed by malevolent and licentious passions ... and sunk in misery by their vices." (as quoted by Sitaram Goel, in his book "History of Hindu-Christian encounters, page 32). Claudius Buccchanan a chaplain attached to the East India Company, went even further: "... Neither truth, nor honesty, honour, gratitude, nor charity, is to be found in the breast of a Hindoo!" what a comment about a nation that gave the world the Vedas and the Upanishads, at a time when Europeans were still fornicating in their caves!

Lord Hastings, Governor General of India from 1813, could not agree more; he writes in his diary on 2nd October of the same year: "The Hindoo appears a being nearly limited to mere animal functions ... with no higher intellect than a dog or an elephant, or a monkey..." No wonder that the British opened the doors wide for missionaries! After the failed mutiny of 1857, the missionaries became even more militant, using the secular arm of the British Raj, who felt that the use of the sword at the service of the Gospel, was now entirely justified. Remember how Swami Vivekananda cried in anguish at the Parliament of Religions in Chicago: "if we Hindus dig out all the dirt from the bottom of the Pacific Ocean and throw it in you faces, it will be but a speck compared to what the missionaries have done to our religion and culture »." These missionaries indeed poisoned the minds of the people they converted, making them hate their own religion, their own country sometimes, cutting them from their own cultural roots. What better example of this than the Anglo-Indians, a race which became neither here nor there, disallowing their Indian-ness, but never being fully accepted as their own by their British masters. Hence they had to slowly disappear, either reverting to their Indian-ness, or settling abroad: evolution does not tolerate a people that loses its soul. It is the same with the "Pondichériens" the French of Tamil origin from Pondichery. Originated from lower castes, they were converted by the early French missionaries and in time assumed French names, French manners and considered themselves as French. But today the French have forgotten them, they cost too much to their government and apart from a few brilliant exceptions, they are also a race which is slowly dying and is gradually engulfed by the Indian Tamils. It is also true that the missionaries, such as "Saint" François Xavier, broke down many "idol" temples to build their churches, although it never had the ruthlessness and ferocity of the Muslims. Nevertheless, the missionaries in India were always a divisive force, which used the Adivasis for advocating covertly a breaking-up of the country. Prof. A.K. Kishu, Secretary General of the Indian Council of Indigenous and Tribal people, has been lobbying hard at the UN so that the Adivasis are recognised as "the original settlers of India." Koenraad Elst writes that the missionaries were ultimately all set to trigger a Christian partition in India: "at the time of Independence, Christian mission centres had dreamed up a plan for a Christian partition in collaboration with the Muslim League. The far north-east, Chotanagur and parts of Kerala were to become Christian states, forming a non-Hindu chain with the Nizam's Hyderabad and with Pakistani Bengal. The secret agreement between the Muslim League and missionaries acting as "representatives of tribal interest," is sometimes used in Muslim propaganda, as proof that "Muslims and tribals are natural allies." Sadly for the Christians, Sardar Patel foiled their plans. (Indigenous Indian Page 229) Even after independence, the missionaries seem to have been involved in secessionist activities in India's north-east, as well as on the Burmese side of the border. Always pretending to act as mediators, they appear to have actually helped the separatists with vital informations. Since then, they have been dictating policies in Nagaland, Megalayam and Mizoram, which recently celebrated with great fanfare its century of Christian rule.

What of today? Moderate Hindu leaders, such as Sri Sri Ravi Shankar, the founder of the Art of Living, feels "that Christianity has often alienated Indian Christians from the mainstream. They are afraid for instance to participate in anything that has a Hindu connotation, or they are made to change their names. And since they get alienated, a certain fear psychosis sets in." And it is true that Christianity also introduced the feeling of guiltiness, of being a sinner, which is absent from Hinduism. "I would even say, adds Sri Sri Ravi Shankar, that it sometimes gave Christians an unfortunate feeling of superiority over Hindus." Christians are also proud that they brought education to India, "but, counters Sri Sri Ravi Shankar, it is not true: there were for instance 125,000 medical institutes in Madras before the British came. Indians never lacked education, the Christians only brought British education to India, which in fact caused more damage to India by westernising many of us."

Then of course, there is the subject of conversions by Christian missionaries, which has triggered a heated debate since the BJP Government came to power. On this topic, Sri Sri Ravi Shankar feels "that when you honour and respect another religion, the culture of conversion is not needed. The Hindus honour the other religions, but unfortunately there is not yet been any sanction to honour similarly other religions in Christianity. The problem with tribals in India is that if the missionaries had just done service there and left the tribals to their indigenous practices, there would not have been so many problems today." We also notice nowadays that Indian missionaries (for there are practically no 'white' missionaries left, have become very smart—they copy Hindu culture and rituals, so as to attract innocent villagers and tribals. Recently they have even had ceremonies that resemble the Ayappa festival!

Finally, no history of the missionary involvement in India, can be complete without mentioning the health and education services they rendered. It is true, that unparalleled selfless service was given and is still rendered all over the country, that Kerala got 100% literacy, thanks in greater part to Christianity, that the best schools in India are Catholic, that the medical care is unique and most advanced. True also that sometimes this service is rendered out of true Christian charity, without any ulterior motive. But nevertheless, there is no doubt about the ultimate purpose of that selfless service. The South Indian Missionary Conference of 1858, set forth very clearly the goals of education in India: "the object of all missionary labour should not be primarily the civilisation, BUT the evangelization of the heathen ... schools may be regarded as converting agencies and their value estimated by the number who are led to renounce idolatry and make an open profession of Christianity..."

Has this policy really changed today? Not that much. The International School of Kodaikanal, under the guise of "religious studies," still tries to convert its students, many of whom are Indians. And nothing symbolises better today the continuing spirit of the missionaries in India than Mother Theresa, although dead for many years, and other missionaries, who have been glorified by the book "the City of Joy" by Dominique Lapierre, a wonderfully written book, which unfortunately gives the impression that a small part of India (the slums of Calcutta), represents the whole of the country.

7.2 Secularism

Many post-independence Indians, particularly the Congress politicians, have always harped on the fact that "The British left no greater legacy in India than secularism." But in the name of secularism, how much irreparable harm has been done to

India, how much damage, slander, stupidity has been heaped upon the land of Bharat!

The beauty and the genius of a truly secular India is indeed appealing. Who would not dream of an India where all would live in harmony: Muslims, Hindus, Christians, Parsis, Buddhists, Jains, Jews, North Indians, South Indians, Assamese, Kashmiris, Sikhs, Nepalese.... Which country in the world can boast of such a diversity, such an incredible mosaic of races, religions, ethnic groups? There would be at the centre a benevolent, non-religious, liberal, reform-oriented, secular government, which would allow for unlimited religious and regional autonomies, so that the soul of each culture, each religion, finds its right expression in the fold of a united India. Is this then the democratic inheritance left by India's erstwhile masters?

In reality, when the British arrived in India, they were only a handful, and realised that they could not govern such a huge country with so few of theirs. They then set upon dividing the nation, pitting each community against the other. In the Muslims they found a ready ear. It would be a total lie to say that the British engineered the Muslim-Hindu enmity and are to be held responsible for the creation of Pakistan. The Muslim-Hindu divide was a problem of religious incompatibility, on the parts of the Muslims, who saw in Hinduism an infidel religion, which had to be wiped-out. Now the clash of swords was no more, and the British were there to pacify everybody; but they very quickly scented blood and felt they could use the ardent wish of Indian Muslims to be separate on their own, now that the bitter realisation had downed upon them that they could not make of India a Dar-ul-Islam, a house of Islam. In the same way, the British were prompt to seize upon the dissatisfaction of the Sikhs, who had fought them ferociously but in peace served them as faithfully, forming with the Gurkhas their best soldiers.

But in treating a minority community, the Muslims (or the Christians), on par with the majority community, the Hindus, the British conveniently forgot that there were more than 300 millions Hindus in India, that Hinduism is more than a religion, it is the very basis, for India's greatness and identity and that which unites all other Indian cultures and even religions: Dharma, the living truth.

7.3 The Indian Elite

When they took over India, the British set upon establishing an intermediary race of Indians, whom they could entrust with their work at the middle level echelons and who could one day be convenient instruments to rule by proxy, or semi-proxy. The tool to shape these « British clones » was *education*. In the words of Macaulay, the « pope » of British schooling in India: « We must at present do our best to form a class, who may be interpreters between us and the millions we govern; a class of persons, Indians in blood and colour, but *English in taste*, in opinions, in morals and in intellects ». Macaulay had very little regard for Hindu culture and education: « all the historical information which can be collected from all the books which have been written in the Sanskrit language, is less valuable than what may be found in the most paltry abridgement used at preparatory schools in England ». Or: « Hindus have a literature of small intrinsic value, hardly reconcilable with morality, full of monstrous superstitions »...

It seems today that India's Marxist and Muslim intelligentsia could not agree more with Macaulay, for his dream has come true: nowadays, the greatest adversaries of an « indianised and spiritualised education » are the descendants of these « Brown Shahibs » : the « secular » politicians, the journalists, the top bureaucrats, in fact the whole westernised cream of India. And what is even more paradoxical, is that most of them are Hindus! It is they, who upon getting independence, have denied India its true identity and borrowed blindly from the British education system, without trying to adapt it to the unique Indian mentality and psychology; and it is they who are refusing to accept a change of India's education system, which is totally western-oriented and is churning out machines learning by heart boring statistics which are of little usefulness in life. And what India is getting from this education is a youth which apes the West: they go to Mac Donald's, thrive on MTV culture, wear the latest Klein jeans and Lacoste T Shirts, and in general are useless, rich parasites, in a country which has so many talented youngsters who live in poverty. They will grow-up like millions of other western clones in the developing world, who wear a tie, read the New York Times and swear by liberalism and secularism to save their countries from doom. In time, they will reach elevated positions and write books and articles which make fun of India, they will preside human-right committees, be "secular" high bureaucrats who take the wrong decisions and generally do tremendous harm to India, because it has been programmed in their genes to always run down their own country. In a gist, they will be the ones who are always looking at the West for approval and forever perceive India through the western prism. It is said that a nation has to be proud of itself to move forward—and unless there is a big change in this intellectual elite, unless it is more conscious of its heritage and of India's greatness, which has begun to happen in a small way, it is going to be very difficult for India to evolve in the 21st century as a real super power.

7.4. Repression, Impoverishment

The British were certainly not the Muslims, whose ruthlessness and atrocities have never been equaled in India's history. Nevertheless, they did their fair share of harm to India, which has not yet really recovered from two centuries of Raj. Their brutality, whether the hangings of Indian nationalists, or the incredible ferocity which followed the great Indian Mutiny, or the massacre of Jalianwala Bagh, are today part of history. They ruled for two centuries with the unshakeable conviction of their own racial superiority which made Fitzjames Stephen, the philosopher of the Indian Civil Service say: "Ours is essentially an absolute government, which has for base not the consent of the Indians, but their conquest. It does not want to represent the concept of the indigenous population of life and government and can never do, because then it would represent idolatry and barbarism. It represents a belligerent civilisation and nothing could be more dangerous than to have in one's administration, at the head of a government founded on conquest-implying in all points the superiority of the conquering race, its institution, its principles, that men who hesitate to impose themselves openly." One of the most important aspects of British India was the development of the British system of education and of the English language as the sole base of university teaching. Only the British diplomas were recognised and permitted to obtain a job. The ancient centres of Hindu culture got gradually bypassed and only the Brahmins kept the knowledge of Sanskrit alive.

Industrially, the British suffocated India, gradually strangling Indian industries, whose finished products, textiles in particular, were of a quality unique in the world, which had made them famous over the centuries. Instead, they oriented Indian industry towards jute, cotton, tea, oil seeds, which they needed as raw materials for their home industries. They employed cheap labour for their enterprises, while traditional artisanat were perishing. India, which used to be a land of plenty, « where milk and honey flowed », started slowly dying. According to British records, One million Indians died of famine between 1800 and 1825; 4 million between 1825 and 1850; 5 million between 1850 and 1875; and *15 million* between 1875 and 1900. **Thus, 25 million Indians died in one hundred years**! The British may be proud of their bloody record. It is probably more honourable and straightforward to kill in the name of Allah, than under the guise of petty commercial interest and total disregard for the ways of a 5000 year civilisation. Thus, by the turn of the century, India was bled dry and had no resources left. Fortunately, visionaries, like Jemshadji Tata, started important industries so that there would be a structure at independence, but in the face of so much resistance by the British. In textiles for example, they imposed the free entry of Lancashire products and slapped a heavy tax on export of Indian textiles. Is it necessary to remind too, how the English "exported" Indian labour all over the world in their colonies, whether to Sri Lanka for the tea plantations, to Fiji, to South Africa, or to the West Indies?

Culturally, there is no need to recall the rape of India. The thousands of art treasures, the diamonds, the priceless statues, stolen, which now adorn the houses of the rich in England, or the Queen's private collections. That the British still do not feel the need to hand back these treasures to India is a shame. The ecological rape of India is also a fact: the tens of thousands of tigers needlessly shot, the great massacre of trees and forests for the voracious railways and the razing of old forts and houses.

Finally, the history of the British would be incomplete without mentioning the positive side. The unification of India by a single language, although it is hoped that it will be eventually replaced by India's true language of the future, acceptable to all. The vast railway system, which more than anything else unified India. The remarkable Postal system, whose structures have survived till today. The roads network of India. But all these were not really meant for the welfare of India, but for a better administration of their own colony.

And ultimately, the question should be asked: "did the British leave India with any understanding, any inkling of the greatness of the country they had lived with for two centuries?" Except for a few souls like Annie Besant or Sister Nivedita, the answer seems to be: **No**. And today's British Prime Minister probably does not understand one bit more about India than Lord Mountbatten did. But then Mountabatten ought to have known better.

CHAPTER 8

The Three Great Disinformations on India

A civilisation is like the human soul: it has a childhood, where it struggles to learn; an adolescence where it discovers—sometimes painfully—the hard facts of life; an adulthood, where it enjoys the fruits of maturity; and an old age, which slowly leads to death and oblivion.

In this manner, since the dawn of human history, civilisations have risen, reached the top, where they gravitate for some time, achieving their enduring excellence—and then slowly begin their descent towards extinction. Usually, old age for these civilisations meant that they fell prey to barbarians, because they had lost the vitality and the inner obedience to their particular genius, which they had possessed at the time of their peak and which had protected them. This has been a natural process and barbarians have played an important role in the evolution of humanity, for they made sure, in the most ruthless manner, that civilisations did not stagnate; because like a human being, a civilisation must die many times before it realises the fullness of its soul and attains divine perfection.

There have been many such great civilisations which rose and fell throughout the ages: Mesopotamia, Egypt, India, Africa, China, Greece, or Rome. Human nature being what it is, most of these civilisations established their might by military conquest and thus imposed their order and their views upon others, a process which some have called civilisation, others colonisation.

The advent of Jesus Christ heralded the rise of the European-Western civilisation, whose forerunners were the Greek and Roman cultures. For long, Europe was only a disunited lot of barbarian tribes fighting each other. The Crusades signalled the earliest attempt at unity, although the French and the British, for instance, kept warring each other long after them. Some of these nations were great seafarers. Thus Spain and Portugal for instance, reached out to the far world and colonised huge chunks of territories in the Americas from the 14th century onwards. But it can be safely said that with the industrial revolution, European civilisation started reaching its maturity at the beginning of the 19th century and that a great civilisation, whose genius was consciousness in the material, developed henceforth. Simultaneously, of course, as all other civilisations had done before, Europe started expanding outwards and imposed its own civilisation on other cultures, which had lost their vitality and were open to conquest. England, particularly, because it mastered the seas, went farther, faster and acquired more territories than other European nations, such as France, who often had to settle for the crumbs. And certainly, Great Britain's prize possession, the jewel in its colonies, must have been India, whose mighty borders extended then from Afghanistan to Cape Comorin.

Western civilisation must be intimately associated with Christianity, even though Christianity took different forms over the ages: Protestantism, Lutheranism, Russian Orthodoxy.... According to the Hindus, Jesus Christ was an "avatar," a direct emanation from God. Christ was surely a great avatar of love, and Christianity certainly had a softening influence on the Western world, where, let's face it, barbarism was the order of the day for many centuries. In the Middle Ages for instance, Christianity was the only island of sanity in a world of rape, black plague, murders and chaos; and as the Brahmins did in India, it was the Christians who preserved the oral and written word for posterity. There have been many great saints in Christianity, men of wisdom, who strove for divine vision in austerity. Such were Saint François of Assisi's, who reached high spiritual experience. Saint Vincent de Paul, who practised true Christian charity. Or Saint Gregory, who attained authentic knowledge. Unfortunately, Christianity, got somehow politicised and fossilised under the influence of corrupt popes and has often become a magma of dogmas, rites, do's and don't.

Generally, because all Christians believed—like the Muslims—that only their God was the true one, The Christian colons sought to impose upon the people they conquered their own brand of religion—and they used the military authority of their armies to do so. It is true that this was done in good faith, that the « soldiers of Christ » thought that the civilisations they stumbled upon were barbarous, pagan and incomprehensible. True also that they sincerely believed that they brought upon these « savages » the virtues of western civilisation: medicine, education and spiritual salvation.

But the harm done by Christian missionaries all over the earth will never be properly assessed. In South America, the Spanish soldiers and priests annihilated, in the name of Jesus, an entire civilisation, one of the brightest ever, that of the Incas and the Aztecs. Everywhere the Christians went, they stamped mercilessly on cultures, eradicated centuries old ways of life, to replace them with totally inadequate systems, crude, Victorian, moralistic, which slowly killed the spontaneity of life of the people they conquered. They were thus able to radically alter civilisations, change their patterns of thinking. And three generations later the children of those who had been conquered, had forgotten their roots, adapted Christianity and often looked upon their conquerors as their benefactors.

Yet the West was able to celebrate the anniversary of Columbus, discoverer of the "New World" with fanfare and pomp. But the New World was already quite old when it was discovered by the young Barbarians, much older in fact than the fledgling Western civilisation. And Columbus, however courageous and adventurous, was a ruthless man, whose 'discovery' of the New World triggered an unparalleled rape in human history.

However, not only the West still deifies Columbus, but no one in the Third World has been capable to challenge coherently that undeserved status. *The truth is that today, not only in the Western world, but also in the entire so-called developing world, we are constantly looking at things and events through a prism that has been fashioned by centuries of western thinking. and as long as we do not get rid of that tainted glass we will not understand rightly the world in general and India in particular.*

For the stamp of Western civilisation will still take some time to be eradicated. By military conquest or moral assertiveness, the West imposed upon the world its ways of thinking; and it created enduring patterns, subtle disinformations and immutable grooves, which play like a record that goes on turning, long after its owner has attained the age of decline. The barbarians who thought they had become « civilized », are being devoured by other barbarians. But today, the economic might has replaced the military killing machine.

8.1 The Fist Disinformation on India: The Aryan Invasions

The theory of the Aryan invasion is still taken as the foundation stone of the History of India. According to this theory, which was actually devised in the 18th and 19th century by British linguists and archaeologists, the first inhabitants of India were good-natured, peaceful, dark-skinned shepherds, called the Dravidians, who had founded what is called the Harappan—or Valley of the Indus civilisation. They were supposedly remarkable builders, witness the city of Mohenjo-Daro in Pakistani Sind, but had no culture to speak-off, no literature, no proper script even. Then, around 1500 B.C., India is said to have been invaded by tribes called the Aryans: white-skinned, nomadic people, who originated somewhere in Western Russia and imposed upon the Dravidians the hateful caste system. To the Aryans, are attributed Sanskrit, the Vedic—or Hindu religion, India's greatest spiritual texts, the Vedas, as well as a host of subsequent writings, the Upanishads, the Mahabharata, the Ramanaya, etc...

This was indeed a masterly stroke on the part of the British: thanks to the Aryan theory, they showed on the one hand that Indian civilisation was not that ancient, and that it was posterior to the cultures which influenced the western world—Mesopotamia, Sumeria, or Babylon—and that whatever good things India had developed—Sanskrit, literature, or even its architecture, had been influenced by the West. Thus, Sanskrit, instead of being the mother of all Indo-European languages, became just a branch of their huge family; thus, the religion of Zarathustra is said to have influenced Hinduism, and not vice versa. And on the other hand, it divided India and pitted against each other the low caste dark-skinned Dravidians and the high caste light-skinned Aryans, a rift which is till enduring.

But today, this theory is being challenged by many new discoveries, archaeological, linguistic, genetic even. Firstly, in the Rig Veda, the Ganges, India's sacred river, is only mentioned once, but the mythic Saraswati is praised FIFTY times. For a long time, the Saraswati river was indeed considered a myth, until the American satellite Landstat was able to photograph and map the bed of this magnificent river, which was nearly fourteen kilometres wide and took its source in the Himalayas. Archaeologist Paul-Henri Francfort, who studied the Saraswati region at the beginning of the nineties, found out that the Saraswati had "disappeared," because around 2200 B.C., an immense drought reduced the whole region to aridity and famine. "Thus, he writes, most inhabitants moved away from the Saraswati to settle on the banks of the Indus and Sutlej rivers." According to official history, the Vedas were composed around 1500 BC, some even say 1200 BC. Yet, the Rig Veda, describes India as it was BEFORE the great drought which dried-up the Saraswati, which means in effect that the so-called Indus, or Harappan civilisation was a CONTINUATION of the Vedic epoch, which ended approximately when the Saraswati dried-up.

A few years back, the famous Indus seals, discovered on the site of Mohenja Daro and Harappa, have been reportedly deciphered by Dr N. Rajaram, a mathematician who worked at one time for the NASA and Dr Jha, a distinguished linguist. In the biased light of the Aryan invasion theory, these seals were presumed to be written in a crude Harappan (read Dravidian) script, although they had never been convincingly deciphered. But according to Rajaram and Jha "the Harappan Civilization, of which the seals are a product, belonged to the latter part of the Vedic Age. It had close connections with Vedantic works like the Sutras and the Upanishads. The style of writing reflects the short aphorisms found in Sutra works. The imagery and symbolism are strongly Vedic. The vocabulary depends heavily on the Vedic glossary Nighantu and its commentary by Yaska known as the Nirukta. The name of Yaska is found on at least two seals ‹ possibly three. There are references to Vedic kings and sages as well place names. Of particular interest are references to Plakshagra ‹ the birthplace of the Sarasvati River, and Sapta Apah or the Land of the Seven Rivers.

This means that the Rigveda must already have been quite ancient by the time of the Harappan Civilization. Since the Harappan Civilization was known to be flourishing in the 3100 1900 BC period, the Rigveda must have been in existence by 4000 BC. This now receives archaeological support following R.S. Bisht's investigation of the great Harappan city of Dholavira. Bisht (and other archaeologists) have concluded that the Vedic Aryans of the Sarasvati heartland were the people who created the Harappan cities and the civilization associated with it."

English or even Indian anthropologists, such as Dr. D.N. Jha, wrote that 'the first Aryans were generally light in color, while the native people were much darker in complexion. The color of their skin must have been an important sign of their identity.' Unfortunately, for Professor Jha and his accomplices, many recent genetic research by anthropologists, such as the famous SR Walimbe, who studied the skeletons of Mohenjo Daro, in comparison with other skeletons taken at random during different periods, have come to the conclusion that there is a genetic continuity between the Harappeans and the Indians who inhabit India today.

Sri Aurobindo, too, India's greatest yogi, poet, philosopher- and surely its most ardent revolutionary—spoke against the

Aryan theory: "We shall question many established philological myths,—the legend for instance of an Aryan invasion from the North, the artificial and inimical distinction of the Aryan and Dravidian which an erroneous philology has driven like a wedge into the unity of the homogeneous Indo-Afghan race.... Like the majority of educated Indians, I had passively accepted without examination, the conclusion of European scholarship" (India's Rebirth, page 103)... He also shatters the myth of the difference of language to support the theory of meeting of races: «But here also my preconceived ideas were disturbed and confounded. For on examining the vocabulary of the Tamil language, in appearance so foreign to the Sanskrit form and character, I yet found myself continuously guided by words, or families of words supposed to be pure Tamil, in establishing new relations between Sanskrit and its distant sister, Latin, and occasionally between the Greek and the Sanskrit. Sometimes the Tamil vocable not only suggested the connection but proved the missing link in a family of connected words. And it was through this Dravidian language that I came first to perceive what seems to me now the true law, origins and, as it were, the embryology of the Aryan tongues.... The possibility suggests itself that they may even have been two diversions, or families derived from one lost primitive tongue».(India's 104)

Hence, it is becoming more and more clear that there **never was** an Aryan Invasion in India, a theory which was imposed upon the subcontinent by its colonisers and is today kept alive by Nehruvian historians, Christian missionaries (it is thus easy to convert the downtrodden tribals and Dravidians, by telling them that Hinduism was a religion thrust upon them by the hated "Brahmin" invaders) and the communists (who hate anything Hindu). History should be rewritten so that Indian children learn to be proud of their ancient and INDIGENOUS civilisation—and the consequences of this new theory applied not only to Asia, but also to the entire history of the whole world. applied not only to Asia, but also to the entire history of the whole world. Here below an attempt at setting new dates for early Indian history.

	Period	Date
1.	End of Saraswati river	2200-1900 BC
2.	Beg. Of Great Drought	2200-2000 BC
3.	The Sulbastras Period	3000-2000
4.	Beg of drying of Saraswati	3100 BC
5.	Peak of Saraswati Civilisation	Before 3200 BC
6.	Introduction of Silver (Kunal)	Appr. 3300 BC
	Period of 2d Vedas and brahmanas	3300 B.C.
7.	End of the Rig Veda Age	3750 BC
8.	Beginning of Vedic Age	Appr. 7000 BC

8.2. The Second Disinformation: The Caste System

Even more than the Aryans-Dravidians divide and the Vedas, the caste system has been the most misunderstood, the most vilified subject of Hindu society at the hands of Western scholars and even today by "secular" Indians. But ultimately if one wants to understand the truth, the original purpose behind the caste system, one must go back to the Vedas. "Caste was originally an arrangement for the distribution of functions in society, just as much as class in Europe, but the principle on which this distribution was based was peculiar to India. A Brahmin was a Brahmin not by mere birth, but because he discharged the duty of preserving the spiritual and intellectual elevation of the race, and he had to cultivate the spiritual temperament and acquire the spiritual training which alone would qualify him for the task. The Kshatryia was Kshatryia not merely because he was the son of warriors and princes, but because he discharged the duty of protecting the country and preserving the high courage and manhood of action, and he had to cultivate the princely temperament and acquire the strong and lofty Samurai training which alone fitted him for his duties. So it was for the Vaishya whose function was to amass wealth for the race and the Shudra who discharged the humbler duties of service without which the other castes could not perform their share of labour for the common, good." (Sri Aurobindo, in India's Rebirth, p. 26).

Many Indian sages have even gone even further than Sri Aurobindo, arguing that in the occult relation India had with the Universal Force, each one was born in the caste **Corresponding** to his or her spiritual evolution. There are accidents, misfits, errors, they say, but the system seems to have worked pretty well until modern times when it got perverted by the vagaries of materialism and western influence. Can one accept such a theory? Sri Aurobindo, while praising the original caste system, does not spare it in its later stages: "it is the nature of human institutions to degenerate; there is no doubt that the institution of caste degenerated. It ceased to be determined by spiritual qualifications which, once essential, have now come to be subordinate and even immaterial and is determined by the purely material tests of occupation and birth... By this change it has set itself against the fundamental tendency of Hinduism which is *to insist on the spiritual and subordinate the material* and thus lost most of its meaning. the spirit of caste arrogance, exclusiveness and superiority came to dominate it instead of the spirit of duty, and the change weakened the nation and helped to reduce us to our present condition.... (India's Rebirth, p 27). And the Barbarians came!

But finally, have the people who dismiss caste as an Aryan imposition on the Dravidians, or as an inhuman and nazi system, ever attempted to understand its original purpose and genius? Is it really worse than the huge class differences you can see nowadays in Europe? And can you really exclude it today off-hand, when it still survives so much in the villages—and even in more educated circles, where one still marries in matching castes, with the help of an astrologer? Does the caste system need to be transformed, to recapture its old meaning and once more incarnate a spiritual hierarchy of beings? Or has it to be recast in a different mould, taking into account the parameters of modern Indian society? Or else, will it finally disappear altogether from India, because it has become totally irrelevant today?

At any rate, Hindus should not allow it to be exploited shamelessly against them, as it has been in the last two centuries, by missionaries, "secular" historians, Muslims, and by pre and post-independence Indian politicians—each for their own purpose.

8.3. The Third Disinformation: The Vedas

The third piece of disinformation concerns the Vedic religion. Ah, the Vedas! So much misconception, so many prejudices, so much distortion have been spewed about this monument of a book, this unparalleled epic. Danielou for instance, maintains that the original Vedas « were an oral Dravidian tradition, which was reshaped by the Aryans and later put down in Sanskrit ». Danielou finds lineage between the Vedic religion and the Persian religion (Zarathustra), as well as the Greek Gods; the problem is that he seems to imply that the Vedic religion may have sprung from the Zoroastrian creed! He also puts down all Vedic symbols as purely physical signs: for instance Agni is the fire that should always burn in the house's altar. Finally, he sees in the Rig-Veda "only a remarkable document on the mode of life, society and history of the Aryans." (Histoire de l'Inde, page 62)

But Danielou must be the mildest of all critics. The real disinformation started again with the missionaries, who saw in the Vedas "the root of the evil," the source of paganism and went systematically about belittling it. The Jesuits, in their dialectical cleverness, brought it down to a set of pagan offerings without great importance. Henceforth, this theory was perpetuated by most Western historians, who not only stripped the Vedas of any spiritual value, but actually post-dated them to approximately 1500 to 1000 years B.C. It is very unfortunate that these theories have been taken-up blindly and without trying to ascertain their truth, by many Indian historians and sociologists such as Romila Tharpar.

And even when more enlightened foreigners like Max Mueller, whose Sanskrit scholarship cannot be denied, took up the Vedas, they only saw "that it is full of childish, silly, even monstrous conceptions, that it is tedious, low, commonplace, that it represents human nature on a low level of selfishness and worldliness and that only here and there are a few rare sentiments that come from the depths of the soul." But, as we saw in the second chapter, as long as India will not realize what a treasure not only for herself, but also for the whole humanity it possesses in the Vedas, the seed of discord planted by the missionaries and the so-called sanskritists will continue its work of ignorance.

Thus, once these three disinformations, that of the Aryans, the caste system and the Vedas, have been set right, one can begin to perceive in its proper perspective the Wonder that WAS India.

CHAPTER 9

The Independence Movement

It is hoped that one day the history of India's independence movement will be totally rewritten. For what is now taught, both in the West and in India, is often the history of the superficial, the apparent, the false even. And those who have least contributed to India's independence, or worse who were partially responsible for its most terrible traumas, occupy a place of honour in those books, while those who had a deeper vision and worked with dedication for a true, wholesome independence, are in the shadow and have been waylaid by Historians.

History wants us to believe that the independence movement started with the Indian National Congress. But originally, the Congress was a tool fashioned by the British for their own use. Witness the fact that it all began in December 1885, with an Englishman, A.O. Hume, with the avowed aim to: "Allow all those who work for the national (read British) good to meet each other personally, to discuss and decide of the political operations to start during the year."

And certainly, till the end of the 19th century, the Congress, who regarded British rule in India as a "divine dispensation," was happy with criticizing moderately the Government, while reaffirming its loyalty to the Crown and its faith in "liberalism" and the British innate sense of justice!!!

Thus for a long time, the Britishers considered sympathetically the Congress and sought to use it to justify their continuing occupation of India. But soon of course it changed into suspicion and downright hostility, as the Congress, realising is folly, turned towards constitutional agitation to obtain from the British Parliament a few laws favourable to India. And the Englishmen did hand over a few crumbs here and there, such as giving Lord Sinha (Lord Sinha indeed!) the honour of becoming the first Indian to be part of the Governor's Executive Council...

So what ?

What must be understood to grasp the whole history of the Congress, is that its pre-independence leaders were anglicised, western educated Indians, whose idealism was at best a dose of liberalism peppered with a bit of socialism "British Labour style." They were the outcrop of an old British policy of forming a small westernised elite, cut off from its Indian roots, which will serve in the intermediary hierarchies of the British Raj and act as go-between the master and the slaves. Thus, not only were these Congress leaders "moderate" (as they came to be called), partially cut-off from the reality of India, from the greatness that Was India, the soul-glory of its simple people, but because their mind worked on the pattern of their masters, they turned to be the greatest Hindu-baiters and haters of them all—as verily their descendants, even until today, still are.

But these westernised moderate Congress leaders, found it difficult to get identified by the vast mass of India which was deeply religious. Thus they encouraged the start of "reformed" Hindu movements, such as the Arya Samaj or the Brahma Samaj, through which they could attack the old Hindu system, under the guise of transforming it, which is perfectly acceptable to all Hindus, as Hinduism has always tolerated in its fold divergent movements. It is these early Congress leaders who began the slow but insidious crushing of the Hindu society. For instance, the Congress Governments, which were installed after July 1937 in most of the provinces, encouraged everywhere the development of education modelled on the British system. And comments Danielou: "the teaching of philosophy, arts, sciences, which constituted the prestigious Indian cultural tradition, became more and more ignored and **could only survive thanks to the brahmins**, without any help whatsoever from the State." When the first true cultural, social and political movements, which had at heart the defence of India's true heritage started taking shape, such as the much decried Hindu Mahashaba, which attempted to counterbalance the Muslim League's influence, or the even more maligned Rama Rajya Parishad, initiated by the remarkable Hindu monk Swamy Karpatri, they were ridiculed by the Congress, which used to amplify the problems of untouchability, castes, or cow worshipping, to belittle these movements, which after all, were only trying to change India from a greatness that was to a greatness to be.

"The Congress, writes Danielou, utilised to the hilt its English speaking press to present these Hindu parties as barbaric, fanatical, ridiculous; and the British media in turn, took-up, as parrots, the cry of their Indian counterparts." (Histoire de l'Inde, p. 345) To this day, nothing has changed in India: the English-speaking press still indulges in Hindu-bashing and it is faithfully copied by the western correspondents, most of whom are totally ignorant of India and turn towards Indian intellectuals to fashion their opinions.

But this strategy was good enough to convince the British that when they left, they would have to hand over power to the "respectable" Congress (after all, we are all gentlemen), even though it constituted a tiny westernised minority, whereas India's true Hindu majority would be deprived of their right.

The Congress did turn radical finally in 1942, when because of Mahatma Gandhi's rigorous non-violence policy, it adopted a non-co-operation attitude towards the war effort. Thus the British declared the Congress illegal, jailed most of its leaders and embarked on a policy of heavy repression. But the truth is that those of the Congress who were imprisoned and are deified today for that fact, went there not directly for India's independence, but because Mahatma Gandhi refused to cooperate in the second world war.

So, ultimately, what was true nationalism? Who were the real revolutionaries, those who had an inner vision of what the British really represented, those who knew what was the genius of India and how it was destined to be great again? Once more, we have a wrong understanding of nationalism, because we are induced in error by the West's opinions about it. In Europe, nationalism means external revolutionary movements, revolutionaries, materialism. But India's greatness has always been her spirituality, her strength was always founded upon her Spirit's hold. Not only her Brahmins, but also her Kshatriyas, Vaishyas and Shudras even, drew their heroism from that fountain. Thus in India, the nationalist movement, the **reawakening** of India's soul started at the source, in her Spirit.

Sometimes a nation's soul is more predominant in one region, in one particular culture. In India's early independence movement, it was Bengal which held high the light of reawakening. This has often been forgotten and justice should be done again. Thus, in Bengal, there was born a man who could not read and write a single word. A man without intellectual training, a man who would be considered totally useless by Britishers, or westernised Indians. But this man's inner strength was so great, his truth so radiating, that from all over India, educated and uneducated, rich and poor, they came to the temple of Dakshineshwar in Calcutta and bowed at the feet of Shri Ramakrishna. The work of salvation, the work of raising India out of her lethargic sleep **had begun**. Narendarnath Dutta, later known as Swami Vivekananda, was the brightest disciple of Ramakrishna, and a true son of India. He was the first spiritualised Indian political leader, an ardent Hindu, who was not afraid to call for Hinduism's adaptation to the modern world. He was also the first to inspire in the Western world a certain respect towards Hinduism, because of his education and his forceful personality.

But the man who was the true visionary of an independent India, the man who worked most of all for her liberation, the man who was a yogi, a saint, an avatar, has been mostly ignored by history. Others, who played only a superficial role and did not have a millionth of his vision took the forefront. That man of course was Sri Aurobindo. Born on the 15th August 1872 in Calcutta, he spends his first years at Rangpur (now in Bangladesh) and at the age of 5 is sent to Loreto Convent school in Darjeeling. His father, who wants him to have a thorough Western education, packs him to England, where he enters St Paul's School in London in 1884 and King's College, Cambridge in 1890. Sri Aurobindo is a brilliant student and passes the I.C.S., but "fails" to appear for the riding test and is disqualified. After 13 years in England Sri Aurobindo returned to India on 6 February 1893 at the age of 20. He joined the Baroda State Service from 1897 to early 1906 and taught French and English at the Baroda college, before eventually becoming its Principal. It was at that time that he started writing a series of articles "New lamps for Old" in the Indu Prakash, a Marathi-English daily from Bombay. Sample of his early writings: "I say of the Congress that its aims are mistaken, that the spirit in which it is proceeding is not a spirit of sincerity and whole-heartedness and that the methods it has chosen are not the right methods, and their leaders in whom it trusts, not the right sort of men to be leaders. In brief that we are at present the blind led, if not by the blind, at least by the one-eyed. (Rebirth of India, p. 10). From 1900 onwards, Sri Aurobindo realised that passive resistance, constitutional agitation "A La Congress," was not the right path to achieve an independent India. In the true spirit of a yogi, he re-enacted the Baghavad Gita's great message: that violence is sometimes necessary, if it flows from Dharma -and today's Dharma is the liberation of India. Thus he began contacting revolutionary groups in Maharashtra and Bengal and tried to co-ordinate their action. One should remember that at that time, and indeed until independence, violence against the oppressive British was not organised; it was the work of a few individuals or a sudden outburst of uncontrolled anger and that the famous freedom fighters of the Congress only went jail because they were passive resisters. At Sri Aurobindo's initiative, P. Mitter, Surendranath Tagore and Sister Nivedita formed the first Secret Council for revolutionary activities in Bengal. But action was accompanied by inner vision: "While others look upon their country as an inert piece of matter, forests, hills and rivers, I look upon my country as the Mother. What would a son do if a demon sat on her mother's breast and started sucking her blood?.. I know I have the strength to deliver this fallen race. It is not physical strength—I am not going to fight with sword or gun, but with the strength of knowledge." (India's Rebirth, p. 16)

In 1905, the terrible Lord Curzon partitioned Bengal. This divide-and-rule move was meant to break the back of Bengali political agitation and use the East Bengal Muslim community to drive a wedge between Hindus and Muslims, a policy that was to culminate in India's partition in 1947. Bengal responded to its partition with massive and unanimous protests in which many personalities took part, such as Rabindranath Tagore, Surendranath Banerjee, Bepin Chandra Pal.... The ideal of Swadeshi, which called for the boycott of British goods, spread widely.

It was at this time that B.C. Pal launched the famous English daily, Bande Mataram; Sri Aurobindo joined it and soon became its editor. Day after day, he jotted down his vision and tried to instill fire and courage in the nation through the pages of Bande Mataram. What was true nationalism for Sri Aurobindo? "Nationalism is not a mere political program; nationalism is a religion that has come from God; Nationalism is a creed which you shall have to live.. If you are going to be a nationalist, if you are going to assent to this religion of Nationalism, you must do it in the religious spirit. You must remember that you are the instruments of God.... Then there will be a blessing on our work and this great nation will rise again and become once more what it was in the days of spiritual greatness. You are the instruments of God to save the light, to save the spirit of India from lasting obscuration and abasement..." (Bande Mataram, P.655)

But Sri Aurobindo had to fight against the Congress Moderates (who, it must be remembered came out openly for complete independence only in 1929) of whom he said: "There is a certain section of India which regards Nationalism as madness and they say Nationalism will ruin the country. They are men who live in the pure intellect and they look at things purely from the intellectual point of view. What does the intellect think? Here is a work that you have undertaken, a work so gigantic, so stupendous, the means of which are so poor, the resistance to which will be so strong, so organised, so disciplined, so well equipped with all the weapons science can supply, with all the strength that human power and authority can give.... (Bande Mataram, p. 656)

Sri Aurobindo was very clear in what was demanded of a leader of India: "Politics is the work of the Kshatriya and it is the virtues of the Kshatriya we must develop if we are to be morally fit for freedom (India's Rebirth, p. 19). Or: "What India needs at the moment is the aggressive virtues, the spirit of soaring idealism, bold creation, fearless resistance, courageous attack." (India's rebirth, p. 22) But if the Moderates dismissed Sri Aurobindo as a "mystic," Lord Minto, then Viceroy of India, made no such mistake, calling him, "the most dangerous man we have to deal with at present." Thus Sri Aurobindo was arrested on May 2d 1908, following a failed assassination attempt on a British judge by a nationalist belonging to his brother's secret society. Sri Aurobindo spent a year in jail, which proved to be the turning point of his life as he went through the whole gamut of spiritual realisations. When he came out, the nationalist movement had nearly collapsed and he set about giving it a fresh impetus, launching a new English weekly, the Karmayogin, as well as a Bengali weekly, Dharma. This following is an extract from his famous Uttarpara speech, where he speaks of his spiritual experiences in jail: "Something has been shown to you in this year of seclusion, something about which you had your doubts and it is the truth of the Hindu religion. It is this religion that I am raising up before the world, it is this that I have perfected and developed through the rishis, saints and avatars, and now it is going forth to do my work among the nations. I am raising this nation to send forth my word.... When therefore it is said that India shall rise, it is the Santana Dharma that shall rise. When it is said that India shall be great, it is the Santana Dharma that shall be great. But what is the Hindu religion? It is the Hindu religion only, because the Hindu nation has kept it, because in this peninsula it grew up in the seclusion of the sea and the Himalayas, because in this sacred and ancient land it was given as a charge to the Aryan race to preserve through the ages. That which we call the Hindu religion is really the eternal religion, because it is the universal religion which embraces all others. If a religion is not universal, it cannot be eternal. A narrow religion, a sectarian religion, an exclusive religion can live only for a limited time and limited purpose ... I say no longer that Santana Dharma is for us nationalism.... Santana Dharma IS nationalism." (India's Rebirth, p.46)

In mid-February 1910, news reached that the British had again decided to arrest Sri Aurobindo and close down the offices of the Karmayogin. By that time Sri Aurobindo had the vision that India was free; for the external events are always preceded by an occult happening, sometimes long before they become "fait accompli." Sri Aurobindo then received an "Adesh," an inspiration that he must go to Pondichery, then under French rule. He settled there, with a few disciples, the number of whom slowly swelled, until it became known as the Sri Aurobindo Ashram. He wrote all his masterpieces and devoted the remaining of his life to bringing down what he called the "supramental manifestation on the earth." The great Sage passed away on 5 December 1950.

Hinduism, true Hinduism was for Sri Aurobindo the basis for India's past greatness, it was also the essence of nationalism, the MEANS of liberating India and ultimately the foundation of the future India. Unfortunately, the leaders of the Indian National Congress did not have the same vision. Of these leaders, history has mostly remembered two, the most famous of all: Jawaharlal Nehru and Mahatma Gandhi.

9.1 Jawaharlal Nehru

Nehru, writes Danielou, "was the perfect replica of a certain type of Englishman. He often used the expression 'continental people,' with an amused and sarcastic manner, to designate French or Italians. He despised non-anglicised Indians and had a very superficial and partial knowledge of India. His ideal was the romantic socialism of 19th century Britain. But this type of socialism was totally unfit to India, where there was no class struggle and where the conditions were totally different from 19th century Europe." (Histoire de l'Inde p. 349) It should be added that Nehru was not a fiery leader, maybe because of his innate "gentlemanship" and often succumbed not only to Gandhi's views, with which he sometimes disagreed, not only to the blackmailing of Jinnah and the fanatical Indian Muslim minority, but also to the British, particularly Lord Mountbatten, whom history has portrayed as the benevolent last Viceroy of India, but who actually was most instrumental in the partition of India, whatever "Freedom at Midnight" a very romanticised book, says. (Remember Churchill's words on learning about Partition: "At last we had the last word"). It may be added that the British had a habit of leaving a total mess when they had to surrender a colony, witness Palestine, Ireland, or India.

Nehru has also been made into a myth by foreign writers, such as French Catherine Clement, who wrote a ridiculous and pompous novel depicting the loves between Nehru and Lady Mountbatten. The problem is not whether they had sex or not together, the problem rather, is that this "affair" only symbolizes the fatal attraction which Nehru had for the White

Skin—for Edwina Mountbatten was certainly not a beauty, but was in fact renowned for her nymphomania and inconsequence—an attraction for the White Skin which the Congress perpetuated faithfully and still incarnated today by Sonia Gandhi, who is able to woo the masses, when she has absolutely no qualifications to lead India. The problem is not whether Mountbatten was made a cuckold or not - but that it was India which was cuckolded, for Nehru was unfaithful to India by letting his weaknesses influence him in accepting partition and the terms dictated by the British.

The Congress has today made an icon out Nehru, which nobody has yet dared to touch, but as we will see in the next chapter and as History will show more and more, Nehru did tremendous harm to India by initiating movements and patterns, which not only did vast damage in their times, but continue to survive and weigh down the Indian nation, long after their uselessness has been realized.

9.2 Mahatma Gandhi

Mahatma Gandhi was indeed a great soul, an extraordinary human being, a man with a tremendous appeal to the people. But, unfortunately, he was a misfit in India. Karma or fate, or God, or whatever you want to call it, made a mistake when they sent him down to the land of Bharat. For at heart, Gandhi was a European, his ideals were a blend of Christianity raised to an exalted moral standard and a dose of liberalism "à la Tolstoy." The patterns and goals he put forward for India, not only came to naught, but sometimes did great harm to a country, which unquestionably he loved immensely. Furthermore, even after his death, Gandhism, although it does not really have any relevance to Modern India, is still used shamelessly by all politicians and intellectuals, to smoke-screen their ineffectiveness and to perpetuate their power. To understand Gandhi properly, one has to put in perspective his aims, his goals, and the results today.

One has to start at the beginning. There is no doubt that after his bitter experiences with racism in South Africa, he took to heart the plight of fellow Indians there. But what did he achieve for them? Second class citizenship! Worse, he dissociated them from their black Africans brothers, who share the same colour and are the majority. And today the Indians in South Africa are in a difficult position, sandwiched between the Whites who prefer them to the Blacks, but do not accept them fully as their own and the Blacks who often despise them for their superior attitudes. Ultimately, they sided with the Moderate Whites led by De Klerk and this was a mistake as Mandela was elected and the Blacks wrested total power in South Africa—and once more we might have an exodus of Indians from a place where they have lived and which they have loved for generations.

The Mahatma did a lot for India. But the question again is: What remains today in India of Gandhi's heritage? Spinning was a joke. "He made Charkha a religious article of faith and excluded all people from Congress membership who would not spin. How many, even among his own followers believe in the gospel of Charkha? Such a tremendous waste of energy, just for the sake of a few annas is most unreasonable," wrote Sri Aurobindo in 1938 (India's Reb 207). Does any Congress leader today still weave cotton? And has Gandhi's khadi policy of village handicrafts for India survived him? Nehru was the first to embark upon a massive "Soviet type" heavy industrialisation, resolutely turning his back on Gandhi's policy, although handicrafts in India do have their place.

Then, nowhere does Gandhi's great Christian morality find more expression than in his attitude towards sex. All his life he felt guilty about having made love to his wife while his father was dying. But guiltiness is truly a Western prerogative. In India sex has (was at least) always been put in its proper place, neither suppressed, as in Victorian times, nor brought to its extreme perversion, like in the West today. Gandhi's attitude towards sex was to remain ambivalent all his life, sleeping with his beautiful nieces "to test his brahmacharya," while advocating abstinence for India's population control. But why impose on others what he practiced for himself? Again, this is a very Christian attitude: John Paul II, fifty years later, enjoins all Christians to do the same. But did Gandhi think for a minute how millions of Indian women would be able to persuade their husbands to abstain from sex when they are fertile? And who will suffer abortions, pregnancy and other ignominies? And again, India has totally turned its back on Gandhi's policy: today its birth control program must be the most elaborate in the world -and does not even utilise force (except for a short period during the Emergency), as the Chinese have done.

For all the world, Gandhi is synonymous with non-violence. But once more, a very Christian notion. Gandhi loved the Mahabharata. But did he understand that sometimes non-violence does more harm than violence itself? That violence sometimes is "Dharma," if it is done for defending one's country, or oneself, or one's mother, or sisters? Take the Cripps proposals for instance. In 1942, the Japanese were at the doors of India. England was weakened, vulnerable and desperately needs support. Churchill sent Sir Stafford Cripps to India to propose that if India participated in the war effort, Great Britain would grant her Dominion status (as in Australia or Canada) at the end of the war. Sri Aurobindo sent a personal letter to the Congress, urging it to accept. Nehru wavered, but ultimately, Gandhi in the name of non-violence put his foot down and the Cripps proposal was rejected. Had it been accepted, history might have been changed, Partition and its terrible bloodshed would have been avoided.

Gandhi also never seemed to have realised the great danger that Nazism represented for humanity. A great Asuric wave had risen in Europe and threatened to engulf the world and it had to be fought -with violence. Calling Hitler "my beloved brother," a man who murdered 6 million Jews in cold-blood just to prove the purity of his own race, is more than just innocence, it borders on criminal credulity. And did not Gandhi also advise the Jews to let themselves be butchered?....

Ultimately, it must be said that whatever his saintliness, his extreme and somehow rigid asceticism, Gandhi did enormous harm to India and this harm has two names: Muslims and Untouchables.

The British must have rubbed their hands in glee: here was a man who was perfecting their policy of rule-and-divide, for ultimately nobody more than Gandhi contributed to the partition of India, by his obsession to always give in to the Muslims, by his obstinate refusal to see that the Muslims always started rioting—Hindus only retaliated; by his indulgence of Jinnah, going as far as proposing to make him the Prime Minister of India. Sri Aurobindo was very clear about Hindu-Muslim unity: "I am sorry they are making a fetish of Hindu-Muslim unity. It is no use ignoring facts; some day the Hindus may have to fight the Muslims and they must prepare for it. Hindu-Muslim unity should not mean the subjection of the Hindus. Every time the mildness of the Hindu has given way. The best solution would be to allow the Hindus to organise themselves and the Hindu-Muslim unity would take care of itself, it would automatically solve the problem. Otherwise we are lulled into a false sense of satisfaction that we have solved a difficult problem, when in fact we have only shelved it." (India's Rebirth, p. 159)

Gandhi's love of the Harijans, as he called them, was certainly very touching and sprang from the highest motivations, but it had also as its base a Christian notion that would have found a truer meaning in Europe, where there are no castes, only classes. Glorifying the scavenger as a man of God makes good poetry, but little social meaning. In the words of Sri Aurobindo: "the idea that it needs a special "punya" to be born a Bhangi is, of course one of these forceful exaggerations which are common to the Mahatma and impress greatly the mind of his hearers. The idea behind is that his function is an indispensable service to society, quite as much as the Brahmin's, but that being disagreeable, it would need a special moral heroism to choose it voluntarily and he thinks as if the soul freely chose it as such a heroic service to the society and as reward of righteous acts—but that is hardly likely. In any case, it is not true that the Bhangi life is superior to the Brahmin life and the reward of special righteousness, no more that it is true that a man is superior because he is born a Brahmin. A spiritual man of pariah birth is superior in the divine values to an unspiritual and worldly-minded Brahmin. Birth counts but the basic value is in the soul behind the man and the degree to which it manifests itself in nature." (India's Rebirth, p.201)

Once more Gandhi took the European element in the decrying of the caste system, forgetting the divine element behind. And unfortunately he sowed the seeds of future disorders and of a caste war in India, of which we see the effects only today.

Non-violence, you say? But Gandhi did the greatest

violence to his body, in true Christian fashion, punishing it, to blackmail others in doing his will, even if he thought it was for the greater good. And ultimately, it may be asked, what remains of Gandhi's non-violence to day? India has fought three wars with Pakistan, had to combat the Chinese, has the second biggest army in the world and has to fight counter-insurgency movements in Punjab, Assam and Kashmir. Gandhi must have died a broken man indeed. He saw India partitioned, Hindus and Muslims fighting each other and his ideals of Charhka, non-violence and Brahmacharya being flouted by the very men he brought-up as his disciples.

However, his heritage is not dead, for it survives where it should have been in the first instance: in the West. His ideals have inspired countless great figures, from Martin Luther King, to Albert Einstein, to Nelson Mandela, the Dalaï-Lama or Attenborough and continue to inspire many others. Gandhi's birth in India was an accident, for here, there is nothing left of him, except million of statues and streets and saintly mouthings by politicians, who don't apply the least bit what Gandhi had taught so ardently.

History will judge. But with Nehru on one side and his westernised concept of India and Gandhi on the other, who tried to impose upon India a non-violence which was not hers, India was destined to be partitioned. Thus when the time came, India was bled into two, in three even, and Muslims took their pound of flesh while leaving. India never recovered from that trauma and today she is still suffering from its consequences. Yet has anybody really understood the lessons of history ?

P.S. The history of India's independence movement would be incomplete without mentioning the West's contribution. Perhaps the redeeming factor for the Britisher's utter insensitiveness, lies in Sister Nivedita's recognising India's greatness and consecrating her life and work not only to India but to its independence. The Theosophical Society started in 1875 by Mrs Blavatsky, a Russian and an American, Colonel Olcott, and brought to glory by Annie Besant, has also done a great deal to further abroad Hinduism's cause. Its philosophy is founded upon the recognition of Hinduism as one of the highest forms of revelation, as Mrs Besant wrote: "The action to pursue is to revitalise ancient India to bring back a renewal of patriotism, the beginning of the reconstruction of the nation." Unfortunately, the Theosophical Society got often bogged down in concentrating on the "magical mystical Orient."

Chapter 10

1947: Independence

India was free. But at what price! Was this the independence that so many nationalists had fought for and for which they had lost their lives? Was this truncated, diminished, partitioned India the true Bharat of old, whose mighty borders once extended from Cape Comorin to Afghanistan?

Moreover, who was responsible for the Partition of India? Yes, the British used to the hilt the existing divide between Hindus and Muslims. Yes, the Congress was weak; it accepted what was forced down its throat by Jinnah and Mountbatten, even though many of its leaders, including Nehru, and a few moderate Muslims, disagreed with the principle of partition. It was also Gandhi's policy of non-violence and gratifying the fanatical Muslim minority, in the hope that it would see the light, which did tremendous harm to India and encouraged Jinnah to harden his demands.

But ultimately, one has to go back to the roots, to the beginning of it all, in order to understand Partition. One has to travel back in history to get a clear overall picture. This is why memory is essential, this is why Holocausts should never be forgotten.

For the Jinnah's, the Zia ul-Hacq's, the Musharraf's and today the Imran Khans, are only the vehicles, the instruments, the avatars, the latest reincarnations of the medieval Muslims coming down to rape and loot and plunder the land of Bharat. They are the true sons of Mahmud Ghaznavi, of Muhammed Ghasi, of Aurangzeb. They took up again the work left unfinished by the last Mughal two centuries earlier: 'Dar-ul-Islam,' the House of Islam. The Hindu-Muslim question is an old one—but is it really a Muslim-Hindu question, or just plainly a Muslim obsession, their hatred of the Hindu pagans, their contempt for this polytheist religion? This obsession, this hate, is as old as the first invasion of India by the original Arabs in 650. After independence, nothing has changed: the sword of Allah is still as much ready to strike the Kafirs, the idolaters of many Gods. The Muslims invaded this country, conquered it, looted it, razed its temples, humiliated its Hindu leaders, killed its Brahmins, converted its weaker sections. True, it was all done in the name of Allah and many of its chiefs were sincere in thinking they were doing their duty by hunting down the Infidel. So how could they accept on 15th August 1947 to share power on an equal basis with those who were their slaves for thirteen centuries? *Either the sole power for ourselves, and our rule over the Hindus as it is our sovereign right, we the adorers of the one and only true God—Or we quit India and found our own nation, a Muslim nation, of the true faith, where we will live amongst ourselves*.

Thus there is no place for idolaters in this country, this great nation of Pakistan; they can at best be "tolerated" as second-class citizens. Hence the near total exodus of Hindus from Pakistan, whereas more than half the Muslim population in India, chose to stay, knowing full well that they would get the freedom to be and to practice their own religion. In passing, the Muslims took revenge on the Hindus—once more—and indulged in terrible massacres, which were followed by retaliations from Sikhs and hard core Hindus, the ultimate horror.

Partition triggered one of the most terrible exodus in the history of humanity. And this exodus has not ended: they still come by the lakhs every year from Bangladesh (it is estimated that there are today *twelve million* illegal Bangladeshis in India), fleeing poverty, flooding India with problems, when the country has already so many of her own. Some even say that they bring with them more fundamentalism, a Third Column, which one day could organise itself in a political, social and militant body.

For Danielou, the division of India was on the human level as well as on the political one, a great mistake. "It added, he says, to the Middle East an unstable state (Pakistan) and burdened India which already had serious problems." And he adds: "India whose ancient borders stretched until Afghanistan, lost with the country of seven rivers (the Indus Valley), the historical centre of her civilisation. At a time when the Muslim invaders seemed to have lost some of their extremism and were ready to assimilate themselves to other populations of India, the European conquerors, before returning home, surrendered once more to Muslim fanaticism the cradle of Hindu civilisation." (Histoire de l'Inde, p.355)

For Sri Aurobindo also, the division of India was a monstrosity: "India is free, but she has not achieved unity, only a fissured and broken freedom.... The whole communal division into Hindu and Muslim seems to have hardened into the figure of a permanent political division of the country. It is to be hoped that the Congress and the Nation will not accept the settled fact as for ever settled, or as anything more than a temporary expedient. For if it lasts, India may be seriously weakened, even crippled; civil strife may remain always possible, possible even a new invasion and foreign conquest. The partition of the country must go.... For without it the destiny of India might be seriously impaired and frustrated. That must not be." (Message of Sri Aurobindo on the 15th of August 1947).

Sri Aurobindo had long seen through the British and Jinnah's games and had warned the nation as early as the beginning of the century. His answer to a disciple on 7 October 1940 is very illustrative of the point:

"Q. But now that our national consciousness is more developed, there is more chance of unity if the British don't bolster up Jinnah and his Muslim claims.

A. Does Jinnah want unity?... What he wants is independence for Muslims and if possible rule over India. THAT IS THE OLD SPIRIT... But why is it expected that Muslims will be so accommodating?"

Nevertheless, Sri Aurobindo thought that although the old spirit of the real warriors of Islam, the Muslim invaders, was still present, the majority of Indian Muslims were unconcerned: "The idea of two nationalities in India is only a new-fanged notion invented by Jinnah for his purposes and contrary to the facts. More than 90% of the Indian Muslims are descendants of converted Hindus and belong as much to the Indian nation as the Hindu themselves. Jinnah is himself a descendant of a Hindu named Jinahbahai.... (India's Rebirth, p. 237)

Sri Aurobindo also sought to dispel the widespread notion that the Muslims brought so much to India: "The Islamic culture hardly gave anything to the world which may be said of fundamental importance and typically its own Islamic culture was mainly borrowed from the others. Their mathematics and astronomy and other subjects were derived from India and Greece. It is true they gave some of these things a new turn, but they have not created much. Their philosophy and their religion are very simple and what they call Sufism is largely the result of Gnostics who lived in Persia and it is the logical outcome of that school of thought largely touched by the Vedanta.... Islamic culture contributed the Indo-Saracenic architecture to Indian culture. I do not think it has done anything more in India of cultural value. It gave some new forms to art and poetry. Its political institutions were always semi-barbaric. (p.189 India's Reb).

How could Partition have been avoided? Sri Aurobindo had advocated firmness: "As for the Hindu-Muslim affair, I see no reason why the greatness of India's past or her spirituality should be thrown into the waste paper basket in order to conciliate the Moslems who would not be conciliated at all by such a policy. What has created the Hindu-Moslem split was not Swadeshi, but the acceptance of a communal principle by the Congress." (India's Rebirth, p. 189). History was going to show the accuracy of Sri Aurobindo's predictions: the Congress' obstinate pandering to Jinnah and his terms, proved to be disastrous and the partition of India was a blow from which the nation has not yet recovered.

All right, Nehru got his 'tryst with destiny', although a truncated tryst. India was free and everything was anew, the sky was the limit and a new glory was awaiting the land of Bharat. But what did Nehru and the Congress proceed to do with this new India? Writes Danielou: "The Hindus who had mostly supported the Congress in its fight for independence, had thought that the modernist ideology of an Anglo-Saxon inspiration of its leaders was only a political weapon destined to justify independence in the eyes of Westerners. They thought that once independence was acquired, the Congress would revise its policies and would re-establish proper respect towards Sanskrit culture, Hindu religious and social institutions, which form the basis of Indian civilisation. But nothing doing, the minority formed by the Congress leaders was too anglicised, to reconsider the value of what they had learnt. Few things changed in Indian administration, only the colour of the skin of the new rulers, who were most of the time lower ranks officials of the old regime." (Histoire de l'Inde, p. 348)

And indeed, on top of the Partition tragedy, there is the other calamity of modern India: namely that under Nehru's leadership, it chose to turn its back on most of its ancient institutions, social and political and adapted blindly and completely the British system, constitutional, social, political, judicial, and bureaucratic. For not only the Greatness that WAS India was ignored, but unconsciously, it is hoped, one made sure that there would never be a greatness that IS India.

Democracy was then the new name of the game for India. But Sri Aurobindo had very clear ideas on "western democracy: "I believe in something which might be called social democracy, but not in any of the forms now current, and I am not altogether in love with the European kind, however great it may be an improvement upon the past. I hold that India, having a spirit of her own and a governing temperament proper to her own civilisation, should in politics as in everything else, strike out her original path and not stumble in the wake of Europe. but this is precisely what she will be obliged to do if she has to start on the road in her present chaotic and unprepared condition of mind." This was written, mind you, on January 5 1920 (India's Reb 143)—and it was exactly what happened. Sri Aurobindo also felt: "The old Indian system *grew out of life*, it had room for everything and every interest. There were monarchy, aristocracy, democracy; every interest was represented in the government. While in Europe the Western system *grew out of the mind*: they are led by reason and want to make everything cut and dried without any chance for freedom or variation. India is now trying to imitate the West. Parliamentary government is not suited to India..."

Socialism certainly has its values, as Sri Aurobindo observed in 1914. "The communistic principle of society is intrinsically as superior to the individualistic as is brotherhood to jealousy and mutual slaughter; but all the practical schemes of Socialism invented in Europe are a yoke, a tyranny and a prison." (India's Reb 99). "At India's independence, Nehru opted for what Danielou calls "romantic socialism." Was socialism best suited for India? It was maybe a matter for the best in the worst, to forestall a complete take-over by communism,* which would have, as in China, entirely killed the soul of India and damaged for ever its Dharma. But if Nehru and the Congress leaders had not been so anglicised and had known a little more of the exalted past of their country, they would have opted for a more indianised system of socialism, such as the ancient panchayat system (which Rajiv Gandhi would attempt to revive later). Their socialism, although it was full of great and noble intentions, created great evils in India. Writes Danielou: "But this socialism was empty of meaning, for there existed no class struggle in India, nor social conditions similar to those in Europe. The controls established by a an incapable and corrupted bureaucracy, the ruin of private property, the incredible taxes slapped on capital, the confiscations, the dictatorial exchange controls, and the heavy custom duties, plunged India in a terrible misery. The lands of the zamindars were distributed to the poor peasants, without any institution of agricultural financing, and farmers depending 100% on the loan shark, got completely ruined and agricultural production went into a slump. The prohibition to export profits as well as the excessive taxes, forced all capitalist to flee the country." (Histoire de l'Inde p. 349)

One of the worst legacies of Nehru and the Congress is political. Like the British, Nehru centralised all the power at the Centre, the states were formed in an arbitrary manner and very little political autonomy was left to them. This created a land of babus and bred corruption. In turn, it triggered in certain states such as Tamil Nadu, whose culture has been preserved much more than in North Indian states, (maybe because it was more sheltered from Muslim incursions by the Deccan plateau), a resentment against the Centre, who was trying to impose Hindi on them, for instance, and fostered a seed of separatism.

Nehru also initiated the entire bureaucratisation of India, which was a terrible mistake, if only because it was a system established by the British who wanted to centralise and control everything from the top. It was all right when the English were there, they were the masters, they made their riches out of plundering the country and had no need to be corrupt. But how do you give so much power to an insensitive babu, who earns only a few thousand rupees a month? Hence corruption and bureaucracy flourished together in India under Nehru. The Soviet-type industrialisation, such as massive state industries, big steel, mills and mega dams, have already proved a failure in the West; yet Nehru and his successors all went for it. India became a state owned country which produced sub-standard quality goods. The only merit it had was to shelter her from a take-over by multinationals and allow her to develop her own products, however deficient.

Nehru's foreign policy was often misguided. Nothing exemplifies this better than his attitude vis a vis Red China. He made the mistake of applying to the letter his famous "Hindi chini bhai-bhai" slogan, when he should have known that China could not be trusted. And indeed the Chinese attacked India treacherously in 1962, humiliated the Indian army and took away 20,000 square kilometers of her territory, which they have not yet vacated. Nehru was generous enough to offer India's hospitality to the Dalai lama and his followers when they fled the Chinese occupation of their sovereign country in 1959. But in order not to offend the Chinese, Nehru and all the successive Prime Ministers, including Narendra Modi, let down Tibet, not only by not helping them to regain their independence, but also by stopping the Dalai lama from any political activity in India, including protesting against the hated Olympic Flame when it came to Delhi in April 2008. Do the Chinese show any gratitude? Not at all! They are still claiming Indian territory, particularly the beautiful Arunachal Pradesh. More than that, India could never see that Tibet was the ideal buffer between her and China, if denuclearised and demilitarised, as the Dalai-lama has proposed in the European Parliament of Strasbourg. And India's betrayal of Tibet will come back to haunt her, as it did recently, when the Indian occupation of Kashmir was equalled with the Chinese occupation of Tibet. The Chinese killed 1, 2 million Tibetans and wiped out in 45 years a wonderful 2000 year old civilisation. On the other hand, in Kashmir, there has been no genocide, only war casualties and India is fighting to retain what has been hers for 5000 years.

Indians are so proud of their judicial system; but isn't it a carbon copy of the British one, with as a consequence, a flurry of problems, whether it is the political interference in the naming of judges, the incredible backlog of pending cases, or the overcrowding of jails? Again, the Indian judiciary relies for his judgments on western values, on European jurisprudence, which are totally unfit for India. Once more, it is proud of its « secular » values and often comes down heavily on the fanatical bigots, meaning the Hindus.

In education, Nehru carried on with the British policy of imposing a westernised English system: more and more the universities and schools of India, many of them run by Christians missions, produced a generation of English speaking diploma holders, who did not belong any more to Hindu society, but only to a fake bureaucratic society with westernised manners.

Finally, Hindu-bashing became a popular pastime under Nehru's rule. Jawaharlal had a great sympathy for communism,* like many men of his generation and indeed of the generations thereafter till today. We have all been duped by communism, whose ideal is so appealing in this world of inequalities, but whose practise was taken over by Asuric forces, whether in Stalin's Russia, or in Maoist China. Nehru encouraged Marxist think-tanks, such as the famous JNU in Delhi, which in turn bred a lot of distinguished "Hindu-hating scholars" like the venomous Romila Thapar, who is an adept at negating Muslim atrocities and running to the ground the greatness of Hinduism and its institutions. Today even, most of the intellectuals, journalists and many of India's elite have been influenced by that school of thinking and regularly ape its theories.

*And so has Sonia Gandhi whose government was propped-up by communists who did great damage to India's interests, such as helping a Maoist government come to power in Nepal, the only Hindu state in the world.

CHAPTER 11

20th Century India: A Self-Denial

Why is it that Indians, particularly its elite - the intelligentsia, the journalists, the writers, the top bureaucrats, the diplomats - hold an image of themselves which is often negative, and have a tendency to run down their own country ?

The self-perception that Indians have of themselves, is frequently *detrimental* to their self-confidence. This is particularly striking amongst Indian journalists, who always seem to look at India through a *western* prism and constantly appear to worry how the foreign press views India, how the foreign countries—particularly the United States of America - perceive India, what the Human Right agencies say about India.... What matters to them is not what might utter India's sages, avatars, gurus, wise men and yogis, who dress Indian, eat Indian, think Indian and even dream Indian, but what the western media, or Amnesty International will think about India. They are not interested at all by what the Bhagavad Gita, probably the world's most revelatory, most comprehensive, most relevant sacred book has to say, or how Sri Sri Ravi Shankar, India's 21st century avatar, could help. No, they would rather turn to Thoreau, Marx or Jean-Paul Sartre, people who have even lost relevance in the West, for a solution to thy immense problems.

Thus, when one reads certain Indian magazines, one has the impression that they could be written by foreign journalists, because not only do they tend to look at India in a very critical manner, but often, there is nothing genuinely *Indian* in their contents, no references to India's past greatness, no attempts to put things in perspective through the prism of India's ancient wisdom.

Therefore, most of the time, their editorial contents endeavour to explain the present events affecting India, such as Ayodhya, or the problem of Kashmir, or the Christian missionaries' attempts at conversion of tribal Hindus, by taking a very small portion of the subcontinent's history— usually the most recent one—without trying to put these events in a broader focus, or attempting to revert back to India's long and ancient history. In a gist, one could say— although things have been changing in the late nineties—that there is hardly any self-pride amongst India's intellectual elite, because they are usually too busy running down their own country. It is done in a very brilliantly manner, it is true— because Indian journalists, writers, artists, high bureaucrats, are often intelligent, witty and talented people—but always with that western *slant*, as if India was afflicted by a permanent inferiority complex. One then has to try to *analyse* the underlying reasons of this negative self-perception that India has of herself, probe the unconscious impulses which give many Indians—Hindus, we should say, as the majority of India's intelligentsia are born Hindus—the habit of always depreciating their own culture and traditions. And certainly, Nehru, his daughter Indira, Rajiv and the subsequent Congress leaders must be held partly responsible for this lack of confidence.

11.1 The Humiliation of 1962

The so-called Kargil war of Kashmir in June 99 has triggered two very positive phenomenons for India. For the first time in a long stretch, it gave the country a bit of nationalism, it made many Indians proud of the heroism and selflessness of their soldiers. Whatever jingoism, or chauvinism there also was, one could feel, from Tamil Nadu to Punjab, that for a time there grew a feeling of togetherness in the nation, the knowledge of one's soldiers fighting it out there, in the harshest and most dangerous conditions and defending Mother India's sacred land. And that was very positive, for unless a nation possesses a bit of nationalism, it cannot keep on growing. And the second very positive aspect is that it has revived in India a notion which has been extinct for a long time : that of the kshatriya spirit. A nation needs warriors, it needs soldiers to defend itself and protect its women, children, and its borders from hostile and asuric elements, which throughout history have negated the Good and the Holy. It is fine to be Gandhian and non-violent, but in the tough and rough world of today, one cannot be too naïve: you need a strong and well-equipped army to be able to defend one's dharma. But a well equipped army is not enough—we have seen how today the United States' army, the most modern and high-tech of the world, is only capable of fighting from a distance, either bombarding from the sky, as they did in Yugoslavia or Afghanistan, or shooting from boats off-shore, a coward's war, as its soldiers have lost the sense of kshatriya, of honour, of dying for one's country. In Kargil, India saw the selflessness of its soldiers, with all the officers in front, climbing in the cold under enemy fire and wrestling peaks in impossible conditions, with little more than blood and tears.

But not only Indians lack self-confidence in their dealings with the West, but they seem to have a permanent fear of the Chinese. Is it because in 1962, the Chinese took advantage of India's naïveté, and attacked treacherously in the Himalayas, humiliating the Indian army and taking away 20.000 square kilometres of her territory, which they have not yet vacated ? India's first Prime Minister, Jawarlahal Nehru, had decided that India and China were the natural 'socialist' brothers of Asia. Shortly before China's attack, the Indian Army Chief of Staff had drafted a paper on the threats to India's security by China, along with recommendations for a clear defence policy. But when Nehru read the paper, he said: "Rubbish. Total Rubbish. We don't need a defence plan. Our policy is non-violence. We foresee no military threats. Scrap the Army. The police are good enough to meet our security needs." We know the results of this very foolish assessment.

But the biggest mistake that Nehru did, as we said earlier, was to betray Tibet, a peaceful spiritualised nation. If there is one thing which all political parties in India share, it is the policy of appeasing China in exchange for a non-interference of the Chinese in Kashmir. But what non-interference? Not only did China give Pakistan the know-how to develop nuclear weapons, but it also provided missiles to deliver them! On top of that, according to the CIA, China has transferred one third of its nuclear arsenal to Nagchuka, 250 kms away from Lhassa, a region full of huge caves, which the Chinese have linked together by an intricate underground network and where they have installed nearly one hundred Intercontinental Ballistic Missiles, many of them pointed at Indian cities. The reason for this is that the Chinese, who are probably among the most intelligent people in the world, have always understood that India is their number one potential enemy in Asia—in military, nuclear and economic terms.

It should be clear that as long as India does not stand-up up to its responsibility towards Tibet and continues to recognise China's unjust suzerainty of it, there will be no peace in Asia. Indian leaders are perfectly aware that the Chinese, a span of fifty years, have killed *1,2 million Tibetans*, razed to the ground 6254 monasteries, destroyed 60% of religious, historical and cultural archives and that one Tibetan out of ten is still in jail. As we enter the Third Millennium, a quarter million Chinese troops are occupying Tibet and there are 7,5 million Chinese settlers for six million Tibetans—in fact, in many places such as the capital, Lhassa, Tibetans are outnumbered two to one ... India has also to wake-up to the plain fact that China needs space and has hegemonic aspirations: it got Tibet, it got Hong Kong, it got part of Ladhak; now it wants Taiwan, Arunachal Pradesh, the Spratly islands and what not! Fifty years ago, during the Korean war, Sri Aurobindo, had seen clearly in the Chinese game: "the first move in the Chinese Communist plan of campaign is to dominate and take possession first of these northern parts and then of South East Asia as a preliminary to their manoeuvres with regard to the rest of the continent in passing Tibet as a gate opening to India."

India should overcome its awe of China and be ready to eventually face once more the Chinese army. The nuclear tests of India, which have been very criticised, because ideally you have to get rid of nuclear weapons if you want a safe world, should be seen in that light. Today, successive governments, such as the one of Narendra Modi, continue to pay visits to China with great fanfare ... and come back empty-handed, as the Chinese have perfected the art of smiling while stabbing you in the back. It is amazing today how China has managed to encircle India: Nepal, the only Hindu country in the world has fallen in the hands of Maoists. There are also very present in Burma because there is a lot of oil and gas there and it is very strategically placed in terms of maritime access to the Far East and from the Far East, westwards. India as usual is getting bypassed, because of inertia, indifference and a lack of a forceful will, although Burma falls within her natural sphere of influence. They have heavily invested in Sri Lanka and practically bought the entire country. In Doklam, the NarendraModi Govt held firm the first time, but quietly started again building a High Way bear Bhutan, that will give them military advantage in this strategically very weak part of Indi. The Chinese may also not directly do anything in Kashmir, but they hold a million square meters in Aksai Chin, given to Pakistan, but which rightfully belong to India....

11.2 Indira Gandhi

Indira certainly had a better understanding of the deeper, rural India than her father. But her legacy is still very bleak: she institutionalized the way the Congress still functions today, with its totally centralised pyramid-like system, with one person at the top wielding absolute power—and paved the way for Sonia Gandhi's absolute one-woman rule and the sycophancy surrounding her for ten years, from 2004 to 2014. Punjab and the Sikh problem however were the undoing of Indira; it poisoned the last years of her reign and finally killed her in the most frightful manner.

Wonderful religion that of Sikhism: the only true attempt ever to synthesise Hinduism and Islam—and who knows what would have happened if it had succeeded. "The Sikh Khalsa, writes Sri Aurobindo, was an astonishingly original and novel creation and its face was turned not to the past but to the future. Apart and singular in its theocratic head and democratic soul and structure, its profound spiritual being, its first attempt to combine the deepest elements of Islam and Vedanta, *it was a premature drive towards an entrance into the third or spiritual stage of human society*, but it could not create between the spirit and the external life the transmitting medium of a rich creative thought and culture. And thus hampered and deficient it began and ended with narrow local limits, achieved intensity but no power of expansion..." (Foundations of Indian Culture, p. 380)

Unfortunately, the Sikhs, because they had to defend themselves against the terrible persecutions by the Muslims, became a *militant* religion, adopting hawkish habits, which even in time of peace they kept. And they also retained some of the more negative side of Islam: intolerance, or feeling of persecution, thus cutting themselves from the mainstream spirit of Hindu tolerance and width- from which they anyway came, and where they might ultimately go back.

Today, but even more during Indira Gandhi's time, Sikhism is on the defensive, or rather displays an aggressive spirit of defence. Why? As Sri Aurobindo points out, Sikhism was a wonderful attempt at synthesising Islam and Hinduism, but because the conditions were not right, it faltered. And today, whatever the loveliness of Sikh rites, the incredible beauty of the Golden Temple and its wonderful atmosphere; Sikhism, like Zoroastrianism of the Parsi community, may be a stagnating religion—whereas Hinduism from which Sikhism sprang in greater part, is very much alive and remains the Dharma, the source of all religions in India. **it may be this unconscious realisation by the Sikhs that their religion is being slowly absorbed back into Hinduism, which triggers their militancy and fundamentalism**. And after all, what is fundamentalism, but going back to the fundamentals, the foundations? And Sikhism strove *best* when it was militant, when it fought the Muslims; thus unconsciously, the separatists of the late seventies went back to that crease, to that glorious epoch to regain their identity. That is all what separatism is, a desperate attempt to regain Sikh identity in the face of the all pervasive and subtle Hindu onslaught. The fact that the British had planted that seed of separatism and that later it was fuelled, financed and armed by Pakistan, certainly did not help. But can the British, or Pakistan, or even Indira Gandhi be credited with having of FABRICATED Sikh separatism? Mrs Gandhi was also accused of having 'created' Bhrindhrawale and made thus responsible for the whole Punjab problem. This is going to extremes; she may have helped politically Bhrindhrawale and thought of using him later to counterbalance her opponents in Punjab. That's bad enough; but Bhrindhrawale's fanaticism and violence was his own, he was just an embodiment of Sikh militancy and frustration; if he had not been there, another Bhrindhrawale would have sprung-up, with or without Mrs Gandhi's help.

Finally, Sikhs and many other Indians have not forgiven Mrs Gandhi for giving the order of storming the Golden Temple. History will judge. But think of it this way: would the French Government have tolerated that for months, Basque separatists, for instance, be holed up in the Notre Dame Cathedral in Paris, the holiest of all Christian shrines, with their weapons, issuing deaths warrants against politicians, and receiving journalists, as Bhrindhrawale did? Certainly not. These Basque militants would not have lasted three days in Notre Dame; the army would have been called—and although great care would have been taken that no harm be done to the wonderful 1000 year old church, it would have been a fight to the finish. Remember also what happened to the 350 militants who took over the Kaba in Mecca in 1989? Most of them were killed when the Saudi government sent its special forces against what is *the most sacred place* of worship in the world to all Muslims. It is a credit to Indira Gandhi and the inherent Indian tolerance, that Bhrindhrawale and his followers were allowed to hole-up for so long in the Golden Temple. No democratic government in Europe or any Arab state would have allowed such a situation to continue. It was unfortunate that the Golden Temple got damaged and so many were killed during the assault; but as the Head of Government, Mrs Gandhi took the correct decision. It was not her fault that the Sikhs allowed their most sacred place to become the shelter of men armed with weapons and with death in their hearts.

It is shameful that many Sikhs rejoiced when she was murdered in such a terrible way by her own Sikh bodyguards, men she had trusted, even though she had been told earlier to have all Sikhs removed from her personal security. To kill a woman lying on the ground with bullets, is a curse to any race that condones it. And ultimately, whatever her faults, Indira Gandhi—as she had predicted a few days before her assassination- did give her blood and her life for the country she loved in her own way. The vengeance of Hindus, backed by Congress leaders, was equally shameful and the culprits should be punished, it is never too late. Its is also sad that the Shiromani Gurdwara Prabandhak Committee (organisation in India responsible for the upkeep of gurdwaras), declared in 2007 Jarnail Singh Bhindranwale as a "martyr", coinciding with the anniversary of Operation Blue Star. Even more surprisingly, Indira Gandhi's murderers were also made into saints by the SGPC.

One can observe today a drifting away of the Sikhs from the mainstream Hindus—That is even more worrying and it should be addressed quickly by the mainstream community, as there are very few differences between these two people.

This is why, FACT-India, an organization, which highlights human rights abuses, which I head, has mounted a project on Sikhism. The objective is to show the Sikhs as the defenders of Indian Dharma. Throughout the ages, Sikhs have protected India from numerous onslaughts by foreign invaders—whether the Mughals or the British. This has not been recognized by society today.

We also need to bring the spirit of *Kshatriyas* back into the people of India, as today it again faces a threat to its culture and traditions from globalization and conversions. This will and courage to defend one's dharma from threats, both within and without, is still very strong in the Sikh community and this should be brought to the forefront and shared with the rest of the people of this country.

This project is in three parts:

1. A documentary film on the 1947 Holocaust when tens of thousands Sikhs and Hindus were slaughtered. Today many of the survivors or those who have been witnesses to the Holocaust are close to dying, so it's important we record their testimonies. We will have two versions: a 13 minutes film for TV's and a 35 minutes one for film festivals abroad.

2. A paintings' exhibition on Sikhism, on the same lines than the one I just did on Aurangzeb (see below the beheading of Guru Teg Bahadur) and the one I am preparing on Shivaji—that is original paintings signed and dated in Moghol miniature style, depicting impeccably documented historical scenes. I am looking for sponsors who could have a share in the exhibition, either in the sales of the paintings when we have shown it in India and the US, or in their ownership.

3. A Coffee Table Book with some of the photos shot during the film plus the paintings of the exhibition, recounting the birth of Sikhism and its history. We will have to find a publisher who will bear the costs.

The Exhibition, "Sikhs, the defenders of Indian Dharma," was inaugurated on 22nd January, 2008 at Delhi's Bangla Sahib Gurudwara by His Holiness Sri Sri Ravi Shankar and the Sikh Gurudwara Management Committee. It ran for twelve days and was viewed by more than a lakh people. It twill travel now across India and will go later to the UK, Canada and the US.

11.3 Rajiv

Rajiv Gandhi was typical of a certain breed of westernised Indians, totally ignorant about their own country, yet full of goodwill. It must be said to his defense that he was never interested in power, content to be a pilot, hobby around and live a quiet life with Sonia and his two children. But fate and his mother's distrust for everybody but her own sons, decided otherwise. It must also be said that the man (and his wife and children) demonstrated poise and dignity at his mother's assassination—and what a horrible way to lose one's mother—which could fill one's heart with hatred and ideas of vengeance. Rajiv showed in his early years goodwill and a sincere aspiration to transform the Indian system. But there were two problems: one was that being totally cut off from the Hindu reality of his country, he applied to his effort misconceived ideas about what India should be. And two, that like Don Quichote battling the windmills, he had to fight the Congress system, its corruption and bureaucracy. In the end he gave-up this unequal battle and had to fall back on advice from the old guard. His ill-advised judgment in the Shah Bano case or his pandering to Palestine, were certainly more in tune with the old Congress policy of flattering the Indian Muslim community, as in the pre-independence Kalhifat movement, than his own opinions, for everything in his upbringing was pro-Western and Israel certainly was no enemy of his. He must have also secretly agreed with the Supreme Court judgment in the Shah Bano case.

If his mother's downfall and ultimate death was due to the Sikh separatist problem, his undoing was Sri Lanka and the Tamil separatist factor there.

11. 4 Sri Lanka

There seems to be little doubt that once upon a time, not so long ago, India and Sri Lanka were linked by a small strip of land, which can still be seen today from the air: Adam's Bridge. Or Rama Setu, a 48 km long stretch of underwater causeway, spoken about in the Ramanayama. And this is how the first Tamils, those who settled in the North, came to Sri Lanka (are they the first inhabitants of Sri Lanka and not the Sinhalese? This is another question!). There is also no doubt—and the Sinhalese recognise it—that they are originally Indians, although some say that they came from Gujurat, others from Bengal. Thus it can be established beyond doubt that Sri Lanka and India are one ethnically, although they differ in religion (but the same can be said within India). And throughout the ages, under one form or the other, Ceylon was under the influence of India. That is why, when the British conquered it in the late 18th century, they chose to attach it to their Indian empire. But when they left in 47, in their desire to see that India never dominates too heavily the subcontinent, they facilitated the creation of Pakistan and handed to Sri Lanka its freedom. And India and Sri Lanka seemed to part way forever, as Tamils and Sinhalese were left to war with each other, until Rajiv sent the IKPF in 1988.

One has to go back a long time to understand what decisive factors shaped the psyche of the island's two communities. And this decisive factor bears the names of two of the world greatest religions: Buddhism and Hinduism. The first one, Buddhism, is a gentle, peaceful creed, that teaches non-violence and brotherhood, even to enemies. Unfortunately, Ceylon, often called the "isle of beauty," has always been too tempting a prey for sea-faring invaders. And indeed, successive colonisers, from Arabs to Africans, from Portuguese to Dutch and finally,

British, preyed on the tiny, defenseless island. In the name of Buddhism and because, the Sinhalese are by nature a fun—loving, gentle people, not only did they hardly resist these invasions, but often, many of their women, mingled freely with the foreign intruders. The result can clearly be seen today on the faces of many Sinhalese women folk, with their African—curled hair, Arabic features and fair skinned faces. As a result, the Sinhalese slowly lost their sense of identity, their feeling of being a collective being, to the point that when the British came, they collaborated wholehearted with them and had to be handed back their independence on a platter, for want of a real freedom movement. Today, democracy and western institutions are just a flimsy cloak that the Sinhalese wear. Lurking underneath the pleasant, sometimes servile attitude towards Westerners, is a sense of hopelessness and a terrible violence. And in reality, since independence, Sinhalese politicians must have been some of the least farsighted of the entire subcontinent: nothing is made in Sri Lanka, everything has to be imported and only tea, tourism and Western grants help the country survive.

On the other hand, Hinduism with its strict caste hierarchy, which forbids much contact with outsiders, particularly sexual contact with foreigners, protected Sri Lankan Tamils from mingling with their invaders. Thus they preserved their identity, their racial purity and their culture. Sinhalese live an easier life in the South, which was always more fertile than the arid North. As a result, Tamils have often been better at studies and more hard-working, (although one should not generalise). This was quickly noticed by the British, who often gave Tamils preference for jobs and university grants, thus angering the Sinhalese, who after all were the majority community.

It is this deep-rooted resentment of the Sinhalese towards the Tamil community which is the cause of most of the troubles. When the British left, the Sinhalese quickly moved in to correct what they saw as an unbalance: they set on depriving the Tamils of most of the rights they had acquired under the British and proceeded to establish a Sinhalese-dominated Ceylon. And every time a Sinhalese politician tried to give the Tamils their just share of power, he quickly had to backtrack under Sinhalese resentment. For years, the Tamils bore the brunt of Sinhalese persecution. But one day, too much became too much and Tamil armed groups started springing up to defend their people. To cut short a long story, the LTTE finally emerged as the most ruthless and sole militant organisation. For those who remember the Tamil Tigers in their early years: young, bright, soft spoken university students, there was no doubt that they had started with a genuine aspiration to secure their just rights. But violence breeds its own violence and soon the Tigers lost all sense of measure and restraint, eliminating ruthlessly all what they think stands in the way of their freedom. Killing Rajiv Gandhi was one of their biggest & most tragic mistakes and they finally paid that karma by being themselves ruthlessly wiped out by the Sinhalese, & Prabhakaran murdered in cold blood.

But the elimination of the LTTE does not solve the Tamil problem in Sri Lanka, as they continue to face discrimination and violence there. Only India has the power and the muscle to impose to Sri Lanka a just solution, which will give the Tamil minority an autonomy which will stop short of total independence. But is the will there? At the moment, the Indian Govt seems pretty helpless or indifferent to the grow Chine military presence in Sri Lanka, with a deep sea water port, that could accommodate Chinese submarines in case of a new Indo-Chinese war.

CHAPTER 12

The Bharatiya Janata Party Years

Western correspondents—and unfortunately also Indian journalists—keep labeling the BJP and organizations to which the BJP owes some of its ideologies—such as the RSS, or the VHP—as "Hindu nationalists," or "Hindu fundamentalists." But this is a totally false and misleading statement, as in the whole history of India, Hindus—who let us remember, are 850 millions today and constitute the overwhelming cultural and political majority of this country—have not only shown that they are extremely tolerant, but Hinduism is probably the only religion in the world which never tried to convert others or conquer other countries to propagate their own religion. This historical tolerance of Hinduism is never taken into account by foreign correspondents covering India and even, unfortunately, by Indian journalists.

On the other hand, Hindus suffered immensely at the hands of the two greatest "monotheists" religions of the world. And it is only in the last eighty years that some "nationalist " movements were born to try to preserve Hindu culture in the face of conversions by Christian missionaries and the rising influence of the Muslim League. These movements, whose descendants today are the RSS, the Shiv Sena or the VHP, may make preposterous statements—although that is debatable—but they have never killed anybody, never massacred anybody in the name of their God. Burning down a few makeshift churches, however reprehensible these acts are, does not make them nazis or even dangerous fundamentalists. Let's respect the proper use of words.

In 1984, the Bharatiya Janata Party bagged only two seats in the general elections, a total humiliation. Twelve years later, in 1996, it became the largest party in India with 186 MP's and came briefly to power, even though it's government was unfairly toppled ten days later. After the disastrous Governments of Gowda and LK Gujral, a well meaning but largely ineffective man.

This is why, after Sonia Gandhi, with the help of Jayalitha, toppled once more the BJP Government, with the covert help of the President of India and the Election Commissioner, the Indian electorate returned to power the BJP and its allies with a stumping majority. Vajpayee boasted two achievements: India tested successfully a nuclear device in the Pokhran desert (and was boycotted thereafter by the entire western world, except for France and fought Pakistani intruders in Kargil. The Indian soldiers performed very bravely in the face of tremendous odds and the international community appreciated India's restraint in not crossing over onto the Pakistani side of the LOC.

But BJP itself did not do as well as expected, specially in Uttar Pradeh, maybe because it had forsaken some of its original ideals, to satisfy its allies. Regrettably, the BJP, in its desire to appear "secular," forsook many of the ideals which had made it dear and unique in the eyes of many of India's voters, thus taking the road charted by the Congress before him. It did not take advantage of the unprecedented popularity it enjoyed once upon a time, of a new feeling of "nationalism" to come-up with some hard decisions, so as to "Indianize" the nation that it may manifest again its true unique soul: give back the power to the villages in the form of Panchayat. Reintroduce Sanskrit as the national language. Rewrite Indian History, which had mostly been devised by White Masters. Revive ancient traditional systems such as pranayama, yoga, and incorporate them in the education system and everyday life. Change the Constitution so that democracy may not be perverted as it is today Privatise the numerous "White Elephants," such as many of the Indian Banks, SAIL, ITDC, etc.... Many of the Hindu groups, like the RSS, are disappointed with the BJP leaders, although some of the Ministers, such as Dr Murli Manohar Joshi did try their best to Indianize culture and education in the face of much resistance.

Today, India is still viewed with suspicion by foreign Governments, although things are beginning to change, because this country is the leading exporter in the world of software programs and Indians abroad are making a mark for themselves. But let us remember how in the sixties, China was to the world a backward nation, the "Red Devil." Richard Nixon's visit there in 1971, changed everything: today, it is a must for Industrialized nations to invest there, even if the returns are very poor and China is bound sooner or later to enter into grave political turmoil when the bloody hand of communism is withdrawn. India's eventual admission in the Security Council of the UN will signal to the world that India is the next superpower of this century, the "other" democratic giant of Asia and that it is time for the West to start doing business with India.

12.1 "Nostradamus and the BJP"

Here below extracts of an article I wrote in 1999 for my Ferengi's column of the Indian Express. Was it prophetic ? Only time will tell....

Michel de Nostre-Dame, better known as Nostradamus (1503-1566), was a famous French astrologer whose predictions—which included the assassination of John Fitzgerald Kennedy, or the premature death of the previous Pope—have proved infallibly accurate.

Last month, unpublished manuscripts of Nostrodamus have been discovered (and authentified) in an old trunk in the French city of Lyon. Curiously, there are two full pages, which deal at length with India, particularly with the Bharatiya Janata Party and the just concluded elections. We are giving here the first words in Latin, the language which he used, along with a rough translation in English.

"Politicus Bharatus Janatus Indicus veni grandus est vingtus unus centurus—Congressus oublium est ..."

The Bharatiya Janata Party will come to dominate India in the 21st century, as the Congress, will slowly sink into oblivion.

"Malheureusus, duo annum millenium trahisonus idealum est Congressus ressemblum, fautum adoptus est. Electionirium Blanca Madamus attaquum..."

Unfortunately, to achieve power, the BJP may gradually forsake some of its idealism and it will not address the real burning changes which India needs to adopt so as to become again a Great Power."

And Nostradamus goes on to enumerate these changes:

"Congressus independantum Blancum copium est; necessarus changum indianus cumum facus est...."

As the Congress had heavily borrowed from the White Man (British?) at Independence, it will become necessary to "Indianize" the nation so that it may manifest again its true unique soul.

"Panchayatum villagum empruntus. Sanskritus introdum

est. Historicum ecritum manus, daemonus est. Yogum, respirationnus introdum est…"

Give back the power to the villages in the form of Panchayat. Reintroduce Sanskrit as the national language. Rewrite Indian History, which had mostly been devised by White Masters. Revive ancient traditional systems such as pranayama, yoga, and incorporate them in the education system and everyday life. Change the Constitution so that democracy may not be perverted as it will be

"Malheureusus, secularus montrarus Congressus devenium est, corptionus introdus cancerus est..."

Unhappily again, goes on to say Nostradamus, the BJP in its eagerness to prove itself secular (secularus is originally a Latin word), will tend to become like the Congress: corruption, bureaucracy, the VIP plague, the madness of subsidies and the hunger for power, may eat its inner core as a cancer…

And this is Nostradamus' scoop—if we may say:

"Politicus Bharatus Janatus interminum dividus duum et novus politicus formus…"

After some time, the Bharatiya Janata Party may split into two. Sincere idealists will form a parallel party which will have as its political platform many of the ideals which the BJP had forsaken.

"Indianus pretus reformus est, Grandus nationus manum…"

India by that time will be ready for the Big Change and the new party will sweep away the polls and implement these reforms.

"Sanskritus savantuus nationalum languus, decentralisum governmentus, aryanus theorum mortuum est, dharmum hinduus devenum. Christianum, Islamus influencum…"

Scholars will sit down to modernize and simplify Sanskrit; government will be decentralised; India will strive to form of a federation of SAARC countries; the theory of the Aryan invasion will be proved false and it will be shown that Indian civilisation is at least ten thousand years old and has influenced all great ancient civilisations and religions such as Christianity and even Islam.

And finally:

"Aurobindus Ghosus realisum est, Indianum Agus ancientus mortum non est.."

And the prophecy of Sri Aurobindo will be fulfilled: "India of the ages is not dead nor has She spoken Her last creative word. And that which She must seek now to awake, is not an anglicised oriental people, docile pupil of the West and doomed to repeat the cycle of the Occident's success and failure, but still the ancient immemorial Shakti recovering Her deepest self, lifting Her head higher towards the supreme source of light and strength and turning to discover the complete meaning and vaster form of Her Dharma."

12.2 Sonia and Rahul Gandhi and the Future of the Congress

When Sonia Gandhi took over the reins of the Congress beginning of 1998, it was thought that the party would revive its fortunes under her leadership. After all, was she not the inheritor of the Gandhi-Nehru dynasty? But under her rule, the Congress did disastrous showings at the polls, particularly during the 1999 elections, where it only got 112 seats, a rout royal; the party did not do well either in recent elections, whether Gujarat or UP. Yet, no voices were raised after these debacles to ask for her resignation, nobody, except Pawar and Sangma dared to challenge her autocratic ways, her absolute control over huge funds and foundations, her aloofness, surrounded that she is by security, sycophants and secretaries. Why is that? Everything possible has been said to explain how Congressmen, big and small, important and humble, are still debasing themselves in front of Sonia Gandhi, even though she is not the Congress President anymore. There is sycophancy, of course : it is an old Congress tradition, although it should be said that Indian sycophancy is a perverted offshoot of bhakti, the great Hindu tradition of worshipping "That" which seems to be above us, regardless of its value; there is obviously self interest—most of the Congress bigwigs, who are much more intelligent that they are credited for, know that without Sonia (or Nehru/or Rajiv/or Indira), they stand to get very little votes; there is the dynasty rule angle—but again, dynasty is a very western word, which applies more to the American soap opera of the same name, than to India, where the concept of bhakti, coupled with the old maharaja tradition, have always ensured respects for "royal" families; there is the foreign angle, naturally: let us not forget that the Congress was founded by a Scot, A.O Hume, and that for long it was manipulated by its British masters to ensure that India stayed with the Crown—with Sonia, another foreigner at its helm, Congress has come a full circle; lastly, there is an element which has been overlooked: the shakti element, which is so strong and prevalent in India, that it allowed Indira Gandhi to govern with an iron hand this male-dominated country for nearly twenty years and that it has even survived in the neighboring Islamic states, such as Pakistan or Bangladesh, witness the late Benazir Bhutto or the two Bangla Begums. But the main cause for this fascination that Sonia Gandhi, whatever her merits (and she did put some order and dignity back in the Congress) exercises on Indians in general, whether they love or hate her, is the Great Myth of the Aryan Invasion of India, of which we have spoken earlier. It is because of this Aryan myth that dark-skinned Indians of humble origin dream of having a white skin; it is because of this myth that even the upper-class Indians think that everything Aryan—read White—is better than their own culture; it is because of this myth that Indians come by droves to witness in person the White Skin of Sonia Gandhi when she comes in their areas to address a rally, even if they might not vote for her…

What is the future of Congress in 21st century India then, now that Rahul has taken over ? If it wants to be a worthy party, it should get rid of its hankering for the dynasty rule, and find within its ranks young and dynamic leaders—and there are quite a few waiting in the wings, more than the BJP even, where leaders are quite old generally. It should also look at the past in a frank and open manner and acknowledge the great blunders it committed since the beginning of the century: the pandering to the Muslim League by Gandhi, specially the horrifying Khalifat episode, the partition of India, for which Gandhi was also greatly responsible, the disastrous "socialist" policies of Nehru, his cowardly attitude towards China and Tibet, which led to the humiliation of the Indian army in 1962, the constant Hindu-baiting by the Nehruvian intelligentsia and Congressmen since 1926, and finally the catastrophic rules of Indira and Rajiv Gandhi, who whatever their goodwill, had no inkling about India's great past and potential spiritual future. Then only will have the Congress a chance to redeem itself and find a meaningful place in History books. Sadly today, it seems that Rahul Gandhi does not seem to have the necessary grip on Indian affairs to be a true successor of his grandmother.

CHAPTER 13

The Threats from Within

Narashima Rao had the misfortune to witness the Ayodhya drama and the internationalisation of the Kashmir problem during his tenure. To be fair to him, he was probably closer to the Hindu point of view on Ayodhya, than say, H.K. Gujral. Yet he was overtaken by the suddenness of events and had to react harshly to bolster up his image as well as India's reputation as a secular country. As for Kashmir, no Prime Minister, from Nehru downwards, dared to tackle the issue headlong, for fear of antagonising the Indian Muslims. Rao was no different. Nevertheless, during Narashima Rao's years, the twin dangers threatening India's disintegration came to the fore and exploded in full view. These dangers facing India today, come first from within, at the hands of Indian Muslims, Indian secularists and the missionary lobby, as well as from without, from hostile nations. If India survives these two life-threatening dangers to her inner soul, from within and without, she has a good chance of preserving her dharma and fulfil her destiny.

13.1 Kashmir

Western correspondents (and unfortunately sometimes Indian journalists) keep lionizing the Kashmiri "freedom fighters" and demonizing the "bad" Indian army. We see today that a Yasin Malik, a proven separatist, is invited at mainstream events, like the India Today Conclave. But Indian journalists should do well to remember Sri Aurobindo, who wrote in 1940: "in Kashmir, the Hindus had all the monopoly. Now if the Muslim demands are acceded to, the Hindus will be wiped out again." (India's Rebirth, p. 220) How prophetic! Because nobody cares to remember today that Kashmiris were almost entirely Hindus or Buddhists, before they were converted by the invading Muslims six centuries ago. True, today these Muslims in Kashmir have not only accepted as their own a religion which their ancestors had rejected, but they have also often taken-up the strident cry of Islam. Does any one remember too, that at the beginning of the century, there still were 25% Hindus in the Kashmir valley and that today the last 350,000 Kashmiri Pandits are refugees in their own land, they who originally inhabited the valley, at least 5000 years ago, a much bigger ethnic cleansing than the one of the Bosnian Muslims or the Albanians in Yugoslavia?

It's a common refrain today in most newspapers to say that since Independence India alienated Kashmiris through years of wrong policies. But those who have been in close contact with Kashmir, even in its heydays of tourism, know for a fact that as a general rule, Kashmiris **never** liked India. There was only one thing that attached them to India, it was the marvellous financial gains and state bounties that they made out of tourism. Even those Kashmiris who are now settled in India make no bones about where their loyalty lies. Talk to them, specially if you are a Westerner, and after some time, they'll open their hearts to you; whether it is the owner of this Kashmir emporium in a five star hotel in Chennai, or the proprietor of that famous travel agency in Delhi: suddenly, after all the polite talk, they burst out with their loathing of India and their attachment to an independent Kashmir. It's a bitter paradox, that Kashmiri Muslims, who don't consider themselves Indians, have taken over the Souvenir business, from Pune to Pondicherry and often spew their venom on innocent westerners.

The Government of India has also often the illusion that ordinary Kashmiris are fed up with the militants after years of fighting, militants' abuses and the partial dry-up of tourism revenues. The army might come-up with some disgruntled girl, who has been raped by the militants and whom they parade to the Indian press; or some family, whose father and sons have been killed by the Hizbullah because they're informers, might be willing to mouth their pro-Indian stance; but these are individual cases. Indeed, if you meet the Kashmiris of today, from the lowly unemployed sikara boatman, to the retired High Court judge, you will find that they are all unanimous in their hatred of the Indian army and their support of the militants. Kashmiris will stick together—and their family system ensures that they will support each other when in need.

Nowadays Farook Abdullah, or Ghulam Nabi Azad wants us to believe that with a certain degree of autonomy, or with the demlitarization of the Valley (Godf forbid!), Kashmiris will be appeased. This was further reinforced by the disastrous alliance of the BJPO with the PDP of Mrs Mufti, which thank God collapsed in 2018. For, basically, there is only one thing which Kashmiris are craving for and that is a plebiscite on whether they want to stay with India or secede...The answer in the Kashmir valley, would be a massive "**no**" to India (98%?). And as for Farook Abdullah, or Ghulam Nabi Azad, they would be quickly eliminated by the militants, who would immediately seize control of Kashmir and attach it to Pakistan.

Most of the Indian Media is after the army in Kashmir, which is accused of all kind of atrocities. But this is war, not a tea party! If India decides to keep Kashmir, it has to do so according to the rules set by the militants: violence, death and treachery are the order of the day. And men are men: after having been ambushed repeatedly, after having seen their comrades die, after weeks and weeks of waiting in fear, one day, they just explode in a burst of outrage and excesses. Amnesty International chooses to highlight "the Indian atrocities" in Kashmir. But Amnesty which does otherwise wonderful work to keep track of political atrocities world-wide, can sometimes become a moralistic, somewhat pompous organisation, which in its comfortable offices in London, judges on governments and people, the majority of whom happen to be belonging to the Third World. Its insistence on being granted unlimited access to Kashmir is a one-sided affair. Did Amnesty bother at all about the support given by the CIA to the most fundamentalists Mujhadins group in Afghanistan and Pakistan, support which led to the bleeding of Afghanistan and the Pakistani sponsoring of terrorism in India? (Without mentioning the fact that most of the Western countries which today sit in judgement of India, raped and colonised the Third World in the most shameless manner; and after all it happened not so long ago).

And this leads to the next question: should then India surrender to international pressure and let Kashmiris decide their own fate? Well it all depends on the Indian people's determination. Each nation has, or has had in the past, a separatist problem. Today, the Spanish have the Basques, the French the Corsicans, or the Turkish, the Kurds. Amnesty International will continue to lambaste India in its reports about human rights violations. But has Amnesty the right to decide what is right or wrong for each nation? Sometimes double standards are adapted by the West. Yesterday it colonised the entire Third World. Today; the United States, under the guise of human rights, is constantly interfering in other's people's affairs, often by force. It uses the United Nations, as it does in Iraq, in Somalia and Yugoslavia and is getting away with it. Can Amnesty International, the United States and the United Nations decide today what is democratic and what they deem anti-democratic and use their military might to enforce their views? But this is the trend today and it is a very dangerous and fascistic trend. Will tomorrow the United Nations send troops to Kashmir to enforce Pakistan's dreams?

Furthermore, there is today another very dangerous habit, which is to fragment the world into small bits and parts, thus reverting to a kind of Middle Age status, whereas small nations were always warring each other on ethnic grounds. It is the West and particularly the United States' insistence to dismantle Communism at all costs—which they managed to do everywhere, except in Cuba, thus encouraging covertly and overtly the breaking up of Russia and Eastern Europe, which started this fashion. But this is a risky game and tomorrow Europe and indirectly the USA will pay the price for it: Kosovo declared its independence and Europe will have to deal not only with Turkey in its fold (if its entry in EU is ever approved), but also with a 'White' Muslim nation in the heart of its territory.

Can India get herself dragged into this mire? Why should India which took so long to unite herself and saw at the departure of the British one third of its land given away to Pakistan, surrender Kashmir? The evolution of our earth tends towards UNITY, oneness, towards the breaking up of our absurd borders, the abolishing of passports, bureaucracies, no man's lands; not towards the building up of new borders, new customs barriers, new smaller nations. India cannot let herself be broken up in bits and parts just to satisfy the West's moralistic concerns, although it does have to improve upon its

Human Rights record, particularly the police atrocities and the misuse of TADA. To preserve her Dharma, India has to remain united, ONE, and even conquer again whether by force or by peaceful means, what once was part of her South Asian body . For this she should not surrender Kashmir, it could be the beginning of the breaking up of India.

13.2 The Indian Muslims

Since the late eighties, a radicalism seems to grip some of the Muslim youth, particularly in Kashmir. Yet, nowhere but in India, they have had so much freedom to practice their faith. Try to be a Hindu, a Buddhist or a Christian in Saudi Arabia or Bangladesh ! And we know that the Pakistani terrorists, such the ones who attacked Mumbai in 2011, could never function without the (very) active participation of some of India's Muslims, although Indian politicians keep mum about it.

Today it is even more acute: to physically attack a woman like Taslima Nasreen, forcing her to go in exile (she is back now, tks to the BJP Govt.), shows the intolerance of Indian Muslims today and how influenced they have been by the hard Wahabite streak that most of them pick up when to work in Gulf countries. Yet, they find it normal when a M.F. Hussain used to paint Hindu Deities naked and fornicating. Is there a logic in it?

The question that Indian Muslims should then ask themselves now is simple: "who are we"? Amongst the 120 millions of Muslims in India, only a tiny percentage descends from the Turks, Afghans, or Iranians who invaded India. The majority of them are converted Muslims. And converted how ? By terror, coercion, force, bloodshed. The ancestors of today's Indian Muslims are probably those who suffered the most from the Arab and Muslim invasions. Those Hindus and Sikhs who chose not to convert, took refuge in their faith, fought together and kept their pride and honor. The first two generations of those who converted must have endured hell: for they certainly did not convert out of conviction, but because they had no choice: their daughters and wives were raped, sons taken into slavery, parents killed. It is sad today that their descendants have sometimes made theirs the intolerant cry of Islam.

It is true that many Indian Muslims were Hindu intouchables. Marxists would like us to believe that they converted because they thought that they would access the more egalitarian society of Islam. What rubbish! Does one think in that way in time of war, terror and tears? Do today's Hindu lower castes convert to Islam when there is no more violent coercion? More likely, the Intouchables were the most vulnerable, the least apt to defend themselves; they had neither the faith of the brahmins, nor the riches of the vaishiyas, nor the military skill of the kshatriyas.

Do Indian Muslims understand that they were part of the richest, most advanced, most tolerant and generous civilization of ancient times. That their culture was so advanced that it had spread all over the world? Do they realize that more and more archeological an historical discoveries are pointing out that the genocide of Hindus by Muslim invaders is without parallel. Surely, many of present day Indian Muslims' ancestors must have been among those slaughtered.

Islam cannot be wished away. As Sri Aurobindo said "Mahomed's mission was necessary, else we might have ended by thinking, in the exaggeration of our efforts at self-purification, that earth was meant only for the monk and the city created as a vestibule for the desert...." Thus Indian Muslims have to keep their faith and any attempt by Hindus to convert them back is not only futile, but counterproductive. But the question to be asked to them is: "what kind of Islam do you want to practice? An Islam which looks westwards, towards a foreign city, the Mecca, swears by a Scripture, the Koran, which is not only not relevant to India, but which was meant for people living 1500 years ago, in a language which is not Indian? Or do they want to practice an Islam which is "Indianized," which accepts the reality of other Gods, as Hinduism and Buddhism accept that there have been other avatars than Ram or Buddha.

Do India Muslims want to worship Babar, a man who destroyed everything which was good, beautiful and holy and lived by the power of violence, or do they want to imbibe the qualities of Ram, who believed in the equality of all, who gave-up all riches and honors of the world because he thought his bother deserved the throne more than him?

Whatever the West says, which is obsessed with China, India, a vibrant, English speaking, pro-western democracy is going to become the superpower of the 21st century. Do Indian Muslims want to participate in that great adventure? Do they want to feel that they are part of India, that they are Indians?

Nowadays it is politically not correct to say anything against Islam. You are immediately labeled anti-Muslim and dismissed as a "rightist." No matter if you are only reporting the fact that there is a real problem with Islam in South Asia: that India is surrounded by fundamentalists sates: Afghanistan and Pakistan, while more moderates like Bangladesh, tend to close an eye to anti-Indian activities; that Indian Muslims sometimes tend to put their religion before their country; and that Kashmiris, far from being the persecuted that the Foreign Press likes to portray, are actually paying the price for having allowed Afghan and Pakistani Sunnis radicalize what used to be a more gentle and tolerant Islam and left their Hindu brothers and sisters being butchered and chased away from their ancestral land.

But the truth is that ultimately, what the Muslim invaders did during the centuries of their domination, was that they planted a seed of division, for at that time, their avowed aim, what was driving their extreme ferocity at converting entire nations at the point of their scimitars, was to turn the whole world into "Dar-ul-Islam," the House of Islam. And today, the seed has matured, whether in Kashmir, in Pakistan, or even in India.

Once more, it must be emphasised at the risk of being accused of boring repetition: the point is not to come down on Islam, whose greatness can never be denied, if only because they represent one third of the world's population. The purpose is not to look back at history for a cry of vengeance. What has been done is done; you cannot wish away the Muslims of Bosnia, or of Kashmir, or the 120 millions Indian Muslims. They are part of history, they each belong to their different communities. The purpose is to look at history **so as to understand it today.** The exercise is to glimpse back in time **so that we don't repeat yesterday's mistakes.** The Jews have taught us that the collective memory, the remembering of the Holocaust, Shoah, Shindler's list are meant for the world not to forget its monstrous aberrations.

And even today, there is no doubt that Islam has never been fully able to give up its inner conviction that its own religion is the **only** true creed and that all others are "Kafirs," infidels. In India it was true 300 years ago, and it is still true today. Remember the cry of the militants in Kashmir to the Pandits: "convert to Islam or die"! And in the words of Sri Aurobindo: "As for the Hindu-Muslim affair, I saw no reason why the greatness of India's past or her spirituality should be thrown into the waste paper basket, in order to conciliate the Moslems who would not at all be conciliated by such policy... (Sri Aurobindo India's Rebirth, page 161)

But when will Indian Muslims understand that they have to be Indians first and then Muslims?

Ayodhya is the perfect example of the unwillingness of the Indian Muslims to come to terms with the Indian reality; it is the symbol of a certain kind of insincerity and double standards.

13.3 Ayodhya

How many of those who have lambasted so many times the "Hindu fundamentalists" and lamented the destruction of the Babri Masjid mosque as the "death of secularism in India," have been to Ayodhya? (not Faizabad, mind you, which is Ayodhya's twin Muslim city). When one arrived in Ayodhya before the destruction of the mosque, one was struck by the fact that it was a Hindu town "par excellence." More than Benares even, it is dotted everywhere with innumerable temples; it has all these old Hindus houses and this lovely river with its ghats which runs through the lower town. And then, forlorn on the top, there was this lone mosque with its two ugly domes, which looked so out of place and unused, that any one with a right sense—and that includes the Muslims- should see that it was not worth making an issue of.

The destruction of the Babri Masjid has evoked—and is still evoking today—such fiery reactions, that the importance of Ayodhya has been totally overlooked: Ayodhya is a **symbol**, through which two India's are facing each other. And the outcome of their confrontation will shape the future of this country for generations to come.

The first India wants to be secular and unite together through an egalitarian, democratic spirit all the minorities, ethnic groups, religions and people of the country.

But the question is: what would be the binding element of this kind of India? Secularism, says the first side. But secularism has a different meaning for each one, as we saw in the preceding chapters. For the British, it was a convenient way to divide and rule, by treating each Indian community on par, although some were in minority and others in majority, thereby planting the seeds of separatisms. For the Congress Party, it has always meant giving in to the Muslims' demands, because its leaders never could really make out if the allegiance of Indian Muslims first want to India and then to Islam—or vice-versa. And for India's intelligentsia, its writers, journalists, top bureaucrats, the majority of whom are Hindus, it means, apart from spitting on its own religion and brothers, an India which would be a faithful copy of the West: liberal, modern, atheist, industrialised, intellectual and western-oriented.

Furthermore, what makes India unique? Certainly not its small elite which apes the West. Nor its modern youth, whom you meet in Delhi's swank parties. Not even its political, bureaucratic and judicial system; it's a copy of the British set up, which is not fully adapted to India's unique character and conditions. What then?

The second India which is confronting the other at Ayodhya is of a course the India of the Hindus. When Imam Bhukari and others state that "we (the Mughals) gave everything to this country, its culture, its manners, its arts (and he adds: "the Hindus by destroying the Babri Masjid show how little gratitude they have"), apart from making a pompous declaration, he proclaims exactly the opposite of the reality. Because the truth is that not only Hinduism is what makes

India unique, so different from all the other nations of the world, but it is the single most important influence in Indian history. In the words of Sri Aurobindo: "The inner principle of Hinduism, the most tolerant and receptive of all religious systems, is not sharply exclusive like the religious spirit of Christianity or Islam ... it is the fulfilment of the highest tendencies of human civilisation and it will include in its sweep the most vital impulses of modern life..."

And indeed, if you look at India today, you find that Hinduism has permeated, influenced, shaped, every part of this country, every religion, every culture. Be it the Christians who are like no other Catholics of the world, or Indian Muslims, who whatever they may say, are utterly different from their brothers in Saudi Arabia. But Hinduism is too narrow a word, it's a corruption of the original word "Indu," for true Hinduism is Dharma, India's infinite and eternal spiritual knowledge, which took shape into so many varied expressions throughout the ages, be it the Vedantas, Buddhism, or the Arya Samaj and which is today still very much alive in India, particularly in its rural masses, which after all constitute 80% of its population.

What one has to grasp is that Ayodhya only makes sense when the immense harm the Muslims did to India is not **negated**, as indeed it has been and still is today, whether in Kashmir, where the last Hindus were made to flee in terror, or in Bangladesh, where the crowds still regularly go on rampage against Hindus and their temples (as told by a Bangladeshi Muslim herself, Talisma Nasreen). It is in this light, that it becomes extraordinary for an impartial observer to see today that when *for once*, the Hindus wanted to displace, not even to destroy, ONE mosque and rebuild the "temple," which they believe was built in this particular place, for one of their most cherished Gods, the one which is loved universally by all, men, women, children, THEY are treated as rabid fundamentalists. The great Mughals must be laughing all the way down their graves! What a reversal of situation! What a turnabout of history! And when the mosque was destroyed, it evoked such fiery reactions, such pompous, overblown, sanctimonious, holier-than-thou, atrocious, ridiculous, sly and totally undeserved outrage, both within India and in the Western world (who should be the last one to give lessons to India), that the importance of Ayodhya as a symbol has been totally overlooked.

The obvious trap is to think that the demolition of the mosque in Ayodhya is something to gloat about and that it is the duty of all good Hindus to see that other important mosques at Mathura, Vanarasi, or elsewhere, be also razed to the ground; or that all cities with a Muslim name be renamed with a Hindu one. This is not true Hinduism, which has always shown its tolerance and accepted in its fold other creeds and faiths. Indeed a true "Indu" India will be secular in the correct sense of the term: it will give freedom to each religion, each culture, so that it develops itself in the bosom of a Greater India, of which dharma, true spirituality, will be the cementing factor.

Nevertheless, the destruction of the Babri Masjid, however unfortunate, has made its point: the occult Mughal hold over Hindu India has been broken and centuries of Hindu submission erased. Hindus have proved that they too can fight. Today we see how hard it is for Sri Sri Ravi Shankar to convince Muslim leaders that it is in their interest to allow for the construction of a Ram temple the side of the razed one.

13.4 The Indian Elite

Does India's elite look down upon its own country?

To a Westerner, it seems very much so. India's upper class, the cream of this nation, the privileged, those very men and women who had the great fortune not to be born in need, appear to enjoy India-bashing. Nothing seems to find grace in their eyes: everything is rotten, the system, the government, the politicians, the bureaucracy. Nothing works, nothing is possible, everything is bleak, worthless, hopeless.

But the truth is that those Indians who constantly negate India, are ashamed of their country. Educated Indians always seem to compare their democracy to Western standards. They want to apply to India the same norms which are used in the industrialised world. And extraordinarily, many of India's elite ridicule what makes this country unique in the world, what no other nation in the word possesses: Dharma, true Hinduism; the knowledge passed down by thousands of sages, saints, yogis, sadhus of the Eternal Truth, that which gives a meaning to this otherwise senseless life and which the West has totally lost: the Wheel of Life, the endless rebirths and ultimately the evolutionary Ascension of man towards the Ultimate Truth.

And why should the Hindus, at any rate, not be proud of Hinduism? It has not only shaped the psyches of Hindus, but also of Indian Christians, Jains, Parsis, even Muslims, who are like no other Muslims in the world. And why should Indians be ashamed of their own civilisation whose greatness was foremost Hindu? Why should they refuse to have their children read the Vedas, which constitute one of the great fountains of spiritual wisdom, or the Bhagavad Gita, which contains all the secrets of eternal life? Or the Ramanaya and the Mahabharata, which teach the great values of human nature: courage, selflessness, spiritual endeavour, love of one's wife and neighbours....

Are the French ashamed of their Greco-Roman inheritance? Not at all ! On the contrary they even think that civilisation started only with the Greeks. Would you call the Germans or the Italians « nationalists » because they have Christian Democrats Parties? Christianity is the founding stone of Western civilisation and nobody dares deny it. Trump goes to the mass and swears on the Bible and none finds anything to say. We French are brought-up listening to the values of Homer's « Iliad », or Corneille's « Le Cid ». It is true that in France there has been a separation of the State and the Church; but that is because at one time the Church misused its enormous political power and grabbed enormous amounts of lands and gold. But no such thing ever happened India. The much maligned Brahmins never interfered in politics and today they are often a neglected lot.

When they took over India, the British set upon establishing an intermediary race of Indians, whom they could entrust with their work at the middle level echelons and who could one day be convenient instruments to rule by proxy or semi-proxy. The tool to shape these « British clones » was EDUCATION. In the words of Macaulay, the « pope » of British schooling in India: « We must at present do our best to form a class, who may be interpreters between us and the millions we govern; a class of persons, Indians in blood and colour, but English in taste, in opinions, in morals and in intellects ». Macaulay had very little regard for Hindu culture and education: « all the historical information which can be collected from all the books which have been written in the Sanskrit language, is less valuable than what may be found in the most paltry abridgement used at preparatory schools in

England ». Or: « Hindus have a literature of small intrinsic value, hardly reconcilable with morality, full of monstrous superstitions »....

It seems today that India's Marxist and Muslim intelligentsia could not agree more with Macaulay or with Charles Grant (1746-1823), Chairman of the East India Company, who said: "we cannot avoid recognising in the people of Hindustan a race of men lamentably degenerate and base...governed by malevolent and licentious passions ... and sunk in misery by their vices."

For the dream of Macaulay has come true: nowadays, the greatest adversaries of the « Indianised and spiritualised education » of Joshi, are the descendants of these « Brown Shahibs »: the « secular » politicians, the journalists, the top bureaucrats, in fact the whole Westernised cream of India. And what is even more paradoxical, is that most of them are Hindus.

It is they who upon getting independence, have denied India its true identity and borrowed blindly from the British education system, without trying to adapt it to the unique Indian mentality and psychology; and it is they who are refusing to accept « an Indianisation, nationalisation and spirtualisation » of India's education system, which is totally western-oriented and is churning out machines learning by heart (Indian children must be amongst those having most homework in the world) boring academics which are of little usefulness in life. And what India is getting from this education is a youth which apes the West: they go to Mac Donald's, thrive on MTV culture, wear the latest Klein jeans and Lacoste T-Shirts, and in general are useless, rich parasites, in a country which has so many talented youngsters who live in poverty. They will grow-up like millions of other western clones in the developing world, who wear a tie, read the New York Times and swear by liberalism and secularism to save their countries from doom.

But then, what does makes India unique? Take the once upon a time BJP's proposal to make Sanskrit compulsory in school. Great idea! Sanskrit is the Mother of all languages, so intricate, so subtle, so rich, that no other language can equal it today. And moreover, it could become the unifying language of India, apart from English, which is spoken only by a tiny minority.

Why should anyone also object to Saraswati, the Goddess of learning, She who bestowed so much Grace on India. In 1939, a disciple had said to Sri Aurobindo that: "there are some people who object to the singing of Vande Mataram as a national song; Sri Aurobindo had replied: "in that case Hindus should give up their culture." But the disciple had continued: "the argument is that the song speaks of Hindu gods, like Durga and that it is offensive to Muslims." Said Sri Aurobindo: "but it is not a religious song, it is a national song and the Durga spoken of is India as the Mother. Why should not the Muslims accept it? In the Indian concept of nationality, the Hindu view should be naturally there. if it cannot find a place, the Hindus may as well be asked to give-up their culture. The Hindus don't object to "Allah-Ho-Akbar."

It is then obvious that Education in India has to be totally revamped. The kind of westernised education which is standard in India, does have its place, because India wants to be on par with the rest of the world, and Indian youth should be able to deal confidently with the West: do business, talk, and relate to a universal world culture. But nevertheless, the first thing that Indian children should be taught **is the greatness of their own culture**. They should learn to revere the Vedas, they should be taught the genius of the Mahabharata and the

Ramanayana; they should be told that in this country everything has been done, that it was an unsurpassed civilisation, when the West was still mumbling its first words, that Indian civilisation reached dizzying heights, which have been since unsurpassed. But overall they should be taught early that India's greatness is her spirituality her world-wide wisdom.

Do not Indians realise that by constantly belittling their own country and seeing it the way the West wants them to perceive it, they are handing over India to her enemies, those who wish her ill? Those who would like to see her humbled, broken, fragmented? Do these people want to see India go the way of Yugoslavia? Don't they realise that they are traitors to their own country, to its uniqueness, to is unparalleled greatness? That ultimately their India-bashing is a colonial leftover? An unconscious inferiority complex, which has been planted in the minds of their ancestors more than two centuries ago?

Nobody in India is more representative of this Hindu-bashing syndrome than some of the Indian Press. it is they who called Narendra Modi a Hitler. Do they have any knowledge of European history: at the worst, Modi just stood by while his people took revenge for the horrible burning alive of 36 Hindus in the Godhra Express. Hitler killed in cold blood 6 millions Jews and crores of other people). It is they who are still at it today, by portraying the Christian community in India as persecuted, when many of the incidents are the result of jealousies between converted and non-converted tribals, or are even engineered by Muslims and forgetting how much harm Christianity has done to this country for three centuries, converting by devious means, crucifying Brahmins in Goa, destroying temples in Pondichery....

True, the Indian Press should also be praised for its incredible diversity, for its inexhaustible reserve of talented writers, for its investigative journalism which makes sense when it helps uncover corruption, injustice, or political despotism. But again, it should learn to look at things NOT through the Western prism, but through the Indian looking glass, and apply to India standards that are Her own and of which she has nothing to be ashamed, because they are unique in the world.

13.5. Missionaries Post-independence: Exploding the Mother Theresa Myth

The Christians are a much quieter force than the Muslims. They do not advocate openly the breaking-up of India, and certainly the great majority of Catholics in India are peaceful Indian citizens. Yet the missionary spirit brought in by the British is still alive in India and goes on quietly about its work, as Arun Shourie demonstrated in his book, "Missionaries in India and as the continuing conversions of low-caste Hindus show clearly. And nothing symbolises this spirit better than Mother Theresa, even after her death.

But firstly, one should say in defence of Mother Theresa that she certainly did saintly work. After all, there is no denying that it takes a Westerner to pick-up the dying in the streets of Calcutta and raise abandoned orphans, a thankless task if there is one. Indian themselves, and particularly the Hindus, even though their religion has taught them compassion for 7000 years, have become very callous towards their less fortunate brethren and there are not enough Hindu organizations doing charitable work as the Christians do, although there is growing awareness amongst Hindu organisations that it's time to put their act together.

This said, one can wonder: what did Mother Theresa really stand for?

Was caring for the dying and orphaned children her only goal? Well, if you have observed her carefully over the years, you will notice that she did not say much. She did speak against contraception and abortion, in a country of more than one billion, where an ever growing population is swallowing whatever little economic progress is made; where the masses make life in India more and more miserable, invading the cities, crowding their streets and polluting their environments; where for 50 years the Indian Government has directed a courageous and democratic birth control programme, (whereas in China demographic control has achieved though autocratic means). She has also been attacked « for being a friend of the despots and accepting their money ». But of course, many Indian intellectuals immediately sprang-up to the defence of Mother Theresa, saying it was « bad faith, bad taste », to speak thus. But still, the question may be asked : (1) what did Mother Theresa really stand for? (2) Why do Indians defend her so ardently? During her whole lifetime, Mother Theresa spoke only of the dying of the streets in Calcutta, of course, of the poor of India left unattended, of the miseries of the cities. Fair enough, but then it should have been pointed out to her, that she projected (and is still projecting today after her death, through the order she has created) to the whole world an image of India which is **entirely negative**: of poverty beyond humanity, of a society which abandons its children, of dying without dignity. OK, there is some truth in it. But then it may be asked again: did Mother Theresa ever attempt to *counterbalance* this negative image of India, of which she is the vector, by a more positive one? After all, she has lived here so long, that she knows the country as well as any Indian, having even adopted Indian nationality. Surely she can defend her own country? She could for example speak about India infinite spirituality, her exquisite culture, the gentleness of its people, the brilliance of its children....

Unfortunately, Mother Theresa said nothing. For the truth is that she stood for the most orthodox Christian conservatism. There is no doubt that ultimately Mother Theresa's goal was utterly simple: to *convert* India to Christianity, the only *true* religion in her eyes.

Did you notice that she never once said a good word about Hinduism, which after all is the religion of 850 millions people of the country she said she loved and has been their religion for 7000 years. This is because deep inside her, Mother Theresa considered, as all good Christians do, particularly the conservatives ones, that Hinduism is a pagan religion which adores a multitude of heathen gods and should be eliminated. We know now that she had even doubts in her later life about her own faith and there has been in 2018 scandals of adoption for money of orphans by her sisters.

For, make no mistake about it, there has been no changes about Christian or Protestant designs on India since they arrived with the Portuguese and the British, remember what Lords Hastings had to say about the Hindus! Mother Theresa was much more clever than Lord Hastings; she knew that on the eve of the 21st century, it would have looked very bad if she had openly stated her true opinions about Hinduism; so she kept quiet. But ultimately is not charitable work, whatever it dedication, a roundabout manner to convert people? For without any doubt, most of the people she saved from the streets did *ultimately* become Christians. And if you ask those « elite » Indians who knew her well, such as photographer Ragu Rai, a great admirer of her, she always came out after some years with: « It is now time for you to embrace the true religion ». (Rai politely declined).

Chapter 14

The Threats from Without

It would be bad enough if India had to suffer threats from within only, at the hands of Kashmiri secessionists, at the mercy of the sometimes doubtful allegiance of its 120 million strong Muslim community, under the onslaught of its westernised "elite" minority, or from its missionary contingent. But India is also under attack from without, not only from its Muslim neighbours, who are all offspring of a once Greater India; but also from her non-Muslim neighbours, from China—and even further away, from the West, particularly the USA, who does not always grasp India's problems and its relevance to Asia and the world.

14.1 Pakistan

Ah, Pakistan, finally, everything reverts to Pakistan, whether you talk about Kashmir, Ayodhya, Kargil, or the advent of Imran Khan. Everywhere the Indian Government says it sees the "Pakistani hand" behind it. It is an hostile hand, they add, active, militant, whose ultimate goal is the destruction of India. Is actually, Pakistan the continuing incarnation of those Muslim invaders who raped India from the middle of the 7th century onwards? Militant Hindus contend that nothing has changed: "their cry is still the same: "Dar-ul-Islam," the house of Islam. Yesterday they used scimitars, today they have the atomic bomb; but the purpose is identical, only the weapons have evolved: to conquer India, to finish what the Mughal

Emperors were not able to achieve." To reason with Pakistan is useless, they conclude, "for once again they are only putting in practice what their religion teaches them every day—that 'the Pagans shall burn forever in the fire of hell. They are the meanest of creatures.' Or 'Slay the infidels, wherever ye find them and take them captive and besiege them and prepare them for all kinds of ambush.' Or again: 'Choose not thy friends among the Infidels till they forsake their homes and the way of idolatry. If they return to paganism then take them whenever you find them and kill them.' All these quotations are taken from the Koran and are read everyday to the faithful by their mollahs. (Koran 98:51-9:5-4:89)

Is Pakistan's war against India then a Muslim "jihad," the ultimate jihad against the Infidel, which if necessary will utilise the ultimate weapon, nuclear bombs? And as in the case of Ayodhya, the whole of Islam might side with Pakistan, for to their eyes India is still the Infidel, the Idolater, which the Koran asks them to slay. Says Elst: "if tomorrow the Pakistani start the Prophet's first nuclear war against an Infidel country (India), a billion Muslims will feel compelled to side with this muhajid struggle and dissenters will be careful not to protest aloud."

But then you also have to understand the Pakistani point of view: take Kashmir for instance. If one goes by the logic of Partition, then at least the Kashmir valley, which is in great majority Muslim, (and it should be emphasised that for long the Hindus Pandits in Kashmir exploited and dominated the Muslims—who are getting back at them today), should have reverted to Pakistan. It should be clear also that Pakistan never forgot the humiliating loss of Bangladesh at the hands of India, although India only helped Bangladesh to gain its freedom in the face of what the Bangladeshis say was Pakistani genocide. Zia's emergence was a result of that humiliation and the whole policy of proxy war by supporting the separatist movements in Punjab and Kashmir, is a way of getting back at India. And the same can be said about the nuclear bomb, for Pakistan has realised, after having lost three wars (four if you count Kargil), that both numerically and strategically, it can never beat India in a conventional conflict.

It is also clear when one goes to Pakistan today, that the country has evolved a soul of its own, has its individual identity and that in fact it has been able to do better than India in many fields. Their politicians are more accessible than in India for instance; their bureaucrats more friendly; and PIA is definitely a better airline than Air India! Finally, can Pakistanis be accused of all ills that befall India? The Indian Press has become possessed of total paranoia when it comes to Pakistan and Kashmir, always pointing a finger at its neighbour. But many of India's problems are of her own making.

Yet, Indians themselves seem to be confused about Pakistan. When Benazir Bhutto was assassinated in 2007, for instance, Prime Minister Manmohan Singh described her as "one of the outstanding leaders of our sub-continent, who always looked for reconciliation between India and Pakistan." Most magazines did cover stories on her and Benazir Bhutto was on the verge of becoming a "martyr of democracy."

It is a sad that a mother of three children was so brutally killed and we all mourned her terrible death. Nevertheless, truth must be told. For, as usual, what the press says is not exactly what happened. Firstly, under Bhutto, anti-Indian terrorism in the Kashmir region was fostered and increased. Benazir was also directly responsible for the ethnic cleansing of Hindus in Kashmir. "She was instrumental in sponsoring jihad, openly inciting militants to intensify terrorism in India," says Ajai Sahni, the executive director of the New Delhi-based

Institute for Conflict Management. “I find it very difficult to discover a single element with her relationship to India that is positive and for the betterment of her country or the region,” he adds. Remember how she was shouting her slogans of *azaadi*, and exhorting the people of Kashmir to cut Jagmohan, then governor of the state, into pieces, as in “jag-jag, mo-mo, han-han.” She would say this while making chopping motions with her right hand as it moved from her left wrist to the elbow, leaving nobody in any doubt as to what she meant.

Secondly, under Benazir Bhutto, the Taliban formed and, helped by Pakistan’s intelligence service, swept across Afghanistan and later hosted Osama bin Laden. It is a bit of an irony that she may have been killed by the very people she helped foster if at all she was murdered.

Thirdly, she deliberately increased tension levels and then threatened India with a pre-emptive nuclear strike. The tension peaked when Benazir repeated her late father’s immortal boast of waging a thousand-year war against India and even Rajiv Gandhi was forced to mock her in Parliament, asking if those who talked of a thousand-year war could last even a thousand hours.

And fourthly, in her last speech before she died, she alluded to India as one of the threats Pakistan had to face, implying that if she wasre-elected she would deal firmly with it. Then why was it that Prime Minister Manmohan Singh called her a friend of India and that Indians mounted candle light vigils in the Gateway of India Mumbai for her?

I interviewed Benazir Bhutto twice, the last one as she was campaigning to be re-elected for a second term. The first question I asked, was about Kashmir, as she was the one who had called for ‘Azad Kashmir’, a Kashmir free from India, which had triggered the ethnic cleansing of most Hindus of the

Valley of Kashmir, 400.000 of them having to flee their ancestral land.

You know, she answered, you have to understand the Pakistani point of view on Kashmir. If one goes by the logic of Partition, then at least the Kashmir valley, which is in great majority Muslim—and it should be emphasised that for long the Hindus Pandits in Kashmir exploited and dominated the Muslims, who are getting back at them today—should have reverted to Pakistan. But let us say that officially we want to help grant Kashmiris their right to self-determination.

That's the only reason, I continued?

No, answered Benazir, it should be clear also that Pakistan never forgot the humiliating loss of Bangladesh at the hands of India, although India claims it only helped Bangladesh to gain its freedom in the face of what the Bangladeshis say was Pakistani genocide. Zia's emergence was a result of that humiliation.

But Zia hanged your father, I interrupted....

Yes and I hate him, and God the Almighty already punished him for that, said Benazir (alluding to Zia's death in a plane crash). But Zia did one thing right, he started the whole policy of proxy war by supporting the separatist movements in Punjab and Kashmir, as a way of getting back at India.

What about Pakistan' nuclear bomb, I asked?

That's my father's work she said proudly. He realized, after having lost the 1965 and 1971 wars with India, that both numerically and strategically, we can never beat India in a conventional conflict. Thus he initiated the programme by saying that "we will get the nuclear bomb, even if we have to eat grass."

But is it not a dangerous weapon if it falls in the hands of the fundamentalists of your country, I asked?

No such danger, Benazir answered. Anyway, it is not only a deterrent against India's military conventional superiority and an answer to India's own nuclear capability, but also the ultimate weapon to reassert Islam's moral superiority.

We in Europe are going to unite in a Common Market, why don't Pakistan and India forget their differences and form some kind of confederation with other South Asia countries, instead of killing each other?

Pakistan and India were never one country, answered the imperious lady. They were only kept together by force, whether by Mauryan, Moghul or British rule. Hindus have recognised the reality of Islam, and we needed our own country to feel free.

I was flabbergasted: here was a lady educated in Oxford and Harvard, who mouthed such irrational statements. She spoke good English, was pretty, articulate and pleased the Press. But when in power, she had to resort to anti-Indianism to please her voters, her husband was known as Mr 10% and she was hounded out of power twice for incompetence and corruption. Was she then a martyr of democracy? History will tell.

On the opposite spectrum, Indians can cry themselves hoarse about Pakistani treachery and see the evil hand of Islamabad everywhere, even sometimes behind events where Pak is not involved. But then the Indian Government should only blame themselves. For have they not recognised at independence the geographical and political reality of Partition and have they not continued to do so up to now? Is there any political leader in India who dares say today that India and Pakistan are ONE? **Is there any voice to proclaim the truth in a loud and clear voice, as Sri Aurobindo** did in 1947: "But the old communal division into Hindu and Muslim seems to have hardened into the figure of a permanent division of the country. It is hoped that the Congress and the nation will not accept the settled fact as for ever settled, or as anything more than a temporary expedient. For if it lasts, India may be seriously weakened, even crippled: civil strife may remain always possible; possible even a new invasion and foreign conquest. **the partition of the country must go....**"

The menace from within cannot be tackled unless the menace from without is solved. India and Pakistan (+ Bangladesh) are ONE. And as long as Partition remains, India will not be able to live in peace: Ayodhya, Kashmir, Kargil, Bangladeshi infiltration and a potential (nuclear?) war with Pakistan, are always possible.

14.2 The Other Neighbours

How is it that India is almost universally disliked, sometimes even hated by her neighbours, whether they are Muslim Bangladeshis, Buddhist Sri Lankans, or even Hindu Nepalese?

Journalists, both in South Asia, as well as in India, are fond of saying that it is because India is a great bully, hegemonistic in her tendencies. Is she really? At least in her past history, she has never shown any hegemonistic inclinations, her religion never tried to convert anybody and her armies never marched into other countries—the same cannot be said about Islam, or Christianity with her Crusades, or even the more peaceful Buddhist missionaries.... Yet at one time India's influence, solely due to the sheer greatness of her culture and Hindu dharma, extended as far as China on one side and on Iran, Greece and even the Europe on the other. Even today, whether in Thailand, Mauritius, Cambodia, or even Bangladesh and Pakistan, there is a tremendous leftover of India's predominance.

The key word must be fear. All these countries are afraid of India, not entirely because she is a great bully, but because they unconsciously realise that they all **sprang** from India's vast bosom- and that one day, sooner or later, they might very well all **return** to that bosom, under whatever form. Nepal is a very good example of that India-hate syndrome. Here is a wonderful country, with simple and friendly people, which is the only Hindu nation in the world, which is so similar in many ways to India, that there is no reason to be antagonistic to a country with which they have so much in common. Yet Nepal is tilting more and more towards China, maybe because this small country, which is landlocked depends so much on India for goods and transport. The Chinese are even planning a railroad from mainland China to the Nepalese border!

The same goes for Bangladesh. Bangladeshis, it is often said, are Bangladeshis first and Muslims second; this is why they separated from Pakistan, where they were treated as second-class citizens. And in truth, Bangladeshis are generally a friendly race, affectionate as all Bengalis, poetic, humorous. Their society used to be—and still is in many ways—one of the most open and tolerant in the world of Islam, which gives its women a unique place. Yet, a Taslima Nasreen, whatever her personal failings (love of publicity, inflated ego, unnecessary shocking of Islamic feelings), when she dares in her book « Laljja », to utter the truth about the atrocities perpetrated on Hindus after the destruction of the Ayodhya mosque, is hunted down by obscure fundamentalists groups, let down by her government, betrayed by her own people.

Same phenomenon in Sri Lanka. Extraordinary country that erstwhile Ceylon; God gave it everything: good climate, lush country, incredible diversity of races and religions, an easy-going and friendly people, who even welcomed its invaders. Yet the sometimes hate that the Sinhalese have for Indians is something to be seen to be believed. Again it is a hate which was fostered by their political leaders who have become adept at using the hate-India carrot every time he got in trouble. But why should India be blamed for Sri Lanka's ills? The Sri Lankans can go on accusing Mrs Gandhi's of having abetted Tamil Militants in the late seventies. But was it Mrs Gandhi who discriminated for 40 years against the Tamil minority of Sri Lanka? Was it Mrs Gandhi who regularly prodded Sinhalese crowds to indulge in pogroms against the Tamils, thereby building-up a wall of hatred, so that today the Tamils in Sri Lanka cannot trust the Sinhalese anymore and want nothing but total independence? Why blame India for Sri Lanka's problems, a nation, who thanks to the lack of foresight of four generations of Sinhalese politicians, produces nothing today but tea -and that even at the mercy of its Tamil workers imported by the British—and lives on tourist industry? Sad that Sri Lanka too, is falling prey to the Chinese thirst for conquering nations, by any means, including practically buying them.

India has also to account for the hostility of the Gulf countries. And very unfortunately, India's hands are bound, because of its millions of nationals, most of them Muslims, who work in the Gulf and regularly send home precious foreign exchange (even if this tendency is nowadays decreasing). But does India realise that this foreign exchange is sometimes a poisoned gift, that these Indian Muslims often bring home a more militant Islam? The blossoming of a million mosques in India, the Muslim women in many of India's villages and cities more and more covered in black from head to toes, the intolerance, are a direct result of the influence of Saudi Arabia and other Gulf countries who export Wahabism.

14.3 China

It is the infamous 1972 "historical trip" of Richard Nixon to Peking which set the trend: henceforth, the West was gradually going to put all its chips on the Chinese, banking that one day, its investments, political and economical, will bring enormous returns. In the process, the West conveniently forgot that the Chinese had killed 1, 2 million Tibetans, one of the worst genocides of humanity. The brutal repression in Tibet, showed openly the totalitarian face of Chinese communism, but the United States preferred to forget it as fast as possible. The Chinese, clever as they are, make from time to time a few Human Right concessions here and there, such as releasing a handful of dissident student leaders (who by the way, have never raised their voices against the Tibetan genocide), and at the same time they harden their tone. Washington pretends to be satisfied and gives again the green light to its army of businessmen, waiting impatiently to place their green dollars in the huge Chinese slot machine.

But is the West ready to pay the price for that impatience? Because finally, economical liberalisation or not, China remains a communist country with a dictatorial leadership, probably the only one worth that name left in the world. And communism means instability, as the sudden crumbling of the Soviet Union and Eastern Europe, has proved. What is going to happen to the billions of dollars of Western investment, if there is tomorrow a counter-revolution in China—or if communism shows again its true totalitarian face?

India, has also always been duped by China. In 1959, Nehru allowed the Dalaï-Lama and his followers to settle in Dharamsala, where thanks to their spiritual leader's guidance, the Tibetans were able to recreate a small Tibet, complete with

Government in exile, schools, monasteries, Tibetan medicine and arts. It is actually the only real thing that is left of Tibetan culture and civilisation today—and if ever the Tibetans recuperate Tibet, it will have to be re-transplanted to what has become a near completely Chinese Tibet. Unfortunately, the Dalai Lama is getting old and the Chine Government is just waiting for him to die to replace him with a 'reincarnation' chosen by them, as they did for the Panchen Lama. Then the fate of Tibet will really be in jeopardy.

Yet the Chinese have never forgiven India for their generosity and compassion towards the Tibetans. And although some progress has been made, the question remains: can Indians trust the Chinese?

There are two superpowers in the making in Asia: India and China. The West seems to have lost the absolute predominance it used to enjoy and with its slow decline, it will drag in recession many of the so-called tigers of Asia, which vitally need US and Western political support for the growth of their economy: after Tibet and Hong-Kong, it might be soon Taiwan which will be swallowed back by China. And ultimately India and China will be the only superpowers left with Japan in their shadow. But one will be a democratic country, and the other still be a communist dictatorship, with a formidable military arsenal—nuclear and otherwise—at her disposal for her greedy appetite. China seems to be the direct adversary of India, both economically and militarily—and not Pakistan as the Indian Government wants its citizens to believe. The new 'Silk Road' that aims to link China to the rest of the world, via Pakistan and Pakistan-held Kashmir is proof enough of Beijing's megalomania, which unfortunately it has the funds to sustain. When will the West realize that the Chinese are a threat and that India is its natural economical and geopolitical ally?

14.4 The West

And finally no chapter on the threat to India from without, can be complete without a mention of the threat from the Western world, particularly the United States, which seems sometimes to unconsciously wish a divided and weakened India. The negative articles of the New York Times, or CNN and its crusade against the BJP and Narendra Modi, are symbolic of the continuing ignorance of the Americans. Yet, as we said above, what better ally in Asia could the United States find to counter the growing economic and military influence of China? One is also worried about the Globalization and Westernization which is taking place at the moment in India at a frantic pace. TV channels and advertisements must be the biggest culprits. Is White the most beautiful color, does having a White Skin make you so hep? Do a cell phone, a suit, or a fancy car, really make you into a man ? This is what millions of innocent villagers or lower middle class viewers are enticed to believe. This is one of the biggest threats India is facing at the moment—and it will be a great loss for the world if India becomes totally westernized.

14.5 The Nuclear Bomb

All weapons of war are a perversion of man's greed and the ultimate symbol of the misuse he has achieved over matter. Thus, ideally, they should all be banned, or else slowly phased out until we all live in a weapon-less world, for the simple reason that they would not be needed anymore and that man would have outgrown their folly.

Therefore, more than anything, the atom bomb symbolises that folly, because at a single stroke, at the simple push of one button by a misguided hand, or though the order of a mad leader, thousands of lives can be obliterated in a single second, entire cities be wiped out in a single flash.

The atom Bomb also demonstrates the limit of man's command over matter. For what use is that material mastery to man, when he has no control over his impulses, when he is still unable not only to love his human brothers, but even to reason with himself not to use his domination over matter to harm others. And ultimately, his might may slip out of his hands, because material mastery without inner control is incomplete and dangerous.

For this and many other reasons, should not India then voluntarily forsake nuclear power and cap its missile programme and become a true non-violent country, in the spirit of the Mahatma Gandhi?

But have those who are pushing this theory forward read properly the Bhagavad Gita? For, what does the Bhagavad tell us? It does not say, as Christians do, or as the Mahatma purported, that all violence is wrong. It asserts that when violence is absolutely necessary, when it is used for defending one's country, one's wife, brothers, sisters, then it becomes **Dharma**—duty—and is acceptable, as long as it is done with the right attitude in one's heart.

India, as we have just seen, is facing multiple threats from without by hostile nations, armed with both conventional and atomic weapons. The Islamic bomb, assembled by Pakistan with Arab financing, is the first one of these.

The other nuclear threat India is facing is coming from China. Nehru's policy of « Hindi-Chini-bhai-bhai » was a disaster: China attacked India by surprise and took away 20,000 square kilometres of her territory. And today India is still making the same mistake of trusting the Chinese and it recognises the Chinese claim on Tibet, a wholly independent country, which always acted the perfect buffer zone between herself and China.

The Indian Government also knows that many Chinese nuclear missiles are positioned on the Tibetan plateau and pointed towards the North Indian cities. For this and many other reasons, India should for the moment develop its nuclear military programme, in spite of the increasing pressure from the West, particularly the United States. India needs again Kshatriyas to defend herself, not businessmen, or intellectuals who will sell down their country' security for a few more million dollars investments and a pat on the back from Uncle Sam.

It is to be hoped that India will realise that surrendering to America's pressure would jeopardise her unity and open her for dismemberment. For her nuclear and missile programmes are not meant for aggression—once gain in her 7000 year history, India was never an aggressor—**but as a deterrent to protect herself**, to show her enemies that she means business and that she will retaliate in case of first attack. It is a sad reality of the world today, and India has got to take it in consideration. Let India be strong, powerful, nuclear even, but as *dharma*, because it is her duty to protect her children.

Chapter 15

« The Horror that is India »

Indians cannot solely blame internal and external threats for their country's ills. For today, the Wonder that was India has become perverted at the hands of Indian themselves. India seems to have forgotten its eternal truth and Indians appear, in spite of Narendra Modi's efforts, to be constantly turning their back to the 7000 year old soul of their nation. Thus, India, at the beginning of this Third millennium, sometimes looks as if it has become an impossible riddle, where corruption, overpopulation, poverty, ugliness, bureaucracy, crass materialism will have the last word. It even feels sometimes as if the wonder that is India, has become « the Horror that is India ». If one were to pick up three domains of today's Indian horror, then certainly politicians, people and ecology would be the ones.

15.1 Politicians

« Spirituality is India's only politics, the fulfilment of Sanatana Dharma its only Swaraj », wrote Sri Aurobindo in 1911 (India's rebirth,89). In the old times, princes and kings were Kshatriyas, their duty was to serve the nation and high ideals were held in front of them by the Brahmins and rishis who advised them. The Buddha's father for instance, was a king *elected* by its own people Yet what has happened to Indian politicians? Today we see, particularly in the small regional parties, or in the Congress, corrupt, inefficient men, who have lost track of the good of the nation they are supposed to serve, who are only interested in minting the maximum money in the minimum of time. Nowadays, Indian politicians have often become a caricature, which is made fun of by the whole country. They are frequently uneducated, gross people, elected on the strength of demagogic pledges, such as promising rice for 8 RS a kilo, a folly which drained many states' coffers, or of playing Muslims against Hindus, Harijans against Brahmins, as in UP and Bihar. Politicians in India (and often elsewhere), are most of the time ignorant; Ministers have customarily no idea about the department they are overseeing. It is the civil servants who control matters, who know their subject thoroughly. You have to work hard to become a civil servant, study, pass exams, then slowly climb up the hierarchy, hereby gaining experience. The politician just jumps from being a lowly clerk, or some uneducated zamindar to become a powerful Minister, lording over much more educated men. There should be also exams to become a politician (but what if they are rigged like in UP !); a minimum of knowledge and skills should be required of the man who says he wants to serve the nation. Of course, they are exceptions: men of talent and integrity, who strive to serve India to the best of their abilities, who are technocrats first and politicians second. Some of the BJP's ministers, such as MR Javadekar, Mrs Sitharaman, or Mr Suresh Prabhu, but even the BJP seems to have happily fallen in the system put in placeby 50 years of Congress rule. Mr Narendra Modi has however shown that the ancient notion of *seva*, selfless work for the nation, can still be revived. India should adapt a Presidential system, where the President can chose his Ministers, who will not be necessarily MP's.

And what about the habit of Indian politicians of declaring holidays at the drop of the hat? India must be the place in the world where there are the most samadhis, where each year, enormous amounts of time and money are wasted to celebrate the death anniversaries of people which have been completely forgotten and who often did not achieve anything worthwhile in their lifetimes. 5 minutes of silence in all offices should be enough to pay respect to the memory of any important figure who dies. In Madhya Pradesh for example, it has been calculated that there are more leave days (holidays, strikes, bandhs, leave), than working days!

There is also nothing which symbolises better the degeneration of Indian politicians than the VVIP syndrome. The protection that most politicians enjoy today, was born out of the trauma of seeing Indira Gandhi killed by her own bodyguards and Rajiv Gandhi wasted by a human bomb; it sprang from a sincere desire to protect future Indian VIP's from such a fate. But *once again perversion has taken over, and man, the political animal, has misused what was in the beginning a genuine movement*. Today, no leader in the world, even the President of the United Sates, is as protected as the Indian Prime Minister. France, which has got its fair share of Islamic fundamentalism—there has been numerous deadly attacks against its railways, shopping plazas, airlines even, has learnt to cope with security in an efficient and discreet manner. President Sarkozy, for instance, does not move around with an army of rude and brutish security men; and one still remembers how Francois Mitterrand, one previous President, used to go out at night to his favourite restaurant with only two bodyguards.

Everything has already been said about the hassles that VVIP security has created in India: the status symbol it has become for people like Mulayam Singh or Mamta Banerjee, who are not particularly targeted by terrorists; how 70% of the

Indian police is tied-up by VIP protection, instead of attending to the problems of its common citizens; how we all suffer at the hands of VVIP's, waiting endlessly in our cars, as the Honourable Sonia Gandhi passes by, or in planes, as the PM's aircraft is landing; or of being rudely treated by these arrogant and useless Blacks Cats, who all of them should be sent to guard Kargil in winter, so they get a taste of what real security is about. And what about the habit of Indian Prime Ministers and Presidents to charter a full jumbo jet from Air India for their travels abroad? And when a technical snag occurs, the PM finds it quite normal to requisition another one on the spot, throwing into disarray hundreds of passengers, including many foreigners, as Air India's planes have a round the clock schedule. Cannot the Prime Minister have his own plane, even if its is more modest than a Jumbo jet? India after all is a poor country... It is true that Mr Modi has made a real effort to tone down the security and relive some of the hassles it creates for ordinary people, but his bureaucrats seem to have prevailed, because even RSS cadres who have come to power, such as the nice Venkaiah Naidu say that their hands are bound by Protocol...

Politicians who are afraid of dying, should remember what Krishna tells Arjuna in the the Bhagavad Gita: "the body is just an envelope and the soul never dies, but is born and reborn again to complete its works." Do they not know that if they are going to die tomorrow at the hands of an assassin, then it will be their karma, that it has been written somewhere in the book of Destiny and that there is nothing that any security in the world, however sophisticated can do about it? How the LTTE always managed to get the Sinhalese and Tamil leaders it targets, although the Sri Lankan, being trained by the Israelis, have one of the best security in Asia? However a good and wise leader they are—most of India's politicians are pretty old—and India being such a vast and ancient country, there will always be other "vibhutis" to replace them if they were to be assassinated. So why fear death? Does India always have to ape the West, when it has such deep knowledge in itself of the reality beyond the reality, of the occult truth behind the appearances? Does not the present government understand that if it would address itself seriously to the problems of VIP security and tone it down DRASTICALLY, including around the Prime Minister, it would acquire the party tremendous goodwill from the people and as many votes as wining a war against Pakistan?

And finally one has to quote again from the great Avatar of our era: « I have no doubt we shall have to go through our Parliamentary period in order to get rid of the notion of western democracy, by seeing in practice how helpless it is to make nations blessed... It is only when this foolishness is done with, that truth will have a chance to emerge and a really strong spiritual movement begin as a prelude to India's regeneration...» (India's rebirth, P. 89)

And truly, India will get rid of her corrupt politicians; only when she accepts that she made a mistake by adapting blindly all the political structures which the British had put in place to govern this country; it is only when India starts experimenting with her own ancient systems, which have been adapted to today's problems, that an efficient and honest government will spring from her bosom, ready to do service to Mother India, in the old Kshatryia spirit. It is only when India will see through the shortcomings of democracy, that she will get rid of the bureaucrats (*) who are eating up her entrails.

15.2 People

Individually, Indians are the most wonderful people in the world: full of hospitality, gentleness, innate spirituality. But whatever happened to the collective consciousness of the nation? The gap between the very rich and the extremely poor is constantly widening nowadays, thanks in part to the economic liberalisation. If only the very fortunate would care for their less flourishing brethren. But it needs Mother Theresas' and books like the City of Joy to remind us that the dirty work in India cannot be done by its own people. In Malabar Hill district in Bombay, which has become one of the most expensive Real Estate property per square foot in the world, people are still dumping their garbage on the street, without a second thought. Next to Malabar, there lies one of the worst slums of Bombay and none of privileged who live in Malabar have a thought for them. In Surat, one of the richest cities of India, thanks to the diamond trade, its citizens let the most filthiest filth accumulate, without thinking twice what it will do to those who live near it. It is true that the Swachh Bharat of Prime Minister Modi has made a difference—for a time. But look around you: the old Delhi railway station is as dirty as before; in Pondicherry, contractors paid by the Government to collect trash, dump at night in the city of Auroville; in Delhi, Bangalore or Pune, plastic bags seem to have multiplied by two… Indeed, India is a vast dump of garbage, not because it is too poor to process it and store it properly, **but because it does not care, because the tamas in this country is so vast, so deeply ingrained in the collective consciousness, that nobody gives a damn for the other.** And did India learn anything from the West? Unfortunately, the answer is no. The country is still as filthy and Indians have not understood that the wealth of the country has to be shared to avoid a human, social and ecological catastrophe.

Indians show also very little civic sense in other domains of their life. Look how they drive. Truck and bus drivers in India, routinely overtake in curves endangering not only their passengers' lives, but also those of incoming traffic. They park most of the time in the middle of the road when they have to stop, without any concern for those who are coming behind They drive us deaf with their constant blaring horns and generally have a total disregard for the others. And does not the way one drive, show a nation's vital soul? When an Israeli, who said that everything happens in his country with guts, asked his Indian counterpart how it was done in India, he was told: with luck! And it is true that there is some divine grace in India, borne out of the centuries of tapasaya o its yogis, to reach safely on its roads from one point to an other. And the bus driver who overtakes in the curve, must be unconsciously knowing it...

Look also how Indians are in the habit of pushing other people, whether it is to enter a plane, or exit a cinema. Or how they so innocently ignore those who have been queuing for hours at some railway counter, by jumping at the head of the queue. And it is not only the poor, but also the rich, who have this habit, witness the checking in at airports.

Dishonesty is also a lack of collective discipline. Glimpse how the Indian man is often cheating, whether it is the cement which is mixed with ashes, the change not tendered exactly, or the rich man who swindles the Income tax, by keeping lakhs of black money, gold and jewels in his house, when he could very well afford to pay a little more taxes and put his money in his bank? Narendra Modi's demonetization was a great and necessary move, but Indians have found new ways of cheating and bypassing the law. Rich businessmen paid few thousands rupees to their employees to replace their old notes for new ones and today black money still reigns.

Indeed, it is said like this that one third of India's wealth is in the black. For make no mistakes, India is a **wealthy** country. In spite of Modi, the poverty is only there because of the mismanagement, the dishonesty, the tamas and the inheritance of wrong structures. For Indians must be with the Jews the best savers in the world. And they don't save in abstract concepts: they go in for solid gold, land, cash—and that from the little shopkeeper to the business magnate. Where is all this money going? Again lack of discipline, lack of concern for the nation, disregard for what one's egoism will do to the country.

And finally, another area where Indians have miserably failed is Sports. One sees the energy of a nation in sports. And what happened in India? It thrives in sports inherited from the British, such as cricket, a game which is a colonial legacy, which is meant to be played in a cool weather on a green English meadow with a few spectators who shout "jolly good" from time to time, while sipping lemonade. It is not a game intended for a tropical country where you stand for hours under a blistering sun with frenzied fans screaming their approval or displeasure. Cricket has become an obsession here and has totally vampirized all the other sports in India. There is so much money, sponsors, televisions and even the Government have concentrated so much only on cricket at the expense of all the other sports, that corruption and cheating have set in and a big scandal emerged when it was revealed that Cronje, the South African captain, had taken money from an Indian bookie to lose a match .

India is nowhere on the international area of sports and its standard is pathetic if not ridiculous in all sports except for another two other British legacies: tennis and hockey. But look at China, in the early eighties it also could not compete in any discipline, bare table tennis, but in a span of thirty years, it has become a sports superpower in all areas, even in some where disciplines not suited to their morphology, such as swimming and they will reap a mountain of gold at their own Olympics in Beijing. Why can't India, the country that gave to the world hata-yoga, which has been copied the world over, or even pranayama, which is now spreading like wildfire all over the planet, have a coherent and comprehensive program which would build world-class athletes in two decades?

Because of cricket! And it is so unfair: athletes, such as long distance runners, will train in miserable conditions, get a pittance as sponsorship and often have to work full or part time in some obscure Government jobs. Compare this to cricketers who are often spoilt brats, who stay in five star hotels, get millions of rupees in sponsorship and advertisement, are often arrogant and still manage to lose most of the time!

The Indian Government should restrict the number of international matches played by Indian cricketers happening both within and outside India. This will ensure automatically that cricketers get less sponsorship and have to concentrate on home turf. And it should evolve a bold and clear plan for developing other sports, trying as much as possible to bypass bureaucracy which stifle and kill all the good plans (it would maybe make sense to privatize some of the areas such as training). Then only will India become a superpower in sports. It is true however that since Modi came to power, there is an improvement in Indian sports: athletes such as Pusarla Sindhu and Kidambi Srikanthin Badmington, Sishil Kumar in wrestling, Himad Das in athletics, etc...

15.3 Is India Heading Towards Ecological Disaster?

All right: thanks to Narendra Modi's two terms, India is going to overcome its colossal indiscipline, her people will rise, her politicians will change; she will also last through all internal and external threats. Thus, whatever foreigners and India's own "secular" Indians say, the land of Bharat, the cradle of the mighty Vedas, the Mother of so many saints, poets, great artists, philosophers, revolutionaries, **will survive**. After all, it has already passed through the unspeakable barbarism of countless Muslim invaders, the soul-stifling British colonial rule—and 60 years of "secular" socialism.

But for what? By the middle of this century there will be no more forest cover left in India. Its population will have long crossed the billion and half mark and will overflow everywhere, stifling any progress, annihilating all efforts. India's cities will be so polluted by their millions of cars that it will be impossible to breathe any more. India's rivers will be so poisoned by industries, that all living life will long have disappeared from it. There will be no drinking water left, except imported mineral water. And India will be littered with so much plastic (bags, bottles, buckets, etc.), that it will be materially impossible to ever get rid of them (indeed the land of Bharat should be renamed « the civilisation of plastic »...) This is 21st century India for you.

Many experts have already pointed out that hardly 11% of India's classified forests have adequate density. In 1950, 1/3 of India's area was still forested; each year India loses through deforesting a territory bigger than France, that is nearly two million hectares. And of these, only 3% is protected... And even that 3% is in deep distress, because of population pressure, big dams (like the Narmada), and industries. The main culprits of the deforestation are the contractors, the ones with big money, particularly the saw mill owners and the Forest Department, which although it claims that it does selective tree felling, has absolutely no understanding of ecological balance.

But without doubt, the greatest culprits of the massive deforestation, the dwindling of animal life, the thinning of underwater tables and the increasing desertification of India, are the politicians, in connivance with the contractors, who in turn bribe the forest officers. Take the Himalayas for instance, and a region like the lovely Kumaon hills. Less than forty years ago, people in Almora, the ancient capital of the Kumaons, still remember the beautiful blue cedars forests. Today, there are no forests left around Almora—they were cut down in the early 70's by contractors from the plains with the full knowledge of the Government—except commercial pine forests, which impoverish the soil and do not hold it properly. Yet, there is terrible shortage of water in Almora, the climate has warmed-up considerably in the last twenty years and wood is fearfully expensive.

There are literally hundreds of NGO's in the Kumaon hills, who are doing lots of women empowerment, lots of village uplifting, lots of weaving this and weaving that ... but absolutely no tree planting. Why? "Because the others do not do it, "is the usual answer, when you ask some of the NGO's or: "because it is too hard work." But the beauty of the Kumaon hills around Almora is fast going: more and more hotels are coming up, cutting more trees, like near the Kassar Devi temple, above Almora, where Vivekananda is supposed to have meditated and which has been bought to make into a resort by a non- resident Muslim who is suspected to have links with Ibrahim Dawood.

But ultimately, is it fair to blame only the politicians, or even the British, who started the massive deforestation for their railways and killed hundreds of thousands of tigers? Is there not something else in the Indian psyche that is to blame? Where is the root of this massive unconcern for one's environment; this total disregard for beauty, whether it is the terrible ugliness of the cities in Punjab, or the appalling filthiness in Tamil Nadu?... And, maybe, for once, the Hindus are to blame. The Ganges seems to be the perfect illustration of a religion which enjoins a thousand purification rites and yet has allowed her own Mother earth to be defiled. Here is a river that Hindus have held most sacred for centuries, nay millenniums; to bathe in it is to purify oneself of all bad karma; to die here is to be reborn in Light. Yet what do all Hindus do with their sacred Ganges? They defecate in it; they throw in all their refuse; they let their dead float down the mighty river, **as if they thought that the spiritual purity of the water can never be obliterated by material dirtiness.** But ask any scientist what is the degree of pollution in the Ganges today and he will also tell you that it is near the point of return. Did you know for instance that the Ganges has shrunk by half since the Tehri dam was opened? How could the Central Government approve of a dam so harmful to India's interests? What will happen to India if it loses the Ganges, which is its very soul?

So, for once, India should copy the West, which has grown a tremendous ecological concern and developed various ways of fighting against the physical degradation of our planet. We have seen for instance how India has been forced to adopt certain environmental measures just out of greed, when European countries refused for instance to accept any textile export which was not ozo free, or leather which was not chemically poisoned. Look at Auroville, the International city near Pondichery founded by the Mother of the Sri Aurobindo Ashram in 1968, and where a 4000 people from 25 countries live together, has shown how fast the earth can be redeemed, even when the task looks hopeless. When the first settlers arrived, Auroville was a barren plateau of red earth, with no trees left, except a few palms and one or two banyans. Yet old temples still showed records of a once abundant land with forests and wildlife. But indiscriminate tree cutting and heavy monsoons, washed away all the good topsoil in the sea, creating huge canyons and the water table had gone extremely low. The early Aurovillians, mostly foreigners, first stopped the rain water from washing into the sea by erecting earth bunds wherever they could. Thus the water table slowly went up again. Then, they proceeded to plant a million trees, protecting them with thorns from goats and cows, which are a mortal danger to India's ecology. When these trees started growing up, they shed their leaves, which with the help of rain water, started rotting on the ground, recreating in a few seasons a fertile topsoil. Today Auroville is a vast forest, animal life has come back, the canyons are slowly filling up, and villagers have so much firewood, that they do not cut trees any more. Yet these same villagers still keep on planting cashewnut crops, a harmful tree, which has to be sprayed many times with deadly pesticides and whose only value is its international market price. Yet villagers still let rain water flow in the sea and use cheap compost, mixed with plastic bags, hospital refuse and other non-disposable trash. EDUCATION is the word; the Indian Government has got to educate its villagers on the value of the sacred land that is India. India is slowly killing its most precious possession, as no Muslim invader or European coloniser, ever managed to do. Without its land, India will be like a great soul without a body, unable to manifest itself.

Chapter 16

India Outside: True Federalism

Pakistan today appears to be the first dilemma which is always confronting India outside. The major challenge she is facing at her borders stems mainly from Pakistan, constantly repeat Indian leaders. Pakistan's hand appears to be everywhere: in Kashmir, of course, although they denied it for years(and got the support in the 90's from journalists like Mark Tully); but also Punjab in the eighties; in the separatist movements in the East, as in Assam; in Bangladesh today; or in Nepal. And even if Pakistan's hand is not there, Indian political leaders always find the shadow of their enemy.

But the greatest shadow over South Asia is the threat of a nuclear holocaust, which would probably be started by Pakistan, as they know they cannot beat India in a conventional war. And this, it is hoped will remind us of Sri Aurobindo's warning in 1947, which we quote again, because of its total relevance today: "India is free, but she has not achieved unity, only a fissured and broken freedom.... The whole communal division into Hindu and Muslim seems to have hardened into a figure of a permanent political division of the country. It is to be hoped that the Congress and the Nation will not accept the settled fact as for ever settled, or as anything more than a temporary expedient. For if it lasts, India may be seriously weakened, even crippled; civil strife may remain always possible, possible even a new invasion and foreign conquest. The partition of the country must go...For without it the destiny of India might be seriously impaired and frustrated. That must not be." (Message of Sri Aurobindo on the 15th of August 1947).

And if you look closely at India's woes since 1947, many of them seem to have sprung from that partition, from the shame of that division, from the cowardly assent to the terrible maiming of Mother India, which most Indian political leaders have accepted as a permanent 'fait accompli'. But, are not Pakistan and India part of the same soul? Are not Pakistanis and Indians of the same colour, culture, ethnic stock? Have they not the same food habits, the same customs in many ways? In truth, you cannot really differentiate one Punjabi from the other Punjabi, or one Sindhi from the other Sindhi, except for his religion. So what if they worship two different Gods, which are but two names for the same Infinite Reality... This is what marks out 120 million Muslims from their 800 million Hindu brothers; yet they have to learn to live together and they WILL cohabit together in the future. Why should Indian and Pakistan, two developing countries, go on spending billions and billions of dollars on getting ready to fight each other, killing each other, they the brothers that lived together through seven millenniums of one of the greatest civilisations of this earth? For are not Pakistanis as much as Indians part of the same 'Indu' soil, which was the land of Bharat, before the Muslims came and forcibly converted so many—who today call themselves Pakistanis, or Indian Muslims?

All right, you cannot change history. Pakistan has evolved its own identity and it stands on his own as a nation, with its particular ethos. **Yet it should become clear to all, that not only the only lasting solution to peace in the**

subcontinent, but the only way to avoid a nuclear conflict in South Asia, which could even drag the world in its horror, is the reunion of India and Pakistan. but also, even more, that the only way India is going to regain her greatness that was, the only manner she can fulfill her dharma as the spiritual leader of the world, is for her and Pakistan to reunite.

The question is: how? It certainly cannot be done in a day and it cannot be accomplished in a hurried and artificial manner. First there has to be an understanding among both the people, an **acceptance** of that possibility, which up to now has not even been thought off seriously. Once the idea has started to work among people, the process may begin—at the heart of the matter, where things are most difficult between India and Pakistan: in Kashmir, for instance.

For Kashmir represents the perfect impossibility, the absolute dead-end, and symbolises the irrevocable enmity between Pakistan and India. India will not surrender Kashmir, because she considers rightly that it has been part of her territory for 7000 years. Pakistan will not surrender its claim on the Valley, because it estimates rightly that the Kashmir valley is 95% Muslim and that under the (mad) logic of partition, it should have reverted to Islamabad. And both countries are trying by force, the one openly, the other covertly, to stake their claims on Kashmir. Thus, there is no issue, except war, a nuclear conflict maybe—and everyone will be the loser: who will have Kashmir then if there is nothing left of India and Pakistan?

If the absurdity of the whole Kashmir business is seen in that light, then India and Pakistan might agree to sit down and hammer out, not an idiotic splitting in two of Kashmir, as they have already done of India, which will solve nothing and only postpone a later confrontation, but a just reunion. **Let both**

India and Pakistan administer Kashmir, which would retain its identity and culture as a member of a greater India confederation. It can start in a gradual way by military observers of both the countries being posted to watch over the peace process. Eventually it can lead to a joint government of Kashmir. Then there could be a tentative reunification of both the Kashmirs, which would be a prelude to an eventual reunification of India and Pakistan in a loose confederation of which the Kashmir joint experiment would be the model and the guinea pig, because we have no illusion that this will be an easy process. The bus link between Srinagar and Muzaffarabad represents a first small step in that direction.

There can be no peace in the subcontinent until India and Pakistan are reunited. For they are part of the same soul, the same body, even if it has different names and boasts of two religions diametrically opposed to each other, Hinduism and Islam, the latter thrown into India by the twist of fate and invasions. But as long as the two countries do not understand the urgency of reunification, there will be wars, a nuclear war maybe, and Ayodhyas and bomb blasts, and separatist movements in both India and Pakistan, fuelled by each other, and bloated military budgets heavily taxing the economy. But the beautiful thing is that Kashmir, although it looks like the perfect dead-end, is there to show the way to the Light.

But the reunification of India and Pakistan will be only the first step, because ultimately the goal is the reunification of ALL that was once the Greater India and which is today only small fragmented countries with no real soul, no direction, no sense. Bangladesh is the exemplary instance of that meaninglessness. Here is a country full of friendly people, with immense possibilities at all levels, but which on its own, has very little resources, except jute. A country which is constantly invaded by floods, which is at the mercy of dictators, or semi-dictators, who embarked upon an islamization programs which has harmed the spontaneous tendencies of the Bengalis. A nation which is near totally dependent on Foreign Aid agencies, with their luxurious houses, their Japanese 4 wheel drive cars, and their money, which ultimately does not solve much, as each natural catastrophe repeats the same story of helplessness. The same can be said for Sri Lanka, a country, as we have seen earlier, which has shown little foresight since independence, whose Tamil-Sinhalese feud cannot be resolved by reason, for it is the consequence of an old hatred and centuries of Sinhalese discrimination against the Tamil minority. A nation which produces hardly anything, relies on tea and tourism and yet is full of infinite possibilities, with its vast mosaic of people, races, religions, its natural beauty and ideal climate. And what of Nepal, one of the poorest countries of the world, with its rapidly depleting forest cover. Nepal was the only Hindu kingdom of the world and should have then naturally a harmonious fruitful relation with India -which is not the case at all, as the king and the communists, have always played the Chinese card against India. Nepal should have nothing to fear from India, as the two countries have so much in common.

If Europe has done it, why not the South Asian countries? For the ultimate solution to all the problems in South Asia, whether an Indo-Pakistan nuclear conflict, or the Tamil separatist dilemma, is FEDERALISM, a united common Government, under whichever form, which will allow each South Asian country to retain its own individuality, to practice in peace its own religion, to manage even its own affairs, but under the political umbrella of a benevolent, spiritualized, non-violent, but nevertheless powerful India, which will protect them, solve their problems and help them. Not the ex-Soviet type of United Republics, whose totalitarianism showed its ultimate failure, but a spiritualized federalism which would be on the lines of ancient India, when all the republics were allowed free play, while recognising the same unifying principle of Dharma. This Federal union of states would comprise India, Pakistan, Bangladesh, Sri Lanka, Myamar, Nepal, the Maldives.

What we see today in the reunification of the two Germanys, of the two Vietnams, of the two Koreas eventually, is a sign of an evolutionary trend which is trying to manifest itself at present.... "The unification of the human world is under way; there is an imperfect initiation organised but struggling against tremendous difficulties. But the momentum is there and it must inevitably increase and conquer. **Here too India has begun to play a prominent part and if she can develop that larger statesmanship which is not limited by the present facts and immediate possibilities, but looks into the future and brings it nearer, her presence may make all the difference between slow and timid and a bold and swift development**. A catastrophe may intervene and interrupt or destroy what is being done, but even then the final result is sure. For unification is a necessity of Nature, an inevitable movement. Its necessity for the nations is also clear, for without it the freedom of the nations may be at any moment in peril and the life even of the large and powerful nations insecure.... (Sri Aurobindo's message on Independence 15.8.47)

The partition of India must go and the Greater India, the land of the 'Indus', Bharat, be born again....

CHAPTER 17

India, Spiritual Leader of the World

Has Western civilisation reached the end of the road? As we know, each culture has its own uniqueness: the Greeks were great thinkers, the Indians unsurpassed spiritualists, the Egyptians superb occultists. The West's genius is undoubtedly *materialism*, its immense capacity to achieve material perfection and its great vitality. But materialism has its shortcomings and ultimately, because it blanked out spirituality, except in a superficial and ritual manner, it may bring in the decline of Western civilisation. The first signs of its weaknesses have already been seen at the beginning of the 21st century: the collapse of communism, the erosion of capitalism with recession and unemployment and the on and off raging wars in Yugoslavia and the ex-USSR republics; these wars are bound to spill-over in mainstream Europe, even if it is in an indirect manner by an influx of refugees. That the United States still survives as a superpower, should not deceive anybody: often the core is weakened, even if the giant stills carries on with a few steps before collapsing to the ground. History does not happen in a few years. Materialism is doomed.

"For my part, wrote Sri Aurobindo in 1910, I see failure written large over all the splendid and ostentatious achievements of Europe. Her costliest experiments, her greatest expenditure of intellectual and moral force have led to the swiftest exhaustion of creative activity, the complete bankruptcy of moral elevation and discouragement of man's once infinite hope.... System, organisation, machinery, have attained their perfection. Bondage has been carried to its highest expression, and from a passion to organising external liberty Europe is slaying her spiritual freedom. When the inner freedom is gone, the external liberty will follow it, and a social tyranny more terrible, more inquisitorial, and relentless than any that caste ever organised in India, will take its place. The process has already begun. The shell of external liberty remains, the core is already eaten away. Because he is still free to gratify his senses and enjoy himself, the European thinks himself free. He does not know what teeth are gnawing in to the heart of his liberty"! (India's Reb P. 75)

The other reason for the failing civilisation of the West, is that it greatly misused the mastery it had achieved over technology and the material. Instead of putting this mastery to the service of truth, instead of turning it towards the spirit of evolution, it used it for domination and the satisfaction of the Western man's senses.

What about Asia then? In Japan, only codified, externalised forms of the past greatness of Shintoism and Zen Buddhism survive. It is hoped that its success as the most powerful industrial nation today will not totally blank whatever remains of old inner genius of Japan (minus the cruelty). But look at China: communism has killed most forms of Buddhism and Confucianism, making of the Chinese one of the most materialistic nations in the world. And behold what the Chinese did to Tibet, eradicating a 2000 year old tradition of tantric Buddhism in a few decades. This is a karma which China will have to repay one day....

And what of India? During these twelve chapters, the reader has been taken through all the dangers, threats, aggressions, pitfalls, perils, mistakes, that the land of Bharata went through in the aftermath of the glorious Vedic epoch. From the disdaining of Matter and the physical by her yogis, which triggered the great Tamas; the stiffening of the caste system; the fossilisation of its society; and the first foreign incursion by Alexander. To the successive Muslim invasions, which would have wiped out any culture, any civilisation in 10 centuries of furious onslaughts. Yet India's spirituality survived, it was preserved by its people in their hearts, when their temples were destroyed, in their flesh when it was burnt, in their souls, when they were killed. And they were reborn again and again, to fight for the continuation of true Hinduism. India also survived the immense threat of European colonialism, which has annihilated the souls of so many countries, some more powerful than India. The British came, conquered ... understood nothing ... left nothing ... and India's spirituality remained. It survived the cruel partition of its ancient land, tearing its limbs into Pakistan and Bangladesh; any other nation might never have recovered from such a maiming. It survived the road to socialism charted by Nehru, the stifling oppression of state bureaucracy and corruption. It survived the dangerous politics of non violence, which Mahatma Gandhi propounded for so long and which activated not only the division of India along Hindu-Muslim lines, but also sowed the seeds of inter-caste fighting. It survived the Mahatma's sterile policies of Charkha, Brahmacharya and Khadi. It survived the Chinese onslaught in 1962. It survives today the Hindu-bashing of its westernised elite, which is all set to wipe out whatever is left of Hinduism, to replace it with prototypes that have already shown the world over their total failure. It is also hoped that it is going to survive economic liberalisation, the onslaught of modernity and the egotism of becoming a powerful nation. And finally that it will also survive the ecological holocaust that is taking place in this country.

And if it survives all these dangers, as it survived other dangers for 7000 years, then India will ride the 21st century not only as a world power, industrially, socially and militarily, but also as the only nation in the world where true spirituality will still be alive.

For we have lost the truth. we have lost the great sense, the meaning of our evolution, the meaning of why so much suffering, why dying, why getting born, why this earth, who are we, what is the soul, what is reincarnation, where is the ultimate truth about the world, the universe.... But India has kept this truth. India has preserved it through seven millennium of pitfalls, of genocides and attempts at killing her santanam dharma. And this will be India's gift to this planet during this new millennium: to restore to the world its true sense. to recharge humanity with the real meaning and spirit of life. India will become the spiritual leader of the world: "It is this religion that I am raising-up before the world, it is this that I have perfected and developed through the Rishis, saints, and Avatars, and now it is going forth to do my work among the nations. I am raising forth this nation to send forth my word...When therefore it is said that India shall rise, it is the Santana Dharma that shall rise, it is the Santana Dharma that shall be great. When it is said that India shall expand and extend herself, it is the Santana Dharma that shall expand and extend itself over the world. It is for the Dharma and by the Dharma that India exists." (India's Reb. p. 46 -Uttara speech)

Rise up, O India of the Vedic ages. Thou livest in the hearts of all thy people. Rise up O Westernised "secular" India, because thou art also the true India. Realise in your hearts the genius of the country which is yours. Stop comparing it to a civilisation, which is crumbling and cease equating it with parameters that are not hers. Wake up to the greatness of thy country. Not only the past greatness, which thou seekest to repossess in its music or in its temples, but the greatness that IS, there, waiting to be grasped again, waiting to be brought down concretely. Rise up O India, to the greatness that IS in you. Rise up O true India.

Ah, we are coming back again full circle to the wonder that WAS India, the India of the Vedas and the Upanishad, which many historians have criticized as being militant and politically disunited. But the truth was that they were united in their diversity, that it was much more democratic and allowed much more freeplay and freedom, individually and collectively, than the India of today allows. Let us again reread history, let us look at India, not through the Western prism, but with the ancient wisdom that She has bestowed upon us.

For indeed, this is one of the most amazing paradoxes of today's world: here you have a country, India, which rates today only as a developing nation, still with some of the poorest people on this planet, which is disregarded by most Western nations (and many of its own people), as irrelevant, backward, too bureaucratic—and lately, as a hotbed of Hindu fundamentalism. Yet, India holds the key to the world's future. For India is the only nation which still preserves in the darkness of Her Himalayan caves, on the luminous ghats of Benares, in the hearts of her countless yogis, or even in the minds of her ordinary folk, the key to the planetary evolution, its future and its hope. This knowledge which once roamed the shores of the world from Egypt to China, is today lost everywhere. Europe has now entered a turbulent Age; it will take a long time before it unites in spite of the near uniformity of its races and religions.

The West, in its thirst for materialism, does not know anymore where it stands and has lost this precious knowledge, which India still holds, alone in the world.

The 21st century then, will be the era of the East; this is where the sun is going to rise again, after centuries of decadence and submission to Western colonialism; this is where the focus of the world is going to shift. And as when India used to shine and send forth Her Dharma all over the Orient: Japan, Thailand, China, Burma, or Cambodia and influence their civilisations and religions for centuries to come, once more She will emit Her light and radiate, Queen among nations: "India of the ages is not dead nor has She spoken Her last creative word; She lives and has still something to do for Herself and the human peoples. And that which She must seek now to awake, is not an anglicised oriental people, docile pupil of the West and doomed to repeat the cycle of the Occident's success and failure, but still the ancient immemorial Shakti recovering Her deepest self, lifting Her head higher towards the supreme source of light and strength and turning to discover the complete meaning and vaster form of Her Dharma. (Sri Aurobindo)

But what will be that true India?

17.1 The True India Within

The political problems which India has faced since Independence are either intense regionalist cravings in her different states; or covert—and sometimes open separatisms. This is due to a too strong centralised and heavy-handed Government at the Centre, who not only wants to know everything, control everything, but whose bureaucracy is so pervasive, so omnipresent everywhere, that it stifles all attempts at trying something new, fresh, out of the old patterns. Today, nothing is decided without the Prime Minister, no major decision such as the naming of a Chief Minister, is made except by him, the result of which is that everything comes to a standstill, because nobody dares to take any initiative and everyone always refers to one's immediate superior and so on till it reaches the top. This old Congress policy of centralising everything in its hands has to go. Even Modi doesn't seem to be able to break this straightjacket. Yet, one has to trust the Indian people, their courage and spirit of initiative. It may be because of this constant heavy-hand since independence, that so many separatisms have sprung-up from Assam to even Tamil Nadu with its Dravidian obsession.

The key to India's oneness is DIVERSITY and the unifying element is found in its ancient Hindu culture— 'Indu'—culture which has influence so much all Indians, be they Hindu, Christians, or even Muslims, witness Bangladesh and Pakistan who have women heads of state. India's Dharma is not Hinduism, it is the knowledge preserved throughout the ages of a Higher plane than surface life, of states of being which superimpose our ordinary mind and lead like a pyramid, towards the highest Reality, Sat-Chit, Truth- Existence. In the words of Sri Aurobindo: "A wider spiritual culture must recognise that the Spirit is not only the highest and inmost thing, but all is manifestation and creation of the Spirit. Its aim must be not only to raise to inaccessible heights a few elect, but to draw all man and all life and the whole human being upward, to spiritual life and in the end to deify human nature." (India's Rebirth).

But you have to give breathing spaces to the vast mosaic which is India. Let Indian Muslims rule their own communities, as long as they recognise India's sovereignty and keep within the framework of the Constitution. Let the

Christians worship in peace in their cathedrals, so long as they do not try to go on converting more Hindus. Once again let us listen to the wisdom of Sri Aurobindo: "India, shut into a separate existence by the Himalayas and the ocean, has always been the home of a peculiar people with characteristics of its own, with its own distinct civilisation, way of life, way of the spirit, a separate culture, arts, building of society. it has absorbed all that has entered into it, put upon all the Indian stamp, welded the most diverse elements into its fundamental unity. but it has also been throughout, a congeries of diverse people, lands, kingdoms and in earlier times republics also, diverse races, sub-nations, with a marked character of their own, developing different brands or forms of civilisation and culture.... India's history throughout has been marked by a tendency, a constant effort to unite all this diversity of elements into a single political whole under a central imperial rule, so that India might be politically as well as culturally one....

The ancient diversities of the country carried in them great advantages as well as drawbacks. by these differences the country was made the home of many living and pulsating centres of life, culture, a richly and brilliantly coloured diversity in unity; all was not drawn up into a few provincial capitals, or an imperial metropolis, other towns and regions remaining subordinated and indistinct or even culturally asleep. the whole nation lived with a full life in its many parts and this increased enormously the creative energy of the whole. There is no possibility any longer that this diversity will endanger or diminish the unity of India. Those vast spaces which kept her people from closeness and a full interplay have been abolished in their separating effect by the march of science and the swiftness of the means of communication. The idea of a federation and a complete machinery for its perfect working have been discovered and will be at full work. Above all, the spirit of patriotic unity has been too firmly established in the people to be easily effaced or diminished and it would be more endangered by refusing to allow the natural play of life of the sub-nations than by satisfying their natural aspirations... India's national life will then be founded on her natural strength and the principle of unity in diversity which has always been normal to her and its fulfilment the fundamental course of her being and its very nature the many in one would place her on the sure foundation of her swabhava and swadharma ... a union of states and regional people would again be the form of a united India." (India's reb. p. 240-241)

17.2 The True India Without

But for this purpose, a new Constitution has to be rewritten. We have said it again and again through these chapters: India has blindly borrowed her Constitution and her democratic institutions from the West. Nehru did not bother to adapt them to India's own particular needs, to the immense diversity of her people, who have shown throughout the ages that they are bound to India by something else, than mere petty nationalism. India's civilisation is at least 7000 years old and should have a Constitution framed after her own history. Not only that, but the whole democratic system of India has to be reshaped to suit that new, that true nation, which will manifest the wonder that IS India.

And what is true democracy for India, but the law of Dharma. It is this law that has to be revived, it is this law that must be the foundation of a true democratic India: "It has been said that democracy is based on the rights of man; it has been replied that it should rather take its stand on the duties of man; but both rights and duties are European ideas. Dharma is the

Indian conception in which rights and duties lose the artificial antagonism created by a view of the world which makes selfishness the root of action and regain their deep and eternal unity. Dharma is the basis of democracy which Asia must recognise, for in this lies the distinction between the soul of Asia and the soul of Europe." (India's Reb p.37- March 16th 1908)

And the most wonderful thing is that, practically, we have in India the seed of a new form of democracy. One should begin with the old Panchayat system in the villages and then work up to the top. The Panchayat system and the guilds are more representative and they have a living contact with the people; they are part of the people's ideas. On the contrary, the parliamentary system with local bodies—the municipal councils—is not workable: these councils have no living contacts with the people. « We had a spontaneous and a free growth of communities developing on their own lines... Each such communal form of life—the village, the town, etc., which formed the unit of national life, was left free in its own internal management. The central authority never interfered with it ... because its function was not so much to legislate as to harmonise and see that everything was going all right... (India's Rebirth 172)

The Judiciary would have to be revised also. It would be absurd to put back the Manu law into practice; but certainly the law of Dharma, of Truth, should be translated into a new Judicial system. Not to judge according to Western standards, its secular values, which have no relevance to India. « The work of the legislators attempted to take up the ordinary life of man and of the community and the life of human desire and aim and interest and ordered rule and custom and to interpret and formulate it in the same complete and decisive manner and at the same time to throw the whole in to an ordered relation to the ruling ideas of the national culture and frame and perpetuate a social system and perpetuate a social system intelligently fashioned so as to provide a basis, a structure, a gradation by which there could be a secure evolution of the life from the vita and mental, to the spiritual motive.. » (Found of Indian Culture p. 283)

There is another problem which India has faced since independence, which is that of a unified language. The Central Government has tried to impose Hindi upon the rest the country, which is typical of the arrogance of too centralised a power. Why should they seek to impose on the whole of India a language which is spoken neither in the East, nor in the West, nor in the South? But then, what could be the unifying language of India, bare English, which is spoken only by a tiny minority, as it has no roots here? The answer is here, so simple and luminous: "Sanskrit ought still to have a future as the language of the learned and it will not be a good day for India when the ancient tongues cease entirely to be written or spoken," admonishes Sri Aurobindo (India's Reb 113). Yes, Sanskrit! Sanskrit the Mother of all tongues, one of the richest languages in the world. A dead language, you say! Impossible to revive? But that's what they argued about Hebrew. And did not the Jewish people, when they got back their land in 1948, revive their "dead" language, so that it is spoken today by ALL Jewish people and has become alive again?... The same thing ought to be done with Sanskrit, but as Sri Aurobindo points out: "it must get rid of the curse of the heavy pedantic style contracted by it in its decline, with the lumbering impossible compounds and the overweight of hair-splitting erudition." Let the scholars begin now to revive and modernise the Sanskrit language, it would be a sure sign of the dawning of the

Renaissance of India. In a few years it should be taught as the second language in schools throughout the country, with the regional language as the first and English as the third. Then will India again have its own unifying language.

Education of course has to be totally revamped. The kind of Westernised education which is standard in India, does have its place, because India wants to be on par with the rest of the world, and Indian youth should be able to deal confidently with the West: do business, talk, and relate to a universal world culture. But nevertheless, the first thing that Indian children should be taught is the greatness of their own culture. They should learn to revere the Vedas, they should be taught the greatness of the Mahabharata and the Ramanayana; they should be told that in this country everything has been done, that it was an unsurpassed civilisation, when the West was still mumbling its first words, that Indian civilisation reached dizzying heights, which have been since unsurpassed. But overall they should be taught early that India's greatness is her spirituality her world-wide wisdom. **India's new education has to be spiritualised it has to be an inner education which teaches to look at things from the inner prism, not through the western artificial looking glass.** India's Dharma, her eternal quest for truth should be drilled in the child from an early age. And from this firm base, everything then can be taught—from the most modern forms of mathematics, to the latest technologies.

"National education ... may be described as the education which starting with the past and making full use of the present, builds up a great nation. Whoever wishes to cut of the nation from its past, is no friend of our national growth. Whoever fails to take advantage of the present, is losing us the battle of life. We must therefore save for India all that she has stored up of knowledge, character and noble thoughts in her immemorial past. We must acquire for her the best knowledge that Europe can give her and assimilate it to her own peculiar type of national temperament. We must introduce the best methods of teaching humanity has developed, whether modern or ancient. And all these we must harmonise into a system which will be impregnated with the spirit of self-reliance, so as to build up men and not machines." (India's Reb 36)

It should also be made clear that Indian history will have to be rewritten. Certainly if not only the Jews, but also the whole world is constantly drilled into the history of the holocaust, so as to remember and not repeat the same mistakes, definitely Indian children should be taught about the rape of their country by successive Muslim invaders and the incredible harm done to India. They should know the truth about Aurangzeb, Babar and Mahmud of Ghazni, instead of the present semi-glorifying of the great Mughal culture and period. They should not be taught to hate of their fellow Muslims in India, but to only know them in their real historical perspective. A certain effort in that direction has already been made by the present Government, which for instance has replaced some of the staunch Marxists, such as Romila Thapar from the Indian Council of Research. But what outcry in the "secular" press it has triggered and a lot more needs to be done.

Because, for instance, the Independence story should be also rewritten and true nationalists given their right place. The Congress should be granted its just share of the movement, but not sanctified as it is now. All Marxist denigration of India should also be banned from the books. Indian students should be taught to look at the world through the Indian prism and see historical events, such as the rape of the Third World by Spanish conquistadors or the colonising and impoverishment of Africa, in their factual colours.

Another symbol of the emergence of a new India will be the universal acceptance of *Vande Mataram* as the national anthem – why should anyone object to Saraswati, the Goddess of learning, She who bestowed so much Grace on India. In 1939, a disciple had said to Sri Aurobindo that: "there are some people who object to the singing of Vande Mataram as a national song; Sri Aurobindo had replied: "in that case Hindus should give up their culture." But the disciple had continued: "the argument is that the song speaks of Hindu gods, like Durga and that it is offensive to Muslims." Said Sri Aurobindo: "but it is not a religious song, it is a national song and the Durga spoken of is India as the Mother. Why should not the Muslims accept it? In the Indian concept of nationality, the Hindu view should be naturally there. if it cannot find a place, the Hindus may as well be asked to give-up their culture. The Hindus don't object to "Allah-Ho-Akbar."

On a national level, there should be a revival of authentic Indian traditional forms of genius, such as ancient medical systems, like Ayurveda, or Siddha, instead of the total dependence on Western antibiotics and their terrible proliferation. Today, these alleopathic medecines are found even in India's remotest villages, making people dependant on harmful drugs which are expensive and only serve to enrich the big foreign multinationals. It takes a Deepak Chopra, an Indian doctor exiled in the United States, to remind the world that Ayurveda is one of the greatest medical systems ever devised; that 5000 years ago, when the rest of the planet lived in total medical ignorance, Indian doctors were already performing plastic surgery, knew that the origin of many diseases were psychosomatic, had found in Mother nature the cure for most of man's ailments and realised that the five natural elements have to be made balanced in the human body for a perfect harmonious life. Not only that, but Indian doctors were also yogis. They perceived that beyond the human body was another divine reality, of which the soul was the vehicle on earth. Today, Western doctors (and many Indian ones) are totally ignorant of the different planes of consciousness which superimpose our terrestrial life. Hence these doctors and the psychiatrists of the West are, as Sri Aurobindo pointed out, « searching with a torch light in the dark caverns of man's Unconscious ».

India is also full of marvelous indigenous arts which are ignored by the officialdom, but actually are at the source of many of the world's wonders. Such is Kerala's kalaripayat, the most extraordinary martial art on this earth, not only because it is the ancestor of all great Asian martial arts, such as judo or karate, because it was taken by Buddhist monks and the famous Boddidharma (founder of Zen Buddhism) to China and Japan, but also because it is the only martial art in the world which regroups all kinds of fighting techniques under one umbrella: sword, knife, spears, bare handed techniques, flexible swords. It is also a great medical knowledge, its masters are yogis and practice a unique form of massage. Unfortunately it is dying because India ignores that she possesses such a wonderful art.

And what about Indian yogic sciences? Pranayama for instance is the most exacting, precise, mathematical, powerful breathing discipline one can dream of. Its effects and results have been observed and categorised by Indian yogis for millenniums. This extraordinary knowledge, brings in very quickly wonderful results in both the well being of the body and the quietude of the mind. Pushed to its extreme, it gives to the disciple deep spiritual experiences and a true inner perception of the world. His Holiness Sri Sri Ravi Shankar has revitalized this science and packaged it in modern terms.

And what about Hata-yoga, also a 5000 year old technique, which has inspired today all kind of aerobic, of so-called yoga techniques and gymnastic drills around the world? Practised properly it brings health, strength and endurance to the body. It is the secret of Indian Yogis' incredible longevity. It may be too, a help to a once and future immortality. And like in Pranayama, its exercises, results and particularities are so well categorised that there is a solution for each problem of the human body, an application for each part of the human anatomy.

And what about meditation, queen of all the yogic sciences, which Maharishi, who just died, brought to the West, giving it a scientific stamp ? That which is above everything, that without which any yogic discipline is impossible. That which interiorizes us, carries us within ourselves, to the discovery of our true soul and nature. There are hundreds of different mediation techniques, simple, cartesian, easy to experience, which have been devised by Indian sages since the dawn of Bharat. Each one has its own characteristics, each one gives particular results, which has been experienced by the billions of aspirants who have practised them since the dawn of Vedic times.

But are all these yogic sciences *dead*, disappeared from India, gone for ever from the earth consciousness? Not at all. India is full of ashrams, of yogis, of masters, who are still keeping alive all those wonderful sciences. From the tip of cape Comorin to Kashmir, you cannot go to a place in this country without finding some spiritual place, some sadhu practicing a particular tapasaya, some course in meditation for householders. You have just to step out of the big cities, its five star hotels, its mad traffic, its hurried businessmen with their ties and briefcases and enter India's country side, and you step again in India's immortal Dharma, you can still feel the line of continuity of 7000 years of sages. This is the Wonder that IS India.

And what do you think would happen if these ancient arts still alive in India were officially recognised by the Indian Government, by Indian themselves and UTILISED in every day life. What do you think would happen for instance if pranayama was systematically taught to sportsmen from the beginning of their training? It would produce *supermen*; it would be difficult to beat Indian athletes, because through this marvelous technique they would have achieved perfect concentration. What would happen if Indian businessmen used too Pranayama? It would double their capacity of work and endow them with enthusiasm for their task. Or if school children were taught at a very early age the combined techniques of pranayama, hata-yoga, meditation and Ayurveda ? It would maybe produce the next human species of our era, a race which is spiritualised in both mind and body. Unfortunately, for the moment, the Christian and Muslim minorities reject them outright as part of the Hindu culture and also modern Indians, whether businessmen, intellectuals, or bureaucrats, disdain this golden treasure of India.

But fortunately for the planetary evolution, India's yogis, gurus, teachers are going all around the world to spread this wonderful knowledge. Some are genuine ones, some are semi-fakes, some are total fakes. But it does not matter, because almost all of them carry abroad the message of yoga. Among these messengers of truth, one could mention the remarkable Vipassana mediation technique of Shri Goenka, which has centres all around the world. Or the prayanama courses of the

Art Of Living of Sri Sri Ravi Shankar, which are fast spreading around the world. Or Iyengars' wonderful hata-yoga techniques. Thanks to them, there are more and more people in the West who know about India. It maybe even that India will have to realise its Wonder when the West will point its finger at it, as happened in a lesser way in Japan with its martial art techniques, Zen Buddhism, rock gardens and Bonzai art, when America took hold of them. Let us hope though, that the true India will emerge soon.

For the India of tomorrow, the spiritual leader of the world, Mother India, Durga: "is not a piece of earth; she is a Power, a Godhead, for all nations have such a Devi supporting this separate existence and keeping it in being..." (Sri Aurobindo, India's Rebirth, p. 235) "Mother Durga! Rider on the lion, giver of all strength, we are seated in thy temple. Listen, O Mother, descend upon earth, make thyself manifest in this land of India..."

CHAPTER 18

The Knowledge of Hindus

What is this Knowledge that is still alive in this wonderful country which we call India, thanks to the Hindus?

Firstly and foremost: "I accept you; I accept that you may be White or Black, Red or Yellow, Christian, Buddhist, or Muslim. I accept that God may manifest at different times, under different names, using different scriptures. Thus God is Krishna, but also Jesus Christ, Buddha or Mohamed. This an extraordinary statement and a marvellous instrument towards world peace, at a time where terrorism is striking everywhere in the world in the name of One God. It is also a Knowledge that only the body dies, but not the soul, which is born and reborn again till it achieves perfection. A Knowledge that whatever you do bears consequences in this life or another. A Knowledge that all human beings are made out of Love, even beneath the hate and the killings… "

And also: "I have inherited from my ancestors the tools to become a better person, whatever my religion, ethnicity and profession: a better Christian, a better Hindu, a better Muslim." What are these tools? Hata-yoga, India's gift to the world, which has been copied and imitated everywhere. Meditation, this extraordinary technique of coming back to one's Self, of settling the mind and the body, which is today practiced by millions around the world—another bequest of

India to humanity. Pranayama, the science of respiration, perfected by Indians for three millenniums. "Does the breath have any religion," asks His Holiness Sri Sri Ravi Shankar, the founder of the Art of Living movement, which has spread today in 140 countries? "Is the air we breathe around us, Muslim, Christian, or Hindu"?

This knowledge thus does not only belong to Hindus, but also to Buddhists, Jains, Christians and Muslims of India. Once upon a time, the Syrian Christians of Kerala, though they remained faithful to the word of Jesus Christ, had incorporated some of the basic tenets of Hinduism such as reincarnation and karma. Once upon a time, great Sufis, such as Dara Sukoh, Shah Jahan's eldest and preferred son (who should have become emperor instead of Aurangzeb), while remaining true Muslims (and not apostate ones), could translate the Upanishads and step into a temple without thinking they were committing a mortal sin. Once upon, a time Sikhism was born out of Dharma, to defend the Hindu Dharma and neither Sikh nor Hindu, saw any difference between themselves. Once upon a time, Buddha, although he did strike against ritualism and hereditary Brahmanism, did not found a religion, but a path that led to the same Ananda he came from.

This knowledge is unique to India. For The West has lost the truth. We have lost the Great Sense, the meaning of our evolution, of why so much suffering, why dying, why getting born, why this earth, who are we, what is the soul, what is reincarnation, where is the ultimate truth about the universe? And this will be India's gift to this planet during this century: to restore to the world its true sense; to recharge humanity with the real meaning and spirit of life. Thus, if you are an Indian settled abroad, whatever your religion, you should carry that identity in your actions and your aura, that you may shine without words, for it is a great privilege and responsibility to be born an Indian. Yet, too often, Indians in the US or Canada, or even the UK for that matter, hide their identities and try to merge into the mainstream culture, becoming more American than an Americans, more British than the British. Sometimes even, Indians are ashamed to say that they are Indians and it is a tragedy to themselves and to their children, who lose the connexion with one of the most ancient cultures in the world, which is not a religion but the last living spirituality on this planet.

You should also know that today this 'Hindu' Knowledge is under attack from all sides. Foremost, from the Globalization and Westernization which is taking place at the moment in India at a frantic pace. TV channels and advertisements must be the biggest culprits. There is also a rapid Christianisation of many of the villages in India, whether in Tamil Nadu, or in the North-East, where innocent tribals are converted with the help million of dollars and it is a tragedy, because they are taught to look down upon their own culture and social habits. What about the radicalism that seems to grip some of the Muslim youth? Nowhere but in India, they have had so much freedom to practice their faith. Try to be a Hindu, a Buddhist or a Christian in Saudi Arabia or Bangladesh ! And we know that the Pakistani or Bangladeshi bombers and killers in Hyderabad, Delhi, or Mumbai could never function without the (very) active participation of some India's Muslims, although Indian politicians keep mum about it.

Lastly Hindu renegades (see Annexe below), those intellectuals who want to cut off at any cost India from her past and make a copy—however brilliant—of a Marxism which has died everywhere else, or of the United Sates of America, where violence, divorce and depression are affecting three persons out of five, are extremely active at the moment, thanks to a Government who chooses to closes its eyes, while this is going on.

Yet, it is for this Precious Knowledge that all Indians, be they Hindu, Muslim, Christian, or Sikh, should retain their dharmic identity, while being faithful to their Creed or Supreme God. Every Diwali thus, should symbolize for all Indians, the rekindling of this Ancient, Universal, All-encompassing, Non-Religious Dharmic Light in their hearts. Let Mother India shine in them and rekindle their common identity beyond their religions.

It is time Indians look again at their own history and understand how it is important to save that Knowledge, the Knowledge of the Hindus.

Addendums

I. A List of the 50 Biggest Enemies of Hindus (Dead or Alive)

Hindus should at least know who are their enemies. Jews have shown us that to remember, helps to make sure that atrocities do not happen again. Let us not forget that the biggest genocide ever—is that of the Hindus—which has been calculated at 100 million victims, from the Hindu Kush to the Mumbai attacks of 2006.

This list, which is compiled without any hatred or malice, is not complete. I am counting on you to raise it to a hundred. If you think I missed someone, facebook it to me, with the name and two or three paragraphs on why you think he or she is an enemy of the Hindus.

I have also made a hit parade of the ten countries that I feel are inimical to Hindus.

HERE THE LIST:

1. **Thomas Babington,** 1st Baron Macaulay. Played a major role in introducing English and western concepts to education in India. This was good and one cannot deny that English gives India an edge, say compared to China, in dealing with the West and conducting business. Yet, Macaulay had very little regard for Hindu culture and education: « all the historical information which can be collected from all the books which have been written in the Sanskrit language, is less valuable than what may be found in the most paltry abridgement used at preparatory schools in England ». Macaulay thus succeeded in fashioning a class of "brown Sahibs," who thought and acted British. Today, much of India's intelligentsia and Media stands proof that Macaulay succeeded: they look down on their own culture and analyse India through the western Prism.

2. **Indian National Congress**. Few people know that the Indian National Congress was founded on 28 December 1885 by a Britisher,

A.O. Hume. Its goals were to « allow all those who work for the national (read British) good to meet each other personally, to discuss and decide of the political operations to start during thc year." And certainly, till the end of the 19th century, the Congress, who regarded British rule in India as a "divine dispensation," was happy with criticising moderately the Government, while reaffirming its loyalty to the Crown and its faith in "liberalism" and the British innate sense of justice"!!! Real nationalist leaders like Sri Aurobindo or Tilak, were side-lined by the 'Moderate' Congress'. Today, we find that the British succeeded in implanting an eternal love of the 'White' in the Congress, witness the sycophancy around Sonia Gandhi.

3. **Jawaharlal Nehru.** Nehru, writes French historian Alain Danielou, "was the perfect replica of a certain type of Englishman. He often used the expression 'continental people', with an amused and sarcastic manner, to designate French or Italians. He despised non-anglicised Indians and had a very superficial and partial knowledge of India. His ideal was the romantic socialism of 19th century Britain. But this type of socialism was totally unfit to India, where the conditions were totally different from 19th century Europe. The Congress has today made an icon out Nehru, which nobody has yet dared to touch, but as History will show more and more, Nehru did tremendous harm to India by initiating movements and patterns, which not only did vast damage in their times, but continue to survive and weigh down the Indian nation, long after their uselessness has been realized.

4. **Babur**. Do you know what Jawaharlal Nehru wrote about Babur the destroyer of the Ram mosque in Ayodhya? "Babur did not like India and preferred to isolate himself in the exquisite gardens he had devised, with their geometrical design, their crossed canals, which evoked to him the rivers of paradise." The truth is that Babur was probably the most ferocious Moghol emperor, indulging in unnecessary massacres and that he razed thousands of temples. His ultimate goal was the destruction and the enslaving of the Hindus. It is sad that today Indian History books do not mention his crimes.

5. **Sonia Gandhi**. It is a fact that Sonia brought discipline, order and cohesion into the Congress party. But the amount of power, that she, a non-Indian, a simple elected MP, like hundreds of others, possessed when the Congress was in power for ten years, should frighten us: a word,

nay a glance of her was sufficient to trigger action by her entourage, using any means—witness how P. Chidambaram would have allowed Narendra Modi to be killed by a Israt Jahan, a known terrorist. Thus, the instruments of power had never been so perverted in India. The CBI blatantly and shamelessly quashed all injunctions against Quattrochi and even allowed him to get away with billions of rupees which he had stolen from India. Yet, without batting an eyelid, and with the Indian Media turning a blind eye, it went ruthlessly after Narendra Modi, the then Chief Minister of the most efficiently run state, the most corruption free. Sonia Gandhi continues to be a danger to Hindus, because if by some freak chance Modi loses in 2019, as Vajpayee did before him, Sonia will again become the empress of India.

6. **The Pope.** Christianity, unfortunately, is still clinging in the belief of a single true God, Jesus Christ, in spite of the feeble attempts at "Ecumenism" of the Church. In fact as church attendance is dropping drastically in the West, as less and less youth are willing to become priests and nuns and as the Church is shaken by paedophilia scandals, the Pope's call "for the Evangelisation of Asia in the Third Millennium" is a clear indication that, like the Tobacco companies having less customers in the West, the Church is looking for new converts in the Third World ! It would be all right if the Church was playing by the rules of the free market, where there is a certain amount of fairness: "you see what advantages my religion is bringing you, compare it with your own and then feel free to chose." But, sadly, the missionaries are using unethical means to convert the poorest of the poor Hindus in India: offering free medical treatment, free schooling, interest-free loans, even going as far as organizing "fake miracles" prayer meetings, as it is regularly done by American Preacher Benny Hinn. They do it in India, but they dare not do it in China, where freedom of religion is curtailed and any missionary caught proselytising is kicked out. Would Hindus dare convert Christians in France, for instance? You are joking: there is not a single Hindu temple in France, as their construction has not been allowed and there is even a minister in charge of hunting down "sects" (meaning what is not Christian-oriented).

7. **Rahul Gandhi.** No doubt Rahul Gandhi is a decent, well meaning man, though totally ignorant of India's culture and spirituality as his father was. But his ignorance makes him a dangerous man. Remember the

Wikileaks cables, where Rahul Gandhi tells the American ambassador that Hindu terrorism was more dangerous than Islamic terrorism: *The bigger threat may be the growth of radicalized Hindu groups, which create religious tensions and political confrontations with the Muslim community.* It seems also that Rahul and his mother wanted to make an example of Colonel Purohit and Sadhvi Pragya to please their Muslim electorate and that direct orders were issued from 10 Janpath to get a confession out of him and Sadhvi Pragya at any cost, even torture.

8. The Communist Party of India. Very few people know that the communists refused to collaborate against the Nazis during the 2nd World War, because Russia was then allied with Germany. Their attitude during the war with China in 1962 was also very ambivalent and today newspapers like the Hindu or Frontline are just mouthpieces of the Chinese points of view. Most Marxists in India are anti-Hindu as a principle (Marx was against religion) and their intellectuals are adept at Hindu bashing. Ata time when Marxism is dead all over the world, including in Cuba and China, India is the last refuge of communism. Though communists have a certain sincerity (they generally are not corrupt and live a simple life, contrary to many Indian politicians), it is not a gift to India, as they contribute very little to India's growth, with their constant strikes and demands. Naxalism which is a great danger for this country is also an offshoot of communism.

9. Pryanka Gandhi. Nobody wants to bother Priyanka Gandhi as long as she leads her life, raises her children and is an Indian like another India. But in case her mother Sonia leaves India or something happens to her, Priyanka—and not Rahul—will be the natural choice of the Congress to take up the reins. Would Priyanka think and act differently from her mother, brother, father and grandfather? Unlikely. She will think like a Christian and a westerner, not like an Indian and adopt Nehru's misplaced socialist and popular idea's, which have bogged down India in corruption and red tape. Plus her husband Robert Vadra, a man who multiplied his wealth by 600 in five years, is an albatross around her neck.

10. Barkha Dutt. Most probably Barkha started like a young and idealistic journalist. But the fact that she was married twice to a Kashmiri Muslim, must have influenced her mind. The power that came with NDTV, as it grew into the most sophisticated TV news channel, and her proximity to the Congress party, also went to her head. From a young journo, Barkha turned into a Hindu basher—you just have to listen to the Radia tapes to understand that. Also, woe to those who disagree with her in her interviews and programs, as she rudely interrupts them when she feels like it. There are also accusations of corruption against her and her boss Prannoy Roy.

11. **Kancha Ilaiah**. Known for his immensely controversial book, 'Why I am not a Hindu', Kancha Ilaiah, is a converted Christian, who hates Hindus, particularly Brahmins, whom he accuses of all the possible evils. This hatred makes him irrational. For instance he recently said that vegetarianism is anti-nationalism: "For me, my nation starts with eating beef. Unfortunately, we gave up eating beef and our brains are not growing now. There is no enough protein,"... How stupid can you be, when many westerners are now turning to vegetarianism?

12. **Aamir Khan**. Once upon a time, Aamir Khan, benefited from the goodwill of all, Muslims as well as Hindus. His TV program on social issues, Satyamev Jayata, even raised his status to a crusader for human rights. Then slowly the mask dropped, and one could see that he was no different from the average Muslim, when it came to Hindus, the BJP and Narendra Modi. His reflection on 'Intolerance ' and that his (Hindu) wife wanted to leave India, alienated him from many of his supporters. His anti-Hindu gurus film, like PK, created too a lot of enmity. Not a friend of Hindus.

13. **Shah Rukh Khan**. As Aamir Khan, Shah Rukh is also married to a Hindu, but raises his kids as Muslims, and whenever it suits him, plays the minority card (Pakistan invited him many times to settle there). What one should understand is that it is like elections in India: Aamir's and Shah Rukh's Muslim fan base in India is so huge, that they don't really care about Hindus. In fact, playing a little anti-Hindu card, pleases their Muslim fans and does no harm to their image, as Hindus anyway never retaliate, even by boycotting their films.

14. **Amartya Sen**. This one is a deadly enemy of Hindus, much more than many, because he got the Nobel Prize, teaches in Oxford and is highly respected in the West. But make no mistake about it: Amartya Sen is a true Marxist and he rode his fame on the back of his false theories about poverty in India and in the West. It is a pity that the Congress Govt. gave him the Nalanda University project for which he did nothing. He should become persona non grata in India.

15. Rajdeep Sardesai. Rajdeep is a nasty guy and not an honest journalist—witness the incident when he sat on a sting interview that showed the Congress paying bribes to BJP MLA's to defect. He was also seen in his true light in New York, where he portrayed himself as a victim of a hard-line Hindu, whereas the video replays showed that in fact he was the aggressor. No doubt, Rajdeep is a personal enemy of Narendra Modi and has never hid his dislike of the BJP. There have been many rumours that his father, converted to Christianity late in life and that may have influenced Rajdeep, for he has definitely a Christian-Marxist view of India and Hindus.

16. Angana Chatterjee. Angana Chatterjee, is one of the most venomous anti-Hindu in the USA. The irony is that she is a Hindu herself and started in an association named after India's avatar, himself a great defender of Hindus, Sri Aurobindo. You need to know that she is married to Richard Shapiro who is Director and Associate Professor of the Grad. Anthropology Program at CIIS, also a very anti-Hindu body. In fact, Shapiro was barred from entering India in 2010. Angana and Richard are of course great defenders of the Kashmiri Muslims and attend every International Kashmir Freedom Conference (IKFC), which only gives the Muslim point of view and ignores the 450,000 Kashmiri Hindus who have become refugees in their own country.

17. Teesta Setalvad. First it should be known that Teesta is a Hindu herself, who like Barkha Dutt, is married to a Muslim, Javed Anand. Javed, is General Secretary of Muslims for Secular Democracy, a virulent anti-Hindu organization. Using her organization Teesta Setalvad's name has come to symbolize everything that is wrong with NGO activism in India. She has used any means to go after Hindus, particularly their leaders and specially Narenda Modi. Unfortunately, Teesta has been repeatedly exposed for having indulged in unethical acts and has cases pending against her in courts for perjury. The truth is that Teesta Setalvad is a law unto herself and has total disregard for the rule of law or for victims. Her anti-Hindu agenda is her source of income from foreign agencies. She has taken the courts for a ride with her perjury and her acts of influencing witnesses. She has misused the lack of education and poverty of victims to file false affidavits to further her own agenda.

18. Aurangzeb. Aurangzeb was a monster not only to Hindus, but also to his own family: he beheaded his brother Dara Shikoh, who was the rightful heir to the throne, poisoned his own father, imprisoned his son… Yet, Romila Thapar, Harbans Mukhia and Bipan Chandra, once upon a time professors at the JNU in New Delhi, the Mecca of secularism and negationism in India, denied the Aurangzeb genocide on Hindus by replacing it instead with a conflict of classes. What are the facts? Aurangzeb (1658-1707) did not just build an isolated mosque on a destroyed temple, he ordered ALL temples destroyed, among them the Kashi Vishvanath, Krishna's birth temple in Mathura, the rebuilt Somnath temple on the coast of Gujarat, the Vishnu temple replaced with the Alamgir mosque now overlooking Benares and the Treta-ka-Thakur temple in Ayodhya.… Thank God Shivaji Maharaj, a true Hindu hero brought him to his knees. Yet Shivaji is treated as a nobody in Indian History books and Aurangzeb like a stern but just emperor.…

19. John Dayal The most virulent and articulate Christian anti-Hindu, John and many other Indian Christian leaders and bishops, is not only practicing a Christianity which had its place 50 years ago in Europe (but is no more today, as Western Christianity is evolving), but are also re-embracing the old colonial missionary concept that Christ is the only 'true' God and that all 'heathens' Hindus have to be converted. John Dayal is all the time lobbying in the West, particularly with the US Congress, testifying that 'Christians are persecuted in India', whereas actually Christians have been the worst persecutors in the world, wiping out ruthlessly entire cultures, like those of the Aztecs in South America.

20. Irfan Habib, At last, Irfan Habib have been side-lined by the Modi Government! He and Romila Thapar ruled supreme for nearly 40 years in devising Indian school curriculum. Together they have falsified Indian History with total impunity and went after the Hindus full steam. Irfan Habib continued the legacy of his father, Mohamed Habib, to rewrite the Chapter of Muslim invasions in India. Habib father and son's books are based on four theories: (1) that the records (written by the Muslims themselves) of slaughters of Hindus, the enslaving of their women and children and razing of temples were "mere exaggerations by court poets and zealous chroniclers to please their rulers." (2) That they were indeed atrocities, but mainly committed by Turks, the savage riders from the Steppe. (3) That the destruction of the temples took place because Hindus stored their gold and jewels inside them and therefore Muslim armies plundered these. (4) That the conversion of millions of

Hindus to Islam was not forced, "but what happened was there was a shift of opinion in the population, who on its own free will chose the Shariat against the Hindu law (Smriti), as they were all oppressed by the bad Brahmins"…!!!

21. Ramachandra Guha, Outlook magazine's favourite columnist, is a renowned Hindu/Hindu gurus/Hindu culture hater, who like Rahul Gandhi, recently said that "Hindu fundamentalism is more threatening than Islamic terrorism." He has written a number of books targeting Hindus and their spiritual leaders. Unfortunately, as many of these leftist intellectuals, he is fairly popular in the West and often quoted by western correspondents based in India.

22. Romilla Thapar. The most renowned Indian historian, who has links with all Indologists in the world, universities and India centers. As Rajiv Malhotra writes: "Hindu spiritual experiences are devalued by Romila Thapar, as pathological. She resorts to a quasi-scholarly speculation of racial hatred as existing in entire Indian traditions, demonizing the 'other', a technique to justify holding such people in contempt and even attacking them." This is exactly the same thesis that is being spread today by Maoist insurgents working among remote tribes in central India, namely, that demons mentioned in Hinduism are actually references to tribal people ». Today even, most of the intellectuals, journalists and many of India's elite have been influenced by that school of thinking and regularly ape its theories. Romila Thapar is a traitor to her own culture and society, for she is a Hindu.

23. N. Ram and the Hindu newspaper. Long time editor of the newspaper the Hindu, who should be renamed the "Anti-Hindu." N. Ram is a fervent disciple of Marxism and communist China. The magazine of the Hindu, Frontline, although well written, as the Hindu, perpetuates a dead ideology. Unfortunately the Hindu is still read by many in India, including westerners in the South of India.

24. Sagarika Ghose and CNN IBN, Rajdeep Sardesai's wife shares his beliefs and hatred for the Hindus. It's a tragedy that CNN IBN is so partial towards Hindus and sympathetic to anybody who is anti-Hindu. Why did CNN, a renowned western television, choose to partner someone who is against the majority community of their country?

25. Mamta Banerjee. It is said that Mamta Banerjee is a Kali worshipper and does regular pujas when she is alone in her house.

Unfortunately Mamta has realized that she can get elected as West Bengal Chief Minister on the sole strength of the Muslim vote. She thus panders to them, turning a blind eye to the atrocities committed on the Hindus by the Bangladeshis refugees, who are given ration cards so that they can vote for Mamta. Sad also that she chose to say 'Allah O Akbar' when she just got re-elected. To what depths will Indian politicians sink to get votes? Hindus are becoming minorities in certain districts of WB, Assam or UP. That is a tragedy and something should be done.

26. Akbaruddin Owais. Proof that India is a democracy lies in the fact that people like Owais and his brother can not only rant against the Hindus and preach near secession, but also get elected. There has to be some limits to preaching hatred and separatism.

27. Geelani and other Kashmiri separatists. How can the Indian Government allow these separatists to openly visit the Pakistani embassy in Delhi or travel to Pakistan to take instructions from their masters? No country tolerates that kind of open separatism, be it France with Corsica, or even England with the faraway Falkland Islands, which geographically belong to Argentina. How to forget too that the Muslims chased out of the Valley of Kashmir 500,000 Hindus who had lived there for generations and had not done any harm?

28. Zakir Naik. Zakir Naik tried to hurt religious sentiments of Hindus by denigrating Shri Ganesh; that too, during the Ganesh Festival. He has given a challenge to Hindus, through the medium of 'Facebook' and 'You-tube', to prove that Shri Ganapati is a Deity. He also made an anti-Hindu statement that 'If your God is unable to recognise his own son, how will he know that I am in danger.' By making such comments Naik has hurt religious sentiments of billions of Hindus. It has also created rage among members of Shiv Sena, BJP and various pro-Hindu organisations, Ganeshotsava Mandals and devout Hindus. Naik also went after Sri Sri Ravi Shankar in the famous debate.

29. Christophe Jaffrelot. This most famous French Indologist, paid by the French Government, who wrote many a nasty books on 'Hindu fundamentalism' and is most responsible for the bad image of the BJP in France. Funnily, he regularly comes to India to release the English translations of his books and is feted by the Press corps and gets all kind of laudatory reviews. So much for secularism in India_ Jaffrelot, Sanjay Subramanyam (who teaches in the prestigious College de France), and others in France—keep harping on India's problems—castes, poverty, so called-Hindu fundamentalism, etc. I know for a fact that in France, it has an influence on the top bureaucrats and the politicians, as every time something important happens in India—elections, catastrophes, riots, etc, their slanted opinions are sought by newspapers radios and televisions.

30. NGO's. NGO's in India are most of the time anti-Hindus. 70% of them work on "woman empowerment," or "uplifting" the villagers in tribal areas, which is good, but should be done in a neutral manner with friendliness to the Indian Govt. It is nowadays fashionable in India to always highlight the downtrodden condition of Indian women and their underprivileged place in Indian society. But no country in the world has granted such an important place to women in its spirituality and social ethos. And even today, behind all appearances—arranged marriages, submission to men, preference of male children in some rural areas (but girls are loved in India like nowhere in the world)—it can be safely said that very often, from the poorest to the richest classes, women control –even if behind the scenes—a lot of the family affairs: the education of their children (men in India are often "mama's boys"), monetary concerns, and husbands often refer to them for important decisions. Countries such as France or the United States, who are often preaching India on "women's rights" never had a woman as their top leader, whereas India had Indira Gandhi ruling with an iron hand for nearly twenty years; and proportionately they have less MP's than India, which is considering earmarking 33% of seats in Parliament for women, a revolution in human history! But this obsession of NGO's with women and village empowerment (usually they take one village and make it like a showcase, for the benefit of visiting donors from abroad) has completely eclipsed the burning issue that would require NGO's attention with the tremendous amount of funds they attract from abroad: afforestation, as there are hardly any forest worth the name left today in India.

31. Karunanidhi. Karunanidhi and before him his mentor, Anna, exploited to the hilt he Dravidian theory. According to this theory, which was actually devised in the 18th and 19th century by British linguists and archaeologists, who had a vested interest to prove the supremacy of their culture over the one of the subcontinent, the first inhabitants of India were good-natured, peaceful, dark-skinned shepherds, called the

Dravidians. Then, around 1500 B.C., India is said to have been invaded by tribes called the Aryans: white-skinned, nomadic people, who originated somewhere in Ural, or the Caucasus. To the Aryans, are attributed Sanskrit, the Vedic—or Hindu religion, India's greatest spiritual texts, the Vedas, as well as a host of subsequent writings, the Upanishads, the Mahabharata, the Ramanaya, etc... And thus English missionaries and later, American preachers, were able to convert tribes and low caste Hindus by telling them: "you, the aborigines, the tribals, the Harijans, were there in India before the Aryans; you are the *original* inhabitants of India, and you should discard Hinduism, the religion of these arrogant Aryans and embrace, Christianity, the true religion." Karunanidhi also exploits this theory and he and Anna have made life for Tamil Brahmins so miserable that many left Tamil Nadu for Delhi or even the US.

32. Wendy Doniger. This American Hindu hater, supposedly, a historian, says that "Rama thinks that sex is putting him in political danger (keeping his allegedly unchaste wife will make the people revolt), but in fact he has it backward: Politics is driving Rama to make a sexual and religious mistake; public concerns make him banish the wife he loves. Rama banishes Sita as Dasharatha has banished Rama. Significantly, the moment when Rama kicks Sita out for the second time comes directly after a long passage in which Rama makes love to Sita passionately, drinking wine with her, for many days on end; the banishment comes as a direct reaction against the sensual indulgence. Her latest book, 'The Hindus: An Alternative History' was written intentionally to mock Hinduism.

33. Akbar. Akbar is one of the goody-goodies in Indian History books, like Ashoka because he was a Buddhist, that Marxist historians like to glorify. No doubt, Akbar was one of the better Mughal emperors, but did you know that when he captured Chittor on 25 February 1568, he ordered that the thirty thousand civil population be butchered, including women and children who has taken shelter in the fort? Destruction of temples also took place on mass scale in Akbar's reign and it is even said that he ordered that a mountain be made of the tufts of the Brahmins' hairs.

34. Michael Witzel, Professor of Sanskrit at Harvard, Witzel must be one of the worst enemies of Hindus in the USA, as shown recently when he tried to prevent the removal of references to India, Hinduism in the curriculum followed by schools in California which parents of Indian origin found to be inadequate, inaccurate or just outright insensitive. Known for aggressively pushing theories forged by Left historians of the Romila Thapar genre that have been long discredited through scientific means, including DNA studies, this 'linguist' is known for promoting himself as a 'historian' in academic circles. His proximity to Left historians in India is no secret. Such is Prof. Witzel's contempt for Indians who live and work in the US that he has not minced words running them down as an ethnic group. On one occasion, he declared: "Hindus in the US are lost or abandoned people."

35. Amnesty International. Amnesty International, which has a large number of Pakistanis in its staff, has always been hostile to Hindus. I remember showing an exhibition on Kashmir in London at the prestigious Commonwealth Club. The south Asia Amnesty in charge, refused to come and see it—although the Club was just a stone throw away from Amnesty's London office. What did the Kashmiri Hindus do that Amnesty considers them untouchable? And how come that the Muslims of the Valley who chased them by terror and made them flee their ancestral lands and homes are not condemned by Amnesty? It triggers a lot of questions about Amnesty's impartiality....

36. Prannoy Roy (CEO of NDTV) No doubt, Prannoy Roy created one of the best TV channels in India, in term of content and professional quality, but from the beginning, NDTV's slant was anti-Hindu. Why? Did you know that Prannoy is married to Radhika Roy, who is the sister of Brinda Karat, one of the leading lights of the communist party of India (CPI(M))? The sad thing is that many BJP leaders always run to NDTV, to be crucified by Barkha Dutt, Pranno's second in command today.

37. Chidambaram. There are many questions asked today about the role of P. Chidambaram when he was in power during the ten years of the Congress. As Finance Minister, he went after Hindus by clamping down on Hindu institutions that had the 100% yoga tax rebate; as Home minister, his role is even more dubious: he had cleared an affidavit in 2009 which described college student Ishrat Jahan as a Lashkar-e-Taiba terrorist involved in a plot to assassinate then Gujarat chief minister Narendra Modi. About a month later, a second affidavit was filed in court in which all references to Ishrat's alleged terror links were missing. Did

Chidambaram, with the knowledge of Sonia Gandhi close his eyes on an assassination plot on the person of Narendra Modi? As the Home Minister of India, it would be a crime.

38. Sitaram Yechury. Yechury is an intelligent man and a brilliant speaker—but he is an enemy of Hindus. He for instance went full steam against Modi's declaration of June 21 as International Yoga, which was supported by the UN General Assembly and which should not cause any problem, as yoga is a universal technique that is practiced all over the world, by millions of Christians. Oh, but the hitch is that Yoga is a Hindu invention—hence Yechury's hostility, who famously said: "under this BJP government's aggressive global campaigns, India appears to be seeking a global positioning not on the basis of its internal strength, economic or otherwise, but on the basis of such 'accomplishments' as having the UN General Assembly declare International Yoga Day on 21 June. "The fact that a senior communist leader in India fails to see the potential to leverage the acceptance and spread of Yoga across the world as a means to further India's global influence and power is a testament to the monumental intellectual bankruptcy inflicting the communists in India.

39. Mother Teresa. Mother Teresa is still the worst publicity for India. No doubt, she did saintly work. This said, one may wonder: What did Mother Teresa really stand for? Was caring for the dying and orphaned children her only goal? Mother Teresa never attempted to counterbalance this negative image of India, of whom she was the vector, by a more positive one. She could have said for instance that she was worshipped in a country of 800 million Hindus. The truth is that she stood for the most orthodox Christian conservatism. There is no doubt that ultimately Mother Teresa's goal was utterly simple: to convert Hindus to Christianity, the only true religion in her eyes.

40. Karan Thapar. Karan Thapar, who owns ITV, which unfortunately produces shows for BBC, is one of the most famous faces of journalism in India. Karan Thapar's father was General Pran Nath Thapar COAS during 1962 war, and his aunt is Romila Thapar. Does that explain why Karan, though a decent man, is known for his anti-Hindu bias? Once he invited me on a program about the painter M.F. Husain, who as you know has depicted Hindus' most revered Gods fornicating or even sodomizing each other. I had brought on the show photocopies of these paintings, a solid evidence of Husain's hatred of Hinduism, but

Karan refused that I showed them on camera. So much for ITV's journalistic impartiality....

41. Javed Akhtar. Though Javed Akhtar came out recently against those who opposed saying 'Bharat Mata Ki Jai', he is also known as a Hindu baiter. I remember him going full steam against Sri Sri Ravi Shankar and Hindu gurus in an Indian Today symposium a few years ago. Akhtar also repeatedly equated the Gujarat 2002 anti-Muslim riots to the Jewish holocaust. As one of his detractors said: "it is impossible to believe that Akhtar isn't aware of the horrors at Auswitz or Sobibor to compare them with rioting in Gujarat"? Does Akhtar also ignore that 56 innocent Hindus, amongst them 32 women and children were burnt to death like animals in the Sabarmati Express at Godhra? And that this was the spark that ignited the riots? Again we see how anti-Hindus twist facts and truth...

42. Shabana Azmi. Aktar's second wife, Shabana Azmi is a fine actress. Nevertheless she is also a Hindu baiter. When she was invited to the international film festival of Deauville in France, I read the numerous interviews where she kept harping about "Hindu fundamentalists," and repeatedly lambasted the "Right Wing" BJP Government and accused them of turning a "blind eye" to the attacks towards India's minorities, while portraying herself as a courageous social activist fighting for freedom of expression. She also only spoke "en passant" about Muslim fundamentalism. Again the old trick to either equate Muslim and Hindu fundamentalism, or even in the case of Azmi, Rahul Gandhi and others, to say that Hindu fundamentalism is more dangerous than the Islamic one. What a joke...

43. Akar Patel. Akar Patel, a subtle but redoubtable Hindu hater, is sadly the head of Amnesty International India (one can see there the perversion of Amnesty, to name a Muslim as its head in a country inhabited by 80% Hindus). Akar indeed always rants against Narendra Modi and the Hindu majority, saying: "one must be neutral." but "we dissent against our own country, because dissent is patriotic." However he adds: "Anyone opposing us (Amnesty International?), is morally deficient and a repugnant human being." Akar Patel's virulent hatred for the majority community is not masked. He wrote: "Most extremists in India are not Muslims , they are Hindu Maoists."

44. Arundhati Roy. Cousin of Pranoy Roy, she was married to Gerard Da Cunha first and than to film maker Pradip Kirishen. Arundhati is a pure product of Christianity hiding under an intellectual mask plus hard-core Marxism. Apart from her first book the 'God of Small things,' Arundhati never wrote again anything of value. She is most happy in the company of maoists, naxalites Tamil Elam and Kashmiri separatists. Roy famously said: "Kashmir has never been an integral part of India and the Indian Govt is at war with Maoists to aid the MNCs." She also says Modi is promoting Brahmanism. After the "intolerance" debate, she returned her National award for screenplay. Nobody cared...

45. Father Cedric Prakash. This Indian Christian priest has been most active in betraying his own country in the US, amongst Congress parliamentary committees. In June 2002, he testified before the US Commission for International Religious Freedom (USCIRF) in Washington, so about the lack of religious freedom in India.... His is a clear case of an Indian citizen asking an alien nation tintervene in India's domestic affairs. Fr. Prakash has been a vocalcritic of Narendra Modi, often in collaboration with John Dayal and Teesta Setalvad.

46. Martha Nussbaum. A virulent anti-Hindu American, no doubt supported by Anjana Chatterjee and her ilk. Her pronouncement: "perpetrators of violence are not Muslims but Hindus," is proof enough of that. Her interest in India started while working for Amartya Sen, with whom she shared an intimate relationship, a fact she herself bragged about. Before the 2014 Parliament elections, Amartya Sen had said that he wouldn't like Modi to be the PM of India. Martha does not have any qualification or training in archaeology, Sanskrit, geology, or metallurgy, yet writes with authority about the dating of the Vedas.

47. Hillary Clinton. Hillary Clinton has no great love for India and often leans towards Pakistan (her vice chairman of the 2016 election campaign is Huma Mahmood Abedin, of Pakistani origin). Maybe the numerous infidelities of her husband Bill, made her into a hard and cynical woman, but if she becomes President of the US, she will be no friend of India and Hindus. Her attitude towards Islam and Muslim fundamentalism is also ambiguous and she is probably closer to Obama's views, than any other presidential candidate. You can expect continuing support, financial and in armaments to Pakistan if she is elected.

48. Medha Patkar. Another NGO, who very selectively targets only Hindus. Her Narmada dam agitation had one target only: Narendra Modi. Yet the dam has proved to be the biggest factor to Gujarat's prosperity, bringing electricity, water, prosperity to all, Hindus as well as Muslims. Medha was also involved in many movements that blocked Mr Modi's visas in the UK and the US and that tried to stop him from becoming Prime Minister.

49. The Mahatma Gandhi? I put it with a question mark, as I consider him as a great soul indeed. But there are many who point out that he never seemed to have realised the great danger that Nazism represented for humanity. Calling Hitler "my beloved brother," a man who murdered 6 million Jews in cold-blood just to prove the purity of his own race, is more than just innocence, it borders on criminal credulity. And did not Gandhi also advise the Jews to let themselves be butchered?... His not condemning Muslims during the Khalifat movement when thousands of Hindus were butchered by Indian Muslims, or his indulgence of Jinnah, going as far as proposing to make him the Prime Minister of India, have not always earned him Hindu goodwill.

Gandhi's love of the Harijans, as he called them, was certainly very touching and sprang from the highest motivations, but once more Gandhi took the European element in the decrying of the caste system, sowing the seeds of future disorders and of a caste war in India, of which we see the effects only today.

50. Hindus Themselves. Hindus, it must be said, are their own biggest enemies. They must be some of the most selfish and individualistic people in the world: rich Hindus never help their poorer brothers and sisters—that's why the Mother Teresa's and Sonia Gandhis are able to flourish in India. A Hindu abroad never acknowledges another Hindu, but pretends he or she does not exist. You can insult Hindus and their Gods and Goddesses as much as you want and nothing will happen to you. A billion Hindus have not raised a finger about the 450,000 Kashmiri Pandits who became refugees in their own country after they were chased out by terror from the Valley of Kashmir in the 90's. Hindus today don't give a damn whether their children know about the Ramayana, the Mahabharata or the Bhagavad Gita, where every truth that needs to be known about life, after life, karma, dharma and soul is taught. Modern Hindu children do not go to temples, pray or know what is a puja. Hindus do not care to have colleges where Hindu values are imparted, like the Muslims have (Aligarh university for instance) The only one ever, the Benares Hindu University, should not be called 'Hindu', as nothing Hindu is taught there anymore.

Chhatrapati Shivaji Maharaj, who alone with a few hundred men, stood his ground against the most powerful emperor of his times, has practically no place in Indian History books and is often described as a petty chieftain or even a plunderer. So is Maharana Pratap, the ONLY Rajput who fought against the Moguls and actually defeated Akbar in Hadilgathi.

Hindus who tend to merge and melt wherever they live—and in the process, lose some their identities and togetherness. And finally the most deadly and vicious intellectuals that we have reviewed above, are Hindus most of them. They are the ones that should be targeted, in a non-violent but firm manner.

Countries

1. **China**. After six decades of bitter experience at the hands of the Chinese, of double talk, betrayal and contempt,—India still gets hoodwinked by the Chinese You should also know that China still occupies one third of Ladhak, which it took during the 62 war, still claims for itself the whole of Arunachal Pradesh and has not only furnished Pakistan with its missiles (c/o North Korea), but has given them the know-how to manufacture nuclear weapons? How can Indians say that China is not a security menace to India? Doesn't he know also that according to the CIA, China has transferred one third of its nuclear arsenal to Nagchuka, 250 kms away from Lhassa, a region full of huge caves, which the Chinese have linked together by an intricate underground network and where they have installed nearly one hundred Intercontinental Ballistic Missiles, many of them pointed at Indian cities? The reason for this is that the Chinese, who are probably among the most intelligent people in the world, have always understood that India is their number one economic, military and nuclear competitor in Asia (remember how China blocks India's accession to the UN's Security Council, which France supports).

2. Pakistan. Pakistan is the continuing incarnation of those Muslim invaders who raped India from the middle of the 7th century onwards. Has anything changed: "their cry is still the same: "Dar-ul-Islam," the house of Islam. Yesterday they used scimitars, today they have the atomic bomb; but the purpose is identical, only the weapons have evolved: to conquer India, to finish what the Mughal Emperors were not able to achieve." To reason with Pakistan is useless, many conclude, "for once again they are only putting in practice what their religion teaches them every day—that 'the Pagans shall burn forever in the fire of hell. They are the meanest of creatures.' Or 'Slay the infidels, wherever ye find them and take them captive and besiege them and prepare them for all kinds of ambush.' Or again: 'Choose not thy friends among the Infidels till they forsake their homes and the way of idolatry. If they return to paganism then take them whenever you find them and kill them.' All these quotations are taken from the Koran and are read everyday to the faithful by their mollahs. (Koran 98:51-9:5-4:89)

3. Bangladesh. In 1947, Muslims constituted only 70% of Bangladesh and Hindus, as well as Christians and Buddhists more than 30%, Today, Muslims are nearly 90 percent, making Bangladesh one of the largest Muslim countries in the world and Hindus, have shrunk to 7%. Successive governments have seized 2.5 million acres of land of the Hindus by using a racist law called the Enemy Property Act (renamed *Vested Property Act* by the secularists). Although finally this racist law was repealed, Khaleda Zia's government has blocked its implementation (*Country Report on Human Rights Practices*—2001, 2003, *US Department of State*).

Through the 5th and 8th Amendments of the constitution the BNP and JP governments, virtually transformed the once secular Bangladesh into an Islamic state. Apart from money laundering and providing terrorists sanctuary, Bangladesh's madrasas have become major recruiting and training centres for militancy. A CIA study says that Bangladeshi villagers are increasingly getting sucked into terrorism out of livelihood. The very porous border between India and Bangladesh is used as an infiltration route of militants to India, including those going to Kashmir and to the Northeast. The Indian Intelligence Bureau estimates that twenty million Bangladeshis live illegally in India, with the greatest concentration in West Bengal and Assam and this is creating havoc to the social, religious and cultural fabric of the North-East. Chief ministers, such as Mamta Banerjee routinely give rations cards to these illegal Bangladeshis so that they can vote. IN West Bengal and Assma, Hindus have become minorities in certain districts are regularly beaten up, their temples ransacked, their women raped. Very few Hindus leaders have taken up their cause, save for Tapan Ghosh in WB.

4. Nepal. Sonia Gandhi, whose government was propped-up by communists, did great damage to India's interests, such as helping a Maoist government come to power in Nepal, the only Hindu state in the world. Here is a wonderful country, with simple and friendly people, which is the only Hindu nation in the world, which is so similar in many ways to India, that there is no reason to be antagonistic to a country with which they have so much in common. Yet the erstwhile kings and now the Maoist leaders in power, are often been able to play a divide and rule game by using the Chinese and blaming India for all the ills of Nepal which as become a haven for Pakistani agents.

5. United States. The United States, seems sometimes to have an unconscious wish for a divided and weakened India. And did not Senator Galbraith say after the exploding of Yugoslavia that "India is next"? President Obama, whom the world hailed as its savior, subjected India to immense pressure to negotiate with Pakistan and to do major concessions on Kashmir, which would endanger India's integrity, as Kashmir is such a sensitive strategic state. The continuing propping up and arming of Pakistan, when its duplicity is so well document today, is also a mystery. One does not understand too how so many US Congress committees keep saying that there is no religious freedom in India, when there is actually more freedom here than in the USA. Luckily the Spratly Islands dispute has brought the US and India slightly closer and Donald Trump seems to have more sympathy for India, although he sometimes acts irrationally. But there is still a long way to go before the USA really appreciates what an island of democracy and freedom India is in an Asia racked by Muslim fundamentalism, Christian unethical conversions and Chinese domination.

6. Afghanistan. India is making great efforts to befriend Afghanistan, so as to balance Pakistan's efforts, which props up the Taliban. But as soon as the US fully leaves this region, Afghanistan will go back to its wild Islamic ways and target India again. It's a pity that once

Afghanistan was part of a great Hindu empire and at some times too Buddhist.

7. **Sri Lanka**. Extraordinary country that erstwhile Ceylon; God gave it everything: extraordinary climate, lush country, incredible diversity of races and religions, an easy-going and friendly people, who even welcomed its invaders. Yet the hate that the Sinhalese have for Indians is something to be seen to be believed. Again it is a hate which was fostered by their political leaders: Most Sinhalese presidents have become great adepts at using the hate-India carrot every time they get in trouble. And why should India be blamed for Sri Lanka's ills? Was it India who discriminated for 40 years against the Tamil minority of Sri Lanka? Was it Indians who regularly prodded Sinhalese crowds to indulge in pogroms against the Tamils, thereby building-up a wall of hatred, so that today the Tamils in Sri Lanka cannot trust the Sinhalese anymore and want nothing but total independence? Today, the LTTE has been apparently wiped out, but make no mistake, the Tamil-Sinhalese divide will reappear under some form or the other.

8. **England**. When Mountbatten left India with the British flag, ending three centuries of colonization, he made sure that India was permanently divided by propping-up Pakistan and establishing a foreign policy of always putting India and Pakistan on the same foot—policy that was taken-up by the US and Europe. Hindus were the British colonizer's biggest enemy, that is why they also propped up Sikhs, Christians and Muslims to divide India. The birth of Khalistan can be traced to the British. Finally the British looted Hindu India and stole million of priceless artefacts which are still found in British Museums.

9. **Canada**. Canada is a subtle enemy of Hindus, solely because it has a huge Sikh population. The Canadians allowed them to breed separatism which led to the Air India Kanishka tragedy. Even then the Canadian government continued to show leniency to the Sikhs and today Trudeau does the same by having a Sikh minister and many Sikh MP's who are friendly to the Khalistani cause.

10. **Norway** has been a backer of the Naxalite movement and the LTTE for a long time. These are mostly NGO's and individuals, who often come to spend sometimes in villages of Andhra Pradesh or Bihar, to 'uplift' villagers, but have the tacit backing of their Government. It's amazing also how Norway gives Peace Nobel Prizes to Indians that fit in

their Protestant mould of thinking, such as and Mother Teresa, Amartya Sen or , and neglects real philantropers, such as Sri Sri Ravi Shankar.

II. Ten Challenges For Hindus in the 21st Century World

It is also true that Hindus must to rise to the challenges of this second millennium. Here they are—in order of difficulty.

1. Break the Polytheist image. One of the most enduring clichés about Hinduism is that Hindus adore a multitude of gods and goddesses, which makes them heathens in the eyes of Christians, thus good to be converted to the 'true' God, often with unethical financial baits; and 'kafirs' for Muslims from all over the world, particularly from neighbouring countries, such as Pakistan, which encourages them to wage a jihad on India.

Yet, Hinduism, whether you want to call it a religion or a spiritual system, is without doubt one of the most monotheist creeds in the world, because it always recognized *that the One is Many and that He incarnates Himself or Herself in a multitude of forms—hence the million of gods and goddesses in the Hindu pantheon*. Vedic Sages (from the Vedas, the oldest and most sacred Scriptures of Hinduism) had understood that man has to be given a multiplicity of different approaches to the Unfathomable. And truly, for the Hindus, the Divine cannot be "this" or "that"—*neti, neti*. In its essence, He cannot be several—or even one—and thus can never be perfectly seized by the human mind. Indeed, Hindus, who were once upon a time the best dialecticians in the world (and this is maybe why they are today the top software programmers of this planet), were able to come-up with this kind of equation: (a) God is in the world; (b) the world is in God; (c) the world is God; (d) God and the world are distinct; (e) God is distinct from the world, but the world is not distinct from God; (f) it is impossible to discern if the world is distinct from God or not... Never has the unique nature of Hindu polytheism been better defined.

Hindus in the world need to emphasize to their western brothers and sisters that they have also always recognized the divinity of other religions, as their concept of the *avatar* (the different forms that the Divine takes at different times to incarnate Himself or Herself in a human form) helped them to accept the reality of other prophets, masters or gurus. It is, for instance, perfectly acceptable for an ordinary

Hindu to have on his wall the image of Krishna, alongside the one of Buddha, one of the Christ, with a few photos of the Mecca or even John Fitzgerald Kennedy! And Hindus have always worshipped at non-Hindu places, such as Velangani, the Christian seat of pilgrimage of South India, or some Sufi shrine in Kashmir or Rajasthan. It should be said too that Hindus *never* tried to convert others to their own religion, not even by peaceful means, as the Buddhists did all over Asia; and their armies never but oh, never, set to conquer other nations to impose their own culture and religion, as Islam and Christianity did, often in a bloody manner. Thus, Hindus in the WORLD, need to be able to counter in a knowledgeable manner, verbally or in writing (letters to editors, etc.) this wrong polytheist image which has harmed them.

2. Dispel the image of poverty attached to India. One of the reasons Hindus are not taken too seriously abroad, is that their country, India, is always associated with poverty. True, there is still poverty in India, social inequality, but since 1947, thanks to the Green Revolution, there has been no famine. Hindus in the world and in India can always counter this pervading untruth in the mind of the westerners, by stating that according to British records, one million Indians died of famine between 1800 and 1825; 4 million between 1825 and 1850; 5 million between 1850 and 1875; and *15 million* between 1875 and 1900. Thus, 25 million Indians died in one hundred years under the benevolent rule of the British Raj!

Poverty in India is also commercially exploited by Hollywood and writers. A book such as 'The City of Joy', by Frenchman Dominique Lapierre, which was a huge success worldwide, gives the impression that India is a vast slum, which is absolutely untrue—and the author, who often comes to India, had to know that he was inducing his readers in error. As for the film "Slumdog Millionnaire," which raked-up so many Oscars, it is even more perverse: it says things which are false, portrays situations that are untrue, such as the young boy throwing himself in excrements, to get an autograph of India's film star Amitabh Bacchan & should have been boycotted by Hindus.

Yet, India is a **wealthy** country. It is said, even today, because of the socialist policies of previous governments and the heavy taxation, that half of India's money is in the black. The poverty is only there because of the mismanagement, the dishonesty, and the inheritance of wrong structures. For Indians must be with some of the best savers in the world. And they don't hoard in abstract concepts: they go in for solid gold, land, cash—and that from the little shopkeeper to the business magnate.

As economic liberalisation is happening in India at this very moment, the rise of India as a superpower will herald the rise of the status of Hindus in the US, UK, Canada and all over the world, for today the assessment that every industrial nation in the world casts on another country, is primarily economical. Thus China is respected so much today in the world, not for its political power, which is overshadowed by immense Human Rights abuses (Mao Tse Tung killed 3 million of his own people during the Cultural revolution and it has been calculated that one million Tibetans have been murdered by the Chinese), but by its economic clout. In the same way, India's image, whose PIB has now overtaken China's, will shed many of the prejudices attached to her, when the world takes notice of the huge investment possibilities there.

3. Explain the caste system to westerners. Caste is still a curse that hangs around India's neck. While it is true that 75% marriages are still arranged in India, Hindus in the US, UK, Canada and elsewhere need to whisper in the ears of their western friends that the Indian Government has made tremendous efforts since 1947 to uplift the lower castes. And it has succeeded in great measure. Tell them that your present Prime Minister comes from one of the lowest castes and was a tea seller, that some of today's Indian Chief Ministers are untouchables, or that one of India's best known saints, Amrita Anandamayi, who has hundreds of thousands of disciples in the WORLD, and millions all over the world, and has built hospitals, universities, housings for the poor, comes from the lowest caste possible in Kerala.

You can also ask your US and European friends if the caste system is really that worse than the huge class differences you can see nowadays in Europe or the USA!

4. Dispel the notion that Hindus can be fundamentalists and violent. Hindus need to repeat again and again to their British brothers and sisters that the only country in the world where Jews were never persecuted is India. Tell them that the genius of this country lies in its Hindu ethos, or rather in the true spirituality behind Hinduism. Explain that the average Hindu that you meet in a million villages, possesses this simple, innate spirituality in his or her genes and accepts your diversity, whether you are Christian, Muslim, or Jain, Arab, French or Chinese. It is this 'Hindu-ness' (which cannot be experienced if you sit in Delhi most of the time) that makes most Indian Christians different, from say a French Christian, or an Indian Muslim unlike a Saudi Muslim. Also that Hindus have given refuge to all persecuted minorities of the world, whether the Syrian Christians, the Parsis (Iranian worshippers of Zarathustra), the Jews, the Armenians, or today the Tibetans (the real Tibet is in India now, as the one in the hands of the Chinese has lost much of its Tibetan character). Thus you cannot find *less* fundamentalist than a Hindu in this world and Hindus in the world should immediately react when they read articles in the western Press (often unfortunately from New Delhi-based correspondents) trying to equate Islamic terrorism, which blow-up innocent civilians, to angry ordinary Hindus who burn churches without killing anybody. Tell them that however reprehensible was the destruction of the Babri Masjid (a Mosque built in the 15th century by Muslim invader Babar on a very ancient and holy Hindu temple dedicated to the God Ram), no Muslim was killed in the process; compare this with the 'vengeance' bombings of 1993 in Mumbai, which wiped-out hundreds of innocent, mostly Hindus. Yet, the Babri Masjid destruction is often described by journalists as the most horrible act of the two. Today, you can argue with your British friends, Hindus are one of the most successful, law abiding and integrated communities in the world. Can you call them terrorists?

5. Tell your western friends about the greatness of Hindu philosophy and Literature. Indian education is a leftover from the British Raj. Nothing wrong with that, except that as a result, Indian students know all about Shakespeare, Napoleon, the Bible, but very little about their great warriors. And there were many: Shivaji Maharaj from Maharashtra, as great as a warrior as Napoleon, who started the first Indian navy, made laws, protected women and children from all religions; Maharana Pratap from Rajasthan, the only Rajput (maharaja, if you wish) who stood up to the Moghol invaders in the 17th century); and even great women warriors, the equals of Jeanne d'Arc: the Rani of Jhansi, who fought the British; Ahilyabai of Indore, who had the first women battalion in India, or Chennama in the South. Tell you British friends that some of the greatest poets who walked on this earth were Hindus: Kalidasa, whose Sanskrit was so pure, than even translated in English it still shines; Vyasa, who composed the Mahabharata, which has been considered by many western authors, of the same epic quality of the Iliad and Odyssey, etc.

Western philosophy and culture trace its sources to ancient Greece... But many famous writers and Indologists have pointed out that Greece was greatly influenced by Hinduism. Famous Indianist Jean Herbert reminds us that "many many centuries before us, India had devised most of the philosophical systems which Europe experienced with later. They contained, at least in its essence, the philosophy of the Greeks, the Alexandrine mystique, the religious speculation of the Middle Ages, the rationalism of the XIXth century and even the most recent incarnations of modern pantheism." In 1782, already, French philosopher Pierre Sonnerat had written: "Ancient India gave to the world its religions and philosophies: Egypt and Greece owe India their wisdom and it is known that Pythagoras went to India to study under Brahmins, who were the most enlightened of human beings."

But it is in XIXth century Europe that an open admiration for ancient India's culture flourished best, particularly in Germany, where philosophers, such a Frederich Shlegel, said that "there is no language in the world, even Greek, which has the clarity and the philosophical precision of Sanskrit," adding "that India is not only at the origin of everything, she is superior in everything, intellectually, religiously or politically—and even the Greek heritage seems pale in comparison"... The great Shopenhauer agrees with him and writes in the preface of his *The World as a Will and as a Representation*: "According to me, the influence of Sanskrit literature on our time will not be lesser than what was in the XVIth century Greece's influence on Renaissance. One day, India's wisdom will flow again on Europe and will totally transform our knowledge and thought." And Nietzsche himself had read the Vedas, which he admired profoundly, could quote from the Law of Manu and thought that "Buddhism and Brahmanism are a hundred times deeper and more objective than Christianity."

6. Hindus in the WORLD should preserve their Indian-ness. Hindus in the US or Britain, or elsewhere, have to ask themselves that question: what is it to be an Indian abroad today? What is meant by Indian-ness? How much of yourself do you give to your British identity—and how much space do you preserve for your Indian-ness? For we see many of the children of Indians who settled in the WORLD twenty or thirty years ago, merge themselves totally in the British way of life, speak with an English accent, eat fish fry, support Chelsea football club ... and in the process forget all about their wonderful Indian culture....

What are those special qualities that confer an Indian-ness? Firstly and foremost: "I accept you; I accept that you may be White or Black, Red or Yellow, Christian, Buddhist, or Muslim." Not only that, "but I am even ready to go and worship in a church or a mosque, besides my temple." "I accept that my Gods are avatars, incarnations of the Divine, but so is Jesus Christ, and also Buddha and even Mohamed." This an extraordinary statement and a marvellous instrument towards world peace, at a time when the two great monotheist religions of the world, Islam and Christianity still say: "there is only one true God in the world—mine- and if you worship any other god, you are an Infidel and a Pagan and it is my right to convert you by any means, or even to kill you." The July 2005 London bombings are nothing but a result of that dangerous theorem. As a result, Indians adapt easily wherever they go, particularly in the West, as they are very open to western culture. Of course, Indians also go to the other extreme: "not only I accept you, but I am going to become exactly like you—no even Whiter than the White: I am going to denigrate my own culture, spit on my religion, belittle my countrymen." This is why you come across so often in the US or UK, or Canada on negative articles on India written by Indians—nay by Hindus.

What second, third or even fourth generations Hindus in the West should also ask themselves today is "How can I repay my debt to India"? After all not only they got a nearly free education in India which was good enough for them to obtain well paid jobs in the US, UK, or elsewhere in the West, but did they not also inherit that certain Indian-ness, which has been a great help to adapt to the western way of life. Or: "In what way can I contribute to this great nation which is India, which is often maligned and side-lined in the US and Europe"?

It would be a blow to both Britain (or the US or Canada, or France) if Hindus would totally blend in their countries of adoption and lose their values of tolerance, gentleness, hospitality and the ability to see the One in the Many, it would be not only a loss to themselves, but also to their countries of adoption, to which they would not bring anything special.

7. Take political power and Unite. You know by now that wherever Hindus exiled themselves, they did well, whether as labourers in Mauritius or doctors in the WORLD or IT engineers in the USA! They pay their taxes, integrate themselves, do not riot, their children top in colleges and universities and generally blend in the culture of the country they adopted. Everybody also knows that some of the biggest multinationals, such as Adobe, Microsoft, Diageo, Mastercard, Google, Pepsi, or others are today headed by Indians—read Hindus.

Yet, Hindus are individualistic people and they tend to look down on politics, as something 'dirty'. This is why they did not always get the politicians they deserve in their home country. We see today that a lot of Muslims are elected in local boroughs or even towns in the US, UK or Canada. That is good and should be praised. But it is also true that often these Muslim leaders tend to think only of their community and sometimes use their offices to enforce the vision of their particular communities, such as segregated swimming pools, or even try to modify western textbooks. Hindus, with their universal outlook will not do such things. But they need to come out of their shells and stand for elections at all levels of the US, British and Canada political system.

Another drawback of Hindus in the West, particularly in the USA, is that they are terribly disunited and are splintered in many groups, along states of origins, profession, or even castes, sometimes even are at odds with each other. Hindus in West should therefore unite under one umbrella organization and the united Hindu diaspora leadership should meet at least once a year with a rotating president.

8. Explain Narendra Modi. There is a lot of disinformation floating around India. We saw how poverty, caste and polytheism still hang around Hindus' necks, but what about political misconceptions? For instance, Hindus in the West should offer some counter arguments on the disinformation about Narendra Modi, India's present prime Minister. They should first remind their friends, that Mr Modi had made of his state, Gujarat, the most efficient, most prosperous and least corrupt of all the states of India. Of course, he is labelled "anti-Muslim and accused him of having engineered the 2002 Gujarat anti-Muslim riots. But remind them that these riots were triggered by the horrifying murder of 57 Hindus, 36 of them innocent women and children, burnt like animals in the Sabarmati Express. Riots of that intensity like in Gujarat, do not happen in a day, they are a result of long term pent-up angers and a spark like the killing of Hindu brothers and sisters, whose only crime was that they believed that the God Ram was born in Ayodhya, is enough the ignite the smouldering fire.

Ask your US, Canadians, French or British friends if it is logical that only Mr Modi is targeted? But who went down in the streets in fury in 2002? Hundreds, if not thousands of Gujuratis, not only from the lower strata of society, not only Dalits, but also middle class, and sometimes even upper middle class! Should they also not be judged and condemned? But then it would be the whole of Gujarat who should be hauled to court, an ancient and noble race, who gave so much to India, including Mahatma Gandhi, and today is still exporting all over the world its upright and successful businessmen, to the West—in the US, for instance, where they own most of the motels. Finally, tell them that it was never proved that Modi waited 24 hours before calling the army to quell the riots.

9. Help India become the alternative to China. Emphasize again and again on western national forums that *India is the natural economic and geopolitical partner of the West and the rest of the civilized world*. For contrary to China, it is democratic, pro-western, liberal, with a middle class as important as China's. Tell them that the Western powers have banked all their investments on China, neglecting India, the other giant of Asia, which is a grave mistake because some social upheaval is bound to happen in China sooner or later, as soon as the authoritarian hold is removed one way or another. Highlight the fact that India is a much safer bet in the long run for western investments. Already India's PIB has overtaken the Chinese, who are facing a lot of economic difficulties. Tell them that at the very least, the US and Europe should balance their chips by investing half of them in India—the Prime Minister, Mr Modi is in the process of liberalizing the economy and making it easier for foreign investors. Tell them that India is the next economic superpower and that it has a much better human rights record than China.

It is also very important that you point out that *India is the natural geopolitical buffer of the West in an Asia* racked by Islamic fundamentalism and the Chinese thirst for hegemony (explain to the British that Beijing is claiming for instance an Indian state as big as England—Arunachal Pradesh). Europe and the US also keep making the mistake of funding and arming Pakistan, even when they fully know that the Pakistanis have unleashed Islamic terrorism not only towards Kashmir, but unto the whole world.

10. Spread Happiness in the West. "India will become the spiritual leader of the world," Swami Vivekananda had predicted. Thus share with your British friends the fact that hatha yoga, today practiced by hundreds of millions in the world, is a Hindu invention. Tell them too that Ayurveda, also taking the West by storm, is the oldest medical system still in practice in the world; that much before the West knew it used plants and minerals to cure people, knew that many illnesses have psychosomatic sources, and that Indian doctors practiced plastic surgery 1000 years before Christ. Talk about Pranayama, the most exacting, precise, mathematical, powerful breathing discipline one can dream of. Its effects and results have been observed and categorised by Indian yogis for millenniums. This extraordinary knowledge, brings in very quickly wonderful results in both the well being of the body and the quietude of the mind. Pushed to its extreme, it gives to the disciple deep spiritual experiences and a true inner perception of the world. Sri Sri Ravi Shankar has revitalized this science and packaged it in modern terms. Help them to practice meditation, queen of all the yogic sciences, that which is above everything, that without which any yogic discipline is impossible. That which interiorizes us, carries us within ourselves, to the discovery of our true soul and nature. There are hundreds of different mediation techniques, simple, cartesian, easy to experience, which have been devised by Indian sages since the dawn of Bharat. Each one has its own characteristics, each one gives particular results, which has been experienced by the billions of aspirants who have practised them since the dawn of Vedic times. This is the Wonder that IS Hinduism, tell them.

In conclusion, when the Hindus strive to shed these prejudices which have been harming their image, they can not only continue to contribute to the WORLD's economic growth, as they have done for several decades, but also, once they participate more intensely in the political power, be recognized as a distinguished community, with a separate and honoured identity.

Bibliography

Negationism in India, by Konrad Elst. Voice of India, New Delhi.

The Wonder That was India, by A.L. Basham, Rupa.

Vande Mataram, by Sri Aurobindo, Sri Aurobindo Ashram Press, Pondichery.

Histoire de l'Inde, by Jean Danielou. Editions Fayard, Paris.

India's Rebirth, Institut de Recherches Evolutives, Paris.

Distributed in India by Mira Aditi Center, 62 Sriranga 1st Cross, 4th Stage Kuvempunagar, Mysore 570023.

The Mother, by Sri Aurobindo, Sri Aurobindo Ashram Press, Pondichery.

Life without death, by Satprem, Mira Aditi center, 62 Sriranga 1st Cross, 4th Stage Kuvempunagar, Mysore 570023.

Indigenous Indians, by Konrad Elst, Voice of India, New Delhi.

The Foundations of Indian Culture, by Sri Aurobindo, Sri Aurobindo Ashram Press, Pondichery.

Hindu Society under siege, by Sitaram Goel, Voice of India, New Delhi.

The Hour of God, by Sri Aurobindo. Sri Aurobindo Ashram Press, Pondichery.

The Supramental Manifestation, by Sri Aurobindo, Sri Aurobindo Ashram Press, Pondichery.

The Secret of the Veda, by Sri Aurobindo, Sri Aurobindo Ashram Press, Pondichery.

The Mother's Agenda, as recorded by Satprem. 13 volumes. Mira Aditi centre, 62 Sriranga 1st Cross, 4th Stage Kuvempunagar, Mysore 570023.

Histoire de l'Inde Moderne, Sous la direction de Claude Markovits, Fayard, 1994.

Le Modèle Indou, by Guy Deleury, Hachette, le Temps and les hommes, 1978.

L'oubli de l'Inde, by Roger-Pol Droit, Puf/Perspectives Critiques, 1989.
Mother India and Her destiny, by the Mother, Sri Aurobindo Ashram Press, Pondichery.
Arise Arjuna, by David Frawley, Voice of India, 1994.
L'Inde où j'ai vécu, Par Alexandra David-Neel, Paris/Plon, 1951.

The author is grateful to the Sri Aurobindo Ashram Trust for permission to quote extensively from Sri Aurobindo and the Mother's works.